W9-BUJ-611

A HANDBOOK FOR THE LECTIONARY

A HANDBOOK
FOR THE
LECTIONARY

by
HORACE T. ALLEN, JR.

Developed by

The Joint Office of Worship
of the
Presbyterian Church in the United States
and
The United Presbyterian Church
in the United States of America

Published by
THE GENEVA PRESS
Philadelphia

Copyright © 1980 The Geneva Press

All rights reserved—no part of this book may be reproduced in any form without permission in writing from the publisher, except by a reviewer who wishes to quote brief passages in connection with a review in magazine or newspaper.

Scripture quotations from the Revised Standard Version of the Bible are copyrighted 1946, 1952, © 1971, 1973 by the Division of Christian Education of the National Council of the Churches of Christ in the U.S.A., and are used by permission.

BOOK DESIGN BY DOROTHY ALDEN SMITH

Published by The Geneva Press®
Philadelphia, Pennsylvania

PRINTED IN THE UNITED STATES OF AMERICA
9 8 7 6 5 4 3 2

Collects are reprinted by permission from:

Lutheran Book of Worship, copyright 1978; adapted from *The Book of Common Prayer*, copyright 1977 by Charles Mortimer Guilbert as custodian.
Page 524 of the English translation of *The Roman Missal* © 1973, International Committee on English in the Liturgy, Inc. All rights reserved.
The Worshipbook—Services and Hymns. Copyright © MCMLXX, MCMLXXII, The Westminster Press.

Library of Congress Cataloging in Publication Data

Allen, Horace T   1933–
   A handbook for the lectionary.

   Bibliography: p.
   Includes index.
   1. Bible—Homiletical use. 2. Bible—Criticism, interpretation, etc. 3. Bible—Liturgical lessons, English. 4. Church year. I. Joint Office of Worship (U.S.) II. Title.
   BS534.5.A43   264'.051   80-19735
   ISBN 0-664-24347-9

To my parents and first teachers of the Bible,
Horace and Dorothy Allen,
And in memory of their beloved Pastor,
The Rev. Alexander Mackie, D.D.

CONTENTS

PREFACE

Churches in the Reformed tradition give high priority to Holy Scripture. Selections from it are read at every service of worship and the proclamation of God's Word is the soul of preaching. A lectionary is an instrument to guide the selection of Bible passages to be used in the worship service. It leads to an orderly and comprehensive approach to the full range of Scripture in all its richness and variety.

This Handbook lists several Scripture readings for each Lord's Day of the year in a three-year cycle. Brief notations on each reading help one to identify the nature of the passage. There is a collect, a psalm, hymns, and anthem suggestions for every week, thus giving the busy pastor significant, practical help in planning the Sunday service.

While a number of persons made contributions to this book, Horace T. Allen, Jr., is listed as the author and rightly so. Without his labor there would have been no book. Part I, "Understanding the Lectionary," is entirely his work. Part II, "Using the Lectionary," draws on the skills of many persons, but Horace was the taskmaster. The notes for each Lord's Day were first published in *Reformed Liturgy and Music*, a publication of the Joint Office of Worship of the Presbyterian Church in the United States and The United Presbyterian Church in the United States of America, of which Horace was formerly director. The names of the various contributors are listed at the end of the Introduction to Part II. Lewis A. Briner compiled the Index of Scripture Lessons.

HAROLD M. DANIELS
Director of the Joint Office of Worship

PART I

UNDERSTANDING
THE LECTIONARY

I. FREEDOM AND ORDER

The authority of the Word and the freedom of the conscience in obedience to that Word constitute the fundamentals of Presbyterian church order. Our constitution declares that "God alone is lord of the conscience, and hath left it free from the doctrines and commandments of men [sic] which are in any thing contrary to his Word, or beside it, in matters of faith or worship."[1]

The other side of this dialectic is stated in the opening paragraphs of the Form of Government of the Presbyterian Church in the United States: "In matters of the worship of God and the government of the Church, there are some circumstances common to human actions and societies, which are to be ordered by reason and Christian prudence, according to the general rules of the Word, which always are to be observed."[2]

This dialectic of law and freedom provides both a caution and an encouragement for ordering the public reading of the Scriptures. The most commonly advanced concern with the use of a lectionary is that such a practice seems to inhibit the freedom of the ministry of the Word.

For this reason the constitutions of both The United Presbyterian Church U.S.A. and the Presbyterian Church U.S. take particular care to guarantee the freedom of the minister of the Word in choosing texts to be read and preached. Thus:

> The Pastor shall have discretion in the choice of Scripture and in the length of the passage read. The Pastor should exercise care to the end that over a period of time the people shall hear the full message of Scripture.[3]

And:

> There are certain responsibilities which belong to the minister as pastor which are not subject to the authority of the session, but which must be exercised by the pastor subject only to the constitutional authority of the presbytery, namely: the selection of the hymns or psalms to be sung at each service, the selection of a passage or passages of Scripture to be read at each service, the leading of the people in prayer, and the preparation and preaching of the sermon.[4]

11

It should immediately be noted, however, that in neither church's view is this freedom absolute. Pastors are accountable to the presbytery and are given this direction: "Over a period of time the people shall hear the full message of Scripture." These limits are not to be taken lightly. They speak of the seriousness with which these churches approach the handling of Holy Writ in the life of the congregation.

To serve precisely that seriousness this Handbook is written, proposing that a lectionary be the instrument of implementation. A lectionary is simply an ordered selection of readings appointed for liturgical use on specific occasions in the church year. In the long history of the church two kinds can be identified. The one, a *lectio selecta*, chooses passages from among the books of the Old and New Testaments appropriate to the day, season, or occasion. The other, a *lectio continua*, takes the books of the Bible themselves as the system, and simply reads them chapter by chapter, week by week. The Directory for Worship of the United Presbyterian Church, enacted in the year 1961, declares that "it is appropriate also that the readings [from both Old and New Testaments] follow, with such latitude as may be proper in varying situations, a set order or lectionary designed to assure that the fullness of God's Word be declared."[5]

A mere two years later the Second Vatican Council of the Roman Catholic Church ruled that

> the treasures of the Bible are to be opened up more lavishly so that a richer fare may be provided for the faithful at the table of God's word. In this way a more representative part of the sacred scriptures will be read to the people in the course of a prescribed number of years.[6]

This action resulted in the production of the three-year lectionary which is the subject of this Handbook. It is already serving in many churches, both Protestant and Roman Catholic. Of this lectionary the respected Methodist liturgist, Prof. James F. White, has said, "Surely, the new Roman Catholic lectionary is Catholicism's greatest gift to Protestant preaching, just as Protestant biblical scholarship has given so much impetus to Catholic preaching."[7]

At issue at the present is not whether the Scriptures shall be read in the midst of the assembled community, but how those readings shall be chosen. We need to consult our Reformed heritage in order to judge whether the adoption of a lectionary, much less a Roman one, can be consistent with our history and polity.

The sixteenth-century Reformers inherited from the Roman Church a *lectio selecta* system consisting of an Epistle and a Gospel for each Sunday (an Old Testament lection long since having dropped out of the picture). The readings followed a calendar that was a complicated mix of traditional Christmas and Easter cycles, with a whole Marian cycle overlaid upon it, and frequent interruptions for special saints' days. According to A. Allan McArthur, this lectionary had come into general use "only from about the ninth century onwards in accordance with the increasing predominance of the Roman rite."[8]

The Reformers rejected this system. In its place they went behind the Roman developments to the early church. They found in the homilies of the Greek and Latin fathers another system: *lectio continua*, the reading and preaching of successive chapters of single books of the Bible. Hughes Oliphant Old reports that "one of the most prominent features of the worship of the Reformed Church has always been the preaching of the Biblical books in course, that is preaching through a book of the Bible or a major section of a book of the Bible starting at the beginning and continuing through, chapter by chapter or even verse by verse, in such a way that the whole message of the sacred writing is presented in an orderly fashion over a series of weeks or months. Zurich, Basel, Strasbourg, and Geneva all adopted the *lectio continua* at an early date in the Reformation and it is unquestionably one of the most clear restorations of the form of worship of the early Church."[9] Dr. Old notes by way of exception that Calvin preached special sermons for Easter and Pentecost, and it was the custom in Geneva to preach from the Passion narrative during the week before Easter.

In both Lutheran and Reformed traditions services combining vernacular Communion with preaching orders were performed without the ceremonial of the Mass, and the church year pericopes were replaced by systematic preaching in course.

Prof. William D. Maxwell quotes from a letter of John Knox dated 1st July 1556 which encourages that in "reading the Scripture, ye sholde joyne some bokes of the Olde and some of the New Testament togeder."[10] Maxwell further states, "In 1644, the Westminster *Directory*, reflecting both English Puritan and Scottish opinion, declared that the reading of the Word in the congregation was 'a part of the publique worship of God,' and ordained that 'ordinarily one chapter of each Testament bee read at euery meeting.' "[11]

Thus in Reformation practice a right ordering of the public reading of the Scriptures included a measure of pastoral freedom and discretion, attention to certain central Christian festivals and celebrations, and the structure of the Scriptures themselves. It clearly did not exclude a fixed or "set" system, as though that in itself would improperly compromise the freedom of the ministry of the Word.

II. HISTORY AND HOPE

In a memorable simile, William Pierson Merrill's hymn "Not Alone for Mighty Empire" sings of "standing in the living present, memory and hope between."[12] This "living present" bounded by history and hope is what the late Karl Barth described as "the time of the community":

The time of the community is the time between the first *parousia* of Jesus Christ and the second. . . . The community exists between His coming then as the risen One and this final coming. Its time is, therefore, this time between. Its movement is from direct vision to direct vision; and in this movement by His Holy Spirit He Himself is invisibly present as the living Head in the midst of it as His body.[13]

This led Professor Barth to coin one of his most graphic metaphors for the church: "The community moves from the one point to the other like a ship—a constantly recurring picture—sailing over an ocean a thousand fathoms deep."[14]

This same sense is conveyed by Paul in his instruction to the Corinthian community: "As often as you eat this bread and drink the cup, you proclaim the Lord's death until he comes" (I Cor. 11:26, RSV). The Christian community in its worship, especially in its eucharistic worship, manifests itself as that ship, making its perilous way across the deep, from the death and resurrection of its Lord to his return and victory. As Holy Scripture is the sole testimony to this journey's origins and endings, so the use of calendar-lectionary for the regular and weekly reading of that testimony in the community has become a kind of chronometer for that journey through time.

Because the Christian community relates in this way to time, it has found calendars and sequential systems for reading Scripture important, if not absolutely necessary. Indeed, the celebration of the passage and cycles of time has always been an essential ingredient of Christian worship. It is a way to recover key events in the past history of revelation. Thus James F. White comments in *New Forms of Worship:*

A basic assumption in Christian worship is that God has disclosed himself to man in past events occurring in the midst of history. Worship becomes a way of regaining the significance of those past events for our present life.[15]

This definition stands in need of some correction from the point of view of a future perspective. Prof. Paul L. Lehmann proposes that in the Christian story "the future shapes the present out of the past. . . . Destiny draws heritage into the human reality and meaning of experience, which is always a compound of happenings, hope and remembrance."[16] The celebration of time, temporal cycles, timely events, and the eventuality of time are all indigenous to Christian worship, as in fact they always were in its Jewish antecedents.

THE ARENA OF GOD'S ACTION

To understand the interaction between calendar and lectionary and the particularities of each, it is necessary to take serious measure of two aspects of the way in which "time" is defined in this context. In the Hebrew-Christian tradition, time and history are accepted as the arena of God's activity. The faith systems of the Old and the New Testament affirm time as the instrument of God's creative and redemptive purpose. It is not a goal of these systems to escape the temporal. This is distinctive from many world religions. In Greek thought, for example, redemption consists in being transferred from existence in this world, bound to the circular course of time, "into that Beyond which is removed from time and is already and always available."[17]

The very structure of creation, as told in Gen. 1:1 to 2:4a, is temporal: seven "days." Each day was "very good," the best being the seventh, the Sabbath. And, as Barth points out, each begins in darkness and ends in light ("evening and morning")—a distinctively joyful way of marking time. In this saga lies the primary temporal cycle of both the Jewish and the Christian tradition: it is the week, with its recurring Sabbath rest. "The biblical meaning of the *Sabbath* is given in Exodus (20:11) as a remembrance of God's resting after the creation, and in Deuteronomy (5:15) as a memorial of liberation from Egypt."[18] In its Christian translation to the first day of the week, "the earliest reason given for celebrating Sunday is that it is the day of the resurrection (*Ep. of Barnabas*, 15:9). . . . From early on too, Sunday has strong eschatological overtones: it is also the eighth day 'on which God inaugurated a new world' (*Ep. of Barnabas*, 15:8), 'the image of the age to come' (Basil, *de Spir. Sanct.* 27); it 'prefigures eternal rest' (Augustine)."[19]

Whatever the historical process whereby the church shifted its weekly celebration from the seventh day to the first, that extraordinary change may be understood within the totality of the Biblical witness. It may also provide us with considerable direction for our celebration of that weekly feast. Professor Barth puts this Old Testament–New Testament unity thus:

> If the Sabbath observed by God was the seventh day for Him, it was undoubtedly the first for man. Man's existence began with the fact that God kept this day, and that He ordained and blessed and sanctified it as a day to be kept by man. . . . What took place [in Christian chronology] was not an innovation but the discovery of the calculation which was already hidden in the calculation of Genesis 1-2*. When God has planned and done everything well in the creation of man and his world, and when He has associated Himself with His creature as the free and living God, then man in free and living fellowship with God can begin his course. What is ostensibly his first day is really (thanks to the preceding grace of God) his second day, and his first real day was really the "Lord's Day."[20]

Thus "day," the succession of days, and the weekly culmination of that succession on Sabbath-Sunday provide the Christian community with its basic occasion, to celebrate both creation and redemption in "rest, freedom, and joy."

This is not the place to enter upon an extended discussion of the other temporal cycle, that of the year (see "III. The Calendar"). It is enough to say here that there is one, for both Jews and Christians. The "natural" division of life and human existence into years is not ignored by these communities. A cycle of feasts and fasts grows up which, like the weekly festival, commemorates both creation and redemption. Central to the Jewish cycle is Passover-Pentecost ("Weeks") and by a historical-theological process similar to that involved in the Sabbath-Sunday shift, for the Christians an annual Easter-Pentecost cycle.

What does this pair of cycles, weekly and annual, tell us about how these traditions regard time? Their double orientation to origins and destiny, to creation and redemption, rules out a cyclical-fatalistic interpretation of time, as ascribed to Greek Platonic philosophy by Professor Cullmann. His alternative is to speak of a "time line" of which Christ is the "mid-point":

> The work of Christ is *primarily* the mid-point of a special happening or process which extends the length of the time line; this process, in the sense early Christianity gives to it, is to be designated as the Christ-process. In a *secondary* way, however, this process, for the Christian, is also the measuring standard of general, so-called "secular," history, which when seen in this light ceases to be secular to him.[21]

So Cullmann affirms a view of time and history for the Biblical tradition which is not circular but linear. Perhaps because his is a New Testament study Cullmann does not take into account the peculiar Old Testament witness which is written in a language that lacks such a linear element as tense (past, present, and future), and whose central temporal festivals, Sabbath and Passover, express a nonlinear immediacy to origins and ends. Passover, for instance, commemorates a past event (the exodus, ca. 1200 B.C.) by declaring that "this is the bread our fathers ate" and concludes with an eschatological affirmation, "Next year in Jerusalem!"[22] Past, present, and future seem to be immediate neighbors, and to play into one another in the midst of the community's liturgical moment. However well one may be able to make such distinctions in Greek, and thus to denominate "Jesus Christ, the same yesterday and today and for ever" (Heb. 13:8), at the center of the Biblical sense for time there seems to be a nonlinear immediacy of all time (which does not necessarily mean timelessness).

Time, particularly in Genesis, is the creation of God. It is his. To him, past, present, and future are equidistant: "For a thousand years in thy sight are but as yesterday when it is past, or as a watch in the night" (Ps. 90:4). Or as the church's annual Easter Vigil liturgy says, "Christ yesterday and today, the beginning and the end, Alpha and Omega; all time belongs to him and all the ages." Only to us, whose lives are measured by fleeting moments, hours, days, and years, time (chronos) may seem linear. To God, however, all time is equally present and immediate. More importantly, for God time (kairos) is "occasion" for decisive action and human response. Incarnation means that in the human being, Jesus of Nazareth, kairos intersects chronos in such a way that past and future become obsolescent categories having been replaced by "promise and fulfillment."

A CELEBRATING COMMUNITY

One further observation must be made. Time is neither circular nor simply linear; it is the "very good" occasion for the gracious intervention of God; it is the vehicle for promise and fulfillment. But for that to be experienced and communicated, there must be . . . the community. This view of time is corporate celebration. As Cullmann says:

> Thus in every Primitive Christian service of worship . . . Christ grants to his congregation assembled at table a survey of the interconnection of the entire redemptive process, and lets the Church share in its fruits.[23]

And again:

> In the Lord's Supper there is a pointing back to the Last Supper of Jesus before his death and to the Easter suppers that were eaten with the Risen One, and there is a pointing forward to the Messianic Banquet, which Christ will eat with his people in the Kingdom of God.[24]

The importance of the weekly assembly is to be found precisely in the Biblical "stories" of the creation and redemption it celebrates and retells in word and action.

This turns us to the unique definition of "time" involved in identifying resurrection and (messianic) return as events in time, for they too are realities which are only present to . . . the community.

The resurrection was not a public event. The return has no date fixed. In what possible sense can these events be called "temporal," "historical"? Only as they condition a historic community's pilgrimage through history.

According to the only witness we have, the documents of the New Testament, the appearances of the risen Christ were limited to a few persons. Most of them are named, but there was one appearance to "more than five hundred of the brothers at the same time" (I Cor. 15:6). Still the witnesses are "brothers," not random believers and unbelievers. So the resurrection may be described as a private rather than a public event, or better, as an event-in-community—that community which understands itself as "the body of Christ." This is not to say that the existence of the church "proves" the resurrection; it is to say, however, that "it is only the matching life of a community that makes it possible for the resurrection to be known."[25] The place and time in which that "knowledge" is embodied is in that Lord's Day assembly for the rehearsal of the Word and sharing of the Meal.

The resurrection was not a public event, although, in the faith of the church, it was constitutive of community. Lying at the origin-boundary of the community's history it is not part of that history (just as the seven "days" are the origin of human history but not part of that history). For the church after Pentecost "there was access only to the fact (of resurrection) as it had been experienced and believed by others, and as it was being enacted in the life of the believing community."[26]

That enactment of resurrection becomes part of human history as the community assembles on the first day for the Word and the Meal, and is sent out "into all the world" to baptize the nations. "The full observance of Sunday, therefore, implies three interdependent realities: religious time, an assembly, and the Eucharist."[27]

THE CHURCH'S TIME

The church's time, however, is the time between resurrection and the Messiah's return. The end of time is no less complex an issue than the resurrection. Our purpose in taking it up, however, is limited. We need only to reflect that the Lord's return has been no more public an event than was his resurrection.

Our concern is to sketch the shape that eschatology gives to the church's "time," its voyage over "the ocean a thousand fathoms deep." The church's self-understanding first develops in response to what must have been one of its most problematic questions: Why was the public return of the Lord delayed?

Even in I Thessalonians, that earliest epistle, the gap, if not contradiction, between the "already" and the "not yet" of the Lord's public *parousia*, begins to be bridged by a subtle combination of ethical and ecclesial emphases. Through these as well as the eucharist, the Christ of the cross and of the coming becomes present as a personal reality in the midst of the history of his people, that intergenerational and transgenerational community called the church.

Historically, I Thessalonians is recognized as the earliest composed book in the New Testament. This places it closer to the source than any other New Testament book. The nonoccurrence of the expected return of the Lord would be considerably more problematic after twenty years than after two hundred or two thousand years. This issue recurs throughout the letter as a result.

Thematically, the letter is doubly interesting. It gives an early look at the young Christian community, still close to its apostolic origins. It also provides us with some of Paul's most earnest pastoral discourse.

Liturgically, I Thessalonians is significant in its appearance in the three-year lectionary in Advent both in years B and C and "in course" for several Sundays in anticipation of Advent in year A.[28] Its relationship to Advent is by reason of its eschatological preoccupation.

I Thessalonians continues the Pauline expectation of the imminent return of the Lord (1:10; 3:13; 4:15-17; 5:2; 5:23). But it gives ample evidence of the difficulty the Lord's nonreturn is already creating. Paul is solicitous for the Thessalonians' "present troubles" (3:3) and "persecutions" (3:4). His instructions concerning "holiness" were being challenged in his absence (4:8). There were clearly questions arising about "those who have died" (4:13) and about "times and seasons" of the Day of the Lord (5:1-2).

These problems put to the church in Thessalonica precisely the question we are addressing: the *meaning* of the present *time* as an increasingly awkward "time between the times" of resurrection and return. How does Paul, the pastor-theologian, meet these problems and terrors?

In addition to numerous reassurances concerning his own affection for the community and his continuing confidence and pride in it there is a recurring exhortation to a particular trinity of gifts: faith, love, and hope. "We always mention you in our prayers and thank God for you all, and constantly remember before God our Father how you have shown your faith in action, worked for love and persevered through hope, in our Lord Jesus Christ" (1:2-3). This triad, placed at the very head of this early letter, led John Calvin to describe this salutation as "a brief definition of true Christianity."[29]

This triad of faith, love, and hope appears often in Paul's correspondence. The almost symphonic way in which it is used here requires that we take it seriously as a summary definition of the character of a true church. This provides content for the more difficult concept of "holiness" which is introduced at 4:3 and concluded at 5:23 ("perfect and holy"). That trinity of Christian virtues guarantees being "kept safe and blameless, spirit, soul and body, for the coming of our Lord Jesus Christ. God has called you and he will not fail you" (by failing to come?!) (5:23).

If that is Paul's ethical bridge between "already" and "not yet," what then is his ecclesial stance?

The first response to be made is to live in community in the exercise of the gifts of faith, love, and hope. This is to be the true church.

Paul goes further in spelling out the sort of relationships and common experiences that pertain to the true church. He testifies to his affection for them and his pride in them. This is balanced by testimony to their faithfulness to his example and teaching (1:2, 6; 2:1, 8, 11-12, 13, 19-20). He exhorts them to continue in this, but now in relation to "those who are [now] working among you and are [now] above you in the Lord as your teachers. Have the greatest respect and affection for them because of their work" (5:12-13). Thus in the Christian community there are (transferable) relationships of trust and teaching, of leading and following.

Secondly, the letter is liberally sprinkled with exhortations to express love within the community and to those without. That was in fact the ground of the concern for those who had died. The question had come to Paul concerning them, not out of grief or simple loss, but apparently from the concern that they might miss out on the Lord's return. Thus Paul assures them that "those who have died in Christ will be the first to rise" (4:16). "Meeting the Lord" will be "together with them" (4:17). And this section comes to its conclusion with the encouragement to "comfort one another" (4:18), whose verb "to comfort," "to encourage," "to console," occurs throughout the letter, as again at 5:11: "give encouragement to each other." And finally: "Be at peace among yourselves" (5:14). The picture emerges in as many metaphors as Paul can find that just as there is a certain kind of leadership love in the community, so also there is a rich peer affection which even transcends the boundary of death. Ecclesial reality is rooted already in *communio sanctorum*. It comes as no surprise then that the letter concludes with the rubric, "Greet all the brothers with the holy kiss" (5:26), the solemn instruction that "this letter is to be read to all the brothers" (5:27), and the greeting of the Lord's grace (5:28).

The presence of the awaited Lord is anticipated in the ethics and the order of the community, marked by the exercise of faith, love, and hope. That is Paul's "bridge over troubled waters" which, in Barth's phrase, are "a thousand fathoms deep."

For the church of Jesus Christ, time is the instrument and the arena within which its Lord becomes present to it. That time within which it lives is neither a fatalistic circle nor an endless, aimless line, because it is bounded immediately by the Lord's resurrection and return. These events themselves partake of that dialectical nature of being in time but not of it, events that are not public so much as events-in-community, or, to put it another way, events that are "already" events-in-community but "not yet" public.

These dialectics underlie the historic cycles of Sunday and the feasts of the Christian year. It must be remembered, therefore, that these two cycles are not, nor have they ever been, simply mechanisms for introducing "special days and months and seasons and years" (Gal. 4:10). Each cycle, in its own way, has functioned as a means whereby the community, in its regular and repeated assembling, celebrates the peculiar kind of time characteristic of its life, defined by creation and redemption, and bounded by resurrection and return. Thus, its calendars, weekly and annual, were the occasion of the systematic and obedient reading of the Word as the witness to creation and redemption, resurrection and return, and the repeated celebration of the Table, the corporate enactment of that "history." Thus do we turn now to those calendars, and to the lectionary itself.

III. THE CALENDAR

In the formation of the Christian calendar two cycles claim attention: the weekly cycle of Sunday to Sunday and the annual cycle

which centers on Christmas and Easter. The former is clearly the
older, and, in that sense at least, prior in significance. The Second
Vatican Council solemnly observed that Sunday "is the foundation
and kernel of the whole liturgical year."[30]

The sequence of Sundays is itself a calendar, a cycle, with its own
integrity and theological significance. As the church's principal
calendar it must be protected both from cultural confusions and from
other cycles which the church itself may celebrate.

Perhaps an even greater threat is the addition of civic and
denominational "days and seasons." A look at any clergy's desk or
pocket calendar will reveal an incredible combination of national,
regional, and denominational celebrations. However worthy these
may be, the question must be asked, Should such emphases be
allowed to infringe upon the church's weekly resurrection celebration
and its annual progression of Christological feasts? Trivial tampering
with the church's time "between resurrection and return" requires
that we take seriously these two basic cycles, forming one calendar:
Sunday, and the Christian Year. So we examine each, in turn.

The Sunday Cycle

The Sunday assembly is central for the life of the church. That
assembly has consistently occurred throughout the centuries which
link the church to the days of its Lord. Yet our minds are dull to the
singular meaning of that assembly.

What this meeting means in its weekly recurrence has been
powerfully expressed by our own generation's most prolific Reformed
theologian, Karl Barth, of Basel:

> The work of construction in which the community is the true Church is
> at its centre. . . . This work is its common worship. It is not only in
> worship that the community is edified and edifies itself. But it is here
> first that this continually takes place. And if it does not take place here, it
> does not take place anywhere. . . . Assembling for divine worship is
> self-evidently the centre and presupposition of the whole Christian life,
> the atmosphere in which it is lived.[31]

Every pastor knows this, and is only tempted to forget it in the
performance of clerical chores. Whatever else happens in the course
of the week, that assembly will recur. Every denomination, with
whatever discipline it has, requires that this meeting recur. Our
Presbyterian standards are quite clear. The Presbyterian Church in the
U.S. states:

> From the days of the Apostles, Christians have observed the first day of
> the week as the Christian Sabbath because on it our Lord Jesus Christ was
> raised from the dead. . . . The people are to abstain from all unnecessary
> labor, and from recreation which violates or interferes with the character
> of the day. . . . They should so arrange their affairs and so use their
> influence that no one will be kept unnecessarily from the public worship

of God and the proper use of the Lord's Day. . . . It is the privilege and obligation of all the people of God on the Lord's Day to participate in the public worship of God.[32]

However much we might want to question the terminology "Christian Sabbath" and the equal pairing of rest and worship as the day's purpose, we can hardly miss the centrality of the celebration in the Directory's view. The Directory for the Worship of God of The United Presbyterian Church in the U.S.A. takes a more directly liturgical and New Testament stance:

Christians can worship God at any time, for all time has been redeemed by him. Their special time of corporate worship is, however, on the Lord's Day, when they commemorate Christ's resurrection. Every public service of worship witnesses to God's continuing power over sin and death.[33]

The difference between these two statements take us to the heart of the question concerning the relationship of the church's first day assembly to the Jewish Sabbath. It will help in providing perspective to recall how the New Testament's epistles, especially those of Paul and Hebrews, deal with the church's relationship to Israel. Just to remember the dialectical way in which tradition has related Gospel and Law, New Testament and Old, is to get some sense for the delicacy of the matter of Sabbath and Sunday. Professor McArthur tackles this issue at the very outset of his study *The Evolution of the Christian Year*:

The Lord's Day, the first day of the week, is the foundation of the entire structure. . . . It is important to notice that the Lord's Day is not the Sabbath. Yet it is the Sabbath which provides the background for the revolutionary development.[34]

The two categories of rest and of worship provide us with a convenient way of describing the meaning of the Sabbath (literally, "seventh") for Judaism of Jesus' day. The Sabbath rest was understood to be commemorative both of creation and of redemption:

Remember the sabbath day and keep it holy. . . . For in six days the Lord made the heavens and the earth and the sea and all that these hold, but on the seventh day he rested; that is why the Lord has blessed the sabbath day and made it sacred. (Ex. 20:8, 11)

And:

Observe the sabbath day and keep it holy, as the Lord your God has commanded you. . . . Remember that you were a servant in the land of Egypt, and that the Lord your God brought you out from there with mighty hand and outstretched arm; because of this, the Lord your God has commanded you to keep the sabbath day. (Deut. 5:12, 15)

The Sabbath was celebrated in acts of worship both domestically and in synagogue services beginning on Friday night at sundown and continuing until sundown on Saturday. Domestic rites included special prayers and blessings at the Friday evening meal, an occasion of particular joy as the Sabbath is welcomed. And "attendance at the Synagogue on Sabbath for the hearing of Scripture lections and sermons, as well as prayer and praise, was incumbent on all Jews."[35] This Sabbath synagogue assembly had not only commemorative significance, but also, as it recurred week by week, anticipatory and eschatological meaning. "In the thought of the Rabbis, the Sabbath is of the essence of the world to come; or, to express the relationship in another way, the world to come is a day that is all Sabbath."[36]

It is not our purpose to trace the relationship between the synagogue service and later Christian worship, although the parallelism between the synagogue Service of the Word—readings, psalmody, sermon, and prayers—and the first half of the Christian Lord's Day service is suggestive enough. Nor is it possible with certainty to describe the precise process whereby the early Christian church, largely Jewish, moved away from its Jewish seventh day to a once each Lord's Day celebration. It is known from New Testament evidence that Jesus and his disciples were faithful in their synagogue attendance on the Sabbath. The early church, including Paul, for a time continued to relate to the synagogue, at least until relationships between the two communities became strained after the destruction of the Temple in A.D. 70. Even then the Sabbath continued as a specific day on the weekly Christian calendar even though increasingly the first day, the Lord's Day with its assembly, becomes dominant. Professor McArthur sums up much of this development in this way:

> The profound revolution which substituted the Christian Sunday for the Jewish Sabbath took place within the first generation of the Church's life. Certainly by the middle of the sixth decade of that century when Paul, writing to the Church at Corinth, refers casually to "the first day of every week" (1 Cor. 16:2), the Lord's Day must long have been supreme.[37]

The etymological evidence for linking Sunday to resurrection lies in the earliest designation for Sunday, in the New Testament; that designation is found in Rev. 1:10, "the Lord's Day" (hē kyriakē hēmera). The only other occurrence of kyriakos is in I Cor. 11:20 in the phrase to kyriakon deipnon, "the Lord's Supper." This conjunction is echoed in the Didache: "On the Lord's day assemble and break bread and give thanks"[38] as well as by Justin and other patristic sources. This brings to mind the meal symbolism involved in the resurrection appearances of the Lord, which the Gospel narratives carefully relate to "the first day of the week." Attention also should be drawn to Paul's injunction to the setting aside of offerings for the saints "every Sunday" (I Cor. 16:2) and the account in Acts concerning his lengthy sermon at Troas which took place "on the first day of the week [when] we met to break bread" (Acts 20:7).

Professor Rordorf links these early ecclesial celebrations with the Last Supper of Jesus and his disciples by way of the Easter appearance meals. Had not those meals been the formative tradition in the church's later first day "breaking of bread" it might reasonably be expected that the Last Supper tradition would have been carried forward on Thursday nights, if weekly, or on the 15th Nisan (the date of Passover), if annually. So, Rordorf concludes, "everything, therefore, seems to indicate that the origin of the observance of Sunday is to be traced directly to the Easter event."[39]

This being the case, even to describe Sunday as a "little Easter" is to get the relationship between the weekly and the annual calendars quite backward. Easter is a "big Sunday," as Sunday is clearly the primitive and prior resurrection celebration, but since it is a weekly event rather than an annual event, it occurs within the ancient Jewish seven-day cycle of creation, redemption, and (messianic) return typology. It is not simply an annual historical commemoration. It makes of resurrection, therefore, not just a speculative event in or above history but a central event-experience for the community whose "Sabbath" is rooted in creation and whose "Sabbath rest" is expressive of eschatological fulfillment.

Another conclusion bears directly upon the character of the sacrament-meal as we have come to celebrate it in the Western and Protestant churches. This primary signification of resurrection-return contrasts sharply with the dominant theme of sin-crucifixion-death which we associate with the meal. This is precisely the rationale for the eucharistic "Service for the Lord's Day" in The Worshipbook (pp. 25-38) in the way the "Invitation to the Lord's Table" is worded. Whereas all classic Reformed rites have included the Pauline Words of Institution from I Corinthians 11 at this point, as a "warrant" for the rite, The Worshipbook substitutes for "I received from the Lord . . ." two other Scriptural passages: Luke 13:29—"They will come from east and west, and from north and south, and sit at table in the kingdom of God"—and a paraphrase of Luke 24:30-31—"When our risen Lord was at table with his disciples, he took the bread, and blessed and broke it, and gave it to them. And their eyes were opened and they recognized him."[40]

Thus The Worshipbook's eucharistic rite introduces the central act of thanksgiving over bread and wine with Scriptural allusions to messianic return (Luke 13:29) and the Lord's resurrection (Luke 24). It reserves the use of the Pauline words from I Corinthians 11 regarding the Lord's betrayal and death until that point in the service when bread is to be broken and the cup shared, since those words directly refer to the symbolism of those actions.

Some practical suggestions might be in order concerning contemporary celebration of the weekly Sunday cycle. The shift of theological focus in the eucharistic liturgy just mentioned has a whole host of implications for the style and mood of our Communion services. An entirely new perspective is thereby provided for such questions as appropriate music, use of color, lights, vestments, presence of children, posture of reception, and the time of the celebration. The time of the resurrection is given in the Gospels as dawn, not 11:00 A.M. Further, the resurrection meals of the early church were evening events; the shift of the eucharist to early morning by the time of Justin is yet another obscure historical development. This does suggest that as cultural conditions change we might want again to think of an evening assembly, either on Sunday as in the New Testament and postapostolic periods, or on Saturday as in much of the Roman Catholic Church today (since in Jewish chronology, Saturday evening is part of the "vigil" of Sunday).

Another implication is the clear significance of meeting, assembling. The meal is vital and so is the architecture, membership, inclusiveness, and mood of the service. The fact that American Protestantism in our day has had to create yet another "minor order" of ecclesiastical office known as "Greeters" indicates how far we are from that central Sunday sacramental meeting. The Quakers have at least kept the word: the Meeting, and the Meeting House. Further, we now find it necessary to engage in an incredibly impersonal "signing of the roll" as a "ritual of friendship." Another sign that all semblance of interpersonal care and responsibility for one another as co-participants in the meeting has either been lost or shifted to the clerical staff (in both meanings of that word: secretarial and ordained).

Finally, to return to the venerable Calvin, the meal must be recovered as the only possible way to fulfill this central and most historic reality of the community of Christ: its commitment to come together "next Sunday." The Lord's Day requires the Lord's Supper. Otherwise, the Day becomes a solemn "bore" and the Supper becomes an occasional "embellishment" to worship. This is what has happened to Reformed worship in our time because of the breakdown of much of what has here been described as the foundation of the Christian year, the weekly celebration of Sunday.

The Annual Cycle

Perhaps the most important single characteristic of the annual calendar presupposed by the ecumenical lectionary is its Christological center. The annual sequence of seasons is actually a pairing of two Christ-celebrations: (1) Christmas and (2) Easter, (1) Incarnation and (2) Redemption. The Christmas celebration is prepared for in Advent and reflected in Epiphany. The Easter celebration is prepared for in Lent and reflected in the fifty days following, which climax in Pentecost. In this sense the Christian Year may be described as the annual rehearsal of the history of our salvation accomplished in the birth, death, resurrection, and return of Jesus Christ.

The Christological center as set forth by the twin foci of Christmas and Easter is yet another point at which the lectionary conforms to explicit constitutional provisions of both the Presbyterian Church in the U.S. and The United Presbyterian Church in the U.S.A. In Chapter 2 of the Presbyterian Church in the U.S. *Directory for the Worship and Work of the Church* the following paragraph occurs:

> It is appropriate that the worship of the Church provide occasion for recalling the birth of our Lord Jesus Christ, his death, resurrection, ascension and coming again, and the sending of the Holy Spirit.[41]

The Directory for the Worship of God of the United Presbyterian Church is even more explicit:

> Although the fullness of the gospel should be expressed in every service of the Word, some special seasons which are appropriate for observance in the public worship of God are: the season of Advent, wherein the Church remembers the coming of Christ and looks forward to his coming again; Christmas, wherein the incarnation is celebrated in the festival of the birth of Christ; the season of Epiphany, wherein God's gift of himself to all of humanity is revealed; the season of Lent culminating in Holy Week, wherein the Church, in joy and sorrow, proclaims, remembers, and responds to the atoning death of Christ; Easter, wherein the resurrection of Christ from the dead is celebrated; ascension, wherein the Church affirms that Jesus Christ is Lord of all times and of all places; and Pentecost, wherein Christians rejoice in the gift of the Holy Spirit to the Church.[42]

It should be noted that the so-called Christian "Year" is really only half of a year. If Advent be taken as its beginning, December may be said to be its first calendar month. The other end of the Christian Year, regulated by the movable date of Easter, is the Day of Pentecost. Since Easter cannot occur after April 25, Pentecost cannot occur after June 13. The Sundays that follow the fifty days, numbered "after Pentecost" or "after Trinity" for convenience' sake, are not properly a season of Pentecost or of the Holy Spirit. No lectionary has ever tried to identify such a large number of lessons from Old and New Testaments which specifically refer to the Holy Spirit. At best one could denominate these weeks as the new *Lutheran Book of Worship* does, "The Time of the Church."[43] This period is really not a season. It has no theme as have Advent, Christmastide, and Lent. These summer and fall Sundays are ordinary Sundays. This explains why the Pentecost color of red is not carried through this sequence of Sundays following Pentecost. Green is designated the color,[44] since that has historically been the "ferial" (ordinary) color.

However closely one follows the seasons and lections of the Christian "Year," there is an extended period of time (June through November) to structure the Biblical and homiletical content of worship otherwise, if one wishes. Our lectionary does fill out all those

Sundays, and does so according to a careful scheme, so it may profitably be followed if one wishes. The point is that even the careful use of the Christian Year does not lock up the entire Biblical and preaching ministry of the church.

Christmas and Easter, the two centers of the Christian Year, developed rather independently and at different times and places. Their origins provide a picture of the ancient church, moving out of its Jewish, Middle Eastern milieu into a Gentile, cosmopolitan context. The origins of the Easter cycle are much embedded in Jewish history and liturgical custom. The origins of the Christmas cycle are related to a more secular, if not pagan, calendar having to do with the winter solstice.

Let us look first at the Passover-Easter cycle.

The Easter Cycle

In our present calendar this cycle includes the six weeks of Lent (starting with Ash Wednesday and including Holy Week), the seven weeks of Eastertide (formerly "Pentecost"), and the Day of Pentecost. This structure, however, is the product of a long and complicated historical process which combined several strands of tradition. To understand the lectionary's proposals for these seasons, it is necessary to disentangle some of that history. There are four strands which must be identified: (1) the establishment of a primitive annual Christian Passover of approximately twenty-four hours' duration, (2) the addition of a preparatory fasting period which became "forty days," (3) the elaboration of the Passover celebration for a fifty-day period culminating in an Ascension-Pentecost Day, and (4) the spread throughout the Christian world of a special set of services observed in Jerusalem during the week before the Christian Passover which came to be known as Holy Week.

By no means did these developments occur sequentially, or in the same way in every place. For the most concise summary of that whole process, see A. Allan McArthur's definitive work *The Evolution of the Christian Year*.

For the sake of trying to make a complex subject understandable we will use the Greek word *pascha* to refer to the whole festival that celebrates Christ's suffering and death. *Pascha* may be used as a noun to refer to the Jewish Passover (its original meaning) and to the Christian festival; or as an adjective to refer to the lamb used in the Jewish festival ("paschal lamb") or to the meal ("paschal meal") which characterized both the Jewish and the Christian festival.

1. The Establishment of the Pascha

The death and resurrection of Christ are described in the Gospels in a profoundly paschal context. The Passover Hallel Psalm 118 was used at the entry into Jerusalem (Matt. 21:9); the Synoptics explicitly designate the Last Supper as a Passover meal (Matt. 26:19 and parallels); and there are passing references to related legislation and custom (Matt. 26:5; 27:15 and parallels).

Although the Fourth Gospel assigns the Supper to the day before Passover, the "Preparation Day" (John 13:1; 19:14), the paschal context remains. Allan McArthur has surmised that the shift may be read as a deliberate device to strengthen the paschal symbolism bringing Christ's crucifixion and the slaughter of the paschal lambs in the Temple into temporal juxtaposition.[45]

The Passover was Israel's annual remembrance of the exodus, a celebration of corporate identity, redemption, and hope. It was celebrated by rites in the Temple and a domestic meal of great joy at which the narrative of the exodus was rehearsed. Although there is no clear New Testament reference to a continuing Christian annual celebration, there is a suggestive word of Paul to the church at Corinth: "Christ, our passover, has been sacrificed; let us celebrate the feast, then, by getting rid of all the old yeast of evil and wickedness, having only the unleavened bread of sincerity and truth" (I Cor. 5:7).

By the early part of the third century clear references and discussions of the annual Pascha, which had already become the occasion for baptism, are to be found. It was celebrated in the East on 14 Nisan (the old Passover date) but elsewhere on the Saturday night–Sunday immediately following. It was an all-night vigil which celebrated the redemption bought by the death and resurrection of Christ. It included both Baptism and the Supper, together with extensive Scripture readings and possibly a service of lights. At least until the latter part of the fourth century there was no distinction between Friday (as a commemoration of the cross) and the Pascha (as celebration of death-resurrection), which was a unitive festival commemorating both the cross and the resurrection. Dom Gregory Dix summarizes the early development of this festival:

> The primitive Pascha has therefore the character of a liturgy of "Redemption" rather than a commemoration of the historical fact of the resurrection of Jesus, such as Easter has with us. . . . The life, death, resurrection and ascension—the paschal sacrifice—of Jesus was, of course, the means by which this redemption was achieved. "In Him" every christian had gone free from slavery to time and sin and death. But these events of the passion, resurrection and ascension did not stand isolated in primitive christian thought.[46]

This might recall our own comments earlier on the particular sort of "time" which characterizes the church's life between resurrection and return, and the coordinate observation that this "time" can only be celebrated in corporate, sacramental assembly. Thus it was that this Paschal Vigil "combined the commemoration of both the death and the resurrection of Christ and the celebration of both baptism and the Eucharist."[47]

2. The "Forty Days"

The earliest references to a forty-day fasting period leading to the Pascha are from the fourth century (Council of Nicaea, A.D. 325; *Festal Letters* of Athanasius, ca. A.D. 330; and *Catechetical Lectures* of Cyril of Jerusalem, A.D. 348). These suggest that the forty-day fast "was meant to apply not only to the candidates [for baptism] but to the Church as a whole. . . . It is quite possible that in practice only the candidates, who were under discipline, and also the more devoted members of the Church . . . observed the whole period of fasting."[48] This way of seeing the "forty days" reverses our later Lenten preoccupation with personal piety and penitence. This ancient practice has much more to do with the solidarity of the Christian community in its sacramental life and with its relationship to society as symbolized in the catechumens. Thus Dr. McArthur says:

> The Church member was expected to approach the Pascha each year in the way he had done when he himself was solemnly preparing for his Baptism.[49]

The Worshipbook reflects this recall of baptism by each member of the church in a prayer provided for the intercessions at baptism:

> Holy God: remind us of the promises given in our own baptism, and renew our trust in you. Make us strong to obey your will, and to serve you with joy; for the sake of Jesus Christ our Lord. Amen.[50]

3. "Pentecost" as the Fifty Days after Pascha

In yet another semantic shift, the "oldest season of the Church's year,"[51] the fifty days after the Pascha, has become our "Eastertide." The more primitive title, Pentecost, is derived from the Jewish festival from which the Christian observance descends. Second only to Passover was the Feast of Weeks (a "week of weeks": 49 days plus 1). Like Passover, it was initially a harvest festival which gathered to itself the historic commemoration of the giving of the Law on Sinai. This provides us with the basis for understanding the use made of the Jewish occasion by the church:

> As the Old Covenant, ratified in the Exodus which the Passover commemorated, was completed on Mount Sinai, so the New Covenant, ratified in the events which the Christian Pascha commemorated, the Cross and the Resurrection, was completed on the festival of Pentecost when the power of the Holy Spirit came upon the disciples of the Lord. So the Christian Pentecost was the birthday of the Church as the new Israel of God.[52]

This season was marked by such joy that the Council of Nicaea "forbade kneeling in prayer 'in the days of Pentecost,' "[53] as that posture was a sign of penitence. It was also forbidden to fast during these days. The instruction of the catechumens was completed so they could then be "let in" on the secrets of the sacraments which had been withheld from them during their pre-baptismal instruction.

This Christian appropriation of the Jewish Pentecost is given expression in Acts 2. The Jewish feast spoke of the gift of the law on Sinai; Acts 2 speaks of the gift of the Spirit in Jerusalem. The Law was given to Israel; the Spirit to "every nation" (Acts 2:5). All Israel was present at Sinai, so on the Day of Pentecost "Peter stood up with the Eleven" (2:14) and added the prophet's word (Joel) to the celebration of the law (Moses). The chapter concludes with the baptism of three thousand and a summary description of the common life of the church, the new Israel (vs. 42-47).

These fifty days were as clear a symbolization of the fulfilled time of the Messiah as church law and liturgics could provide. Resurrection to Return was the message of this perfect and perfected "time of the church." If the Saturday preceding the Pascha (the completion of the "forty days" fast) was the "great Sabbath," then "Pentecost" (the fifty days) was the "great Sunday." Again we discover the symbolic primacy of the weekly cycle wherein Sabbath becomes Sunday.

4. Holy Week

In the context of the pattern thus far described, Holy Week is a "late" and rather "incongruous" addition. Holy Week's presuppositions are both historically and geographically foreign to the paschal complex. Holy Week introduces a literal daily historicism of Entry-Supper-Crucifixion-Entombment-Resurrection, on the basis of "stational" services celebrated in the Holy City Jerusalem in the fourth century. "Now for the first time we find Palm Sunday and Good Friday."[54] The Spanish nun, Egeria, describes the ceremonies celebrated at the holy sites in Jerusalem in a most convincing way. As a result, these services began to appear throughout the Western world, even though the physical stations in Jerusalem were absent. The rise of Holy Week celebrations testifies to the development of worship as a dramatic remembrance of past, historic events rather than as a participation by corporate and sacramental means in an unfolding, eschatologically oriented new age.

This somewhat literalist preoccupation has given us a "forty days" that begins on Wednesday (Ash Wednesday), whereas for centuries Lent began on a Monday. Palm Sunday becomes preoccupied with the "triumphal entry," making it a little Easter rather than an entry into the Passion. Maundy Thursday is guilt-ridden by its preoccupation with betrayal. We have a Good Friday of unrelieved gloom, an empty Saturday, an Easter Day preoccupied with an empty tomb.

This is the historical and theological background to modern efforts to revise the celebration of Passiontide and Holy Week. The Roman Church, for example, has conflated Passion Sunday and Palm Sunday. Formerly Passion Sunday began a two-week intensification of Lent in which Palm Sunday was actually the Second Sunday of

Passiontide, but which, in nonliturgical churches, had lost all relationship to the Passion by reason of its dramatic rehearsal of the triumphal entry of the Lord into Jerusalem. By conflating the two Sundays, Palm Sunday regains its relationship to the Passion. For a more thorough discussion of this day, together with a suggested order of worship, the reader is referred to this writer's contributions to *Reformed Liturgy and Music*, Vol. XII, No. 4 (Fall 1977).[55]

The historicism of Holy Week, which has become a distinct liability in an age not characterized by weekday worship, needs the correction of tradition's wisdom regarding the Sunday before Easter as a Passiontide occasion. Basically, that means reading one of the Passion narratives, in its entirety, on that Sunday, reducing the palm procession to an entry rite.

The one proposal that transcends all others, however, is that the Vigil of Easter, i.e., the primitive Pascha, be recovered. Far better this early celebration of redemption Holy Saturday, the "Great Sabbath," than a romantic, dramatic appropriation of the discredited Roman Tenebrae on Thursday or Friday! Excellent orders for the Great Vigil of Easter are found in *The Book of Common Prayer* of the Protestant Episcopal Church (1979) (pp. 284-295) and the *Lutheran Book of Worship*, Ministers Edition (pp. 143-153).

The Paschal Vigil lies at the heart of all Christian worship. It deserves a revival. Its revival would provide two Easter essentials now often missing: (1) a fully sacramental and evangelical Christian celebration (in contrast to the usual Easter morning festival of loud music and loud apparel), and (2) an evangelical alternative to nature-oriented sunrise services. Its magnificent multilayered symbolism of darkness-light, fast-feast, death-life, baptism-eucharist, and Biblical readings covering the entire sweep of salvation history, immerses the congregation in the infinitely greater drama of creation-resurrection-return. It is not by chance that Easter Vigil is called "the mother of feasts."

THE CHRISTMAS CYCLE

Among Western Christians, Christmas seems to be the true "mother of feasts." At least, it is the most popular. However many reasons there may be for this, prominent among them must be the fact that the central commemoration of Christmas is an event close to humanity: a birth. Affection for that sort of commemoration can hardly be written off as sentimentalism: therein lies the secret power of the doctrine of incarnation. The origins of December 25 as the Festival of the Birth of Jesus Christ lie in what might be called "folk religion." December 25 in Rome, where Christmas originated (sometime between A.D. 274 and A.D. 336)[56] was the winter solstice and was popularly observed as the birthday of the sun. This might suggest that the Christian festival was either a missionary device or a defensive mechanism. It has been pointed out, however, that the theological conception of Christ as the Light shining in darkness does not derive from the pagan background of 25th December. . . . Its true origin is in the New Testament when theological reflection turns to the Incarnation, especially in the first chapter of St. John's Gospel.[57]

January 6, the solstice in the East, reminds us that there is in the calendar a somewhat puzzling "doublet" of Christmas: Epiphany. Our traditional practice in the West of assigning that day to the Magi strains even the historical credulity of little children. Whence this feast?

Its Greek name suggests an origin east of Rome. McArthur posits such in the Constantinople, Asia Minor, Antioch region, but considerably earlier than Christmas. He does so by an ingenious and complex analysis of patristic lectionaries and sermons which seem to " converge on John 1:1 - 2:11,"[58] including themes of Christ as light, his coming into the world and baptism, and turning water into wine.

According to McArthur, this "unitive" festival of incarnation begins to break down by the introduction into the East of the Western Christmas (by A.D. 380). This introduction was probably related to the Christological controversies of the time and in particular the necessity of balancing birth and baptism as a line of defense against Adoptionism.

A reverse process may have been responsible for the Eastern Epiphany migrating to the regions of North Italy, Gaul, and Spain and the West, from which Rome received only one of its components: the Magi.

One further detail is necessary in order to account for Advent as a preparatory season: In the East, Epiphany became a normal day for baptism, while in the West, baptism was never administered then. In Gaul, however, which was much influenced by the East, from Christmas to Epiphany did become a baptismal season. It is significant that in Gaul "we first hear of a forty-day period of preparation for it,"[59] parallel of course with the Lenten preparation for the Easter baptisms.

Evidence of Advent is found as early as the sixth century and becomes more universal, in the West, in the seventh and eighth centuries. It varies in length from three to six Sundays, the majority of instances being of six or five Sundays. And even though the present Western Advent is but four Sundays, it will be noticed that the lections for the latter Sundays "after Pentecost" tend to anticipate the Second Coming and thus provide just such a lengthened "Advent."

Advent's historic theme has been eschatology, not, as one hears these days, "getting ready for Christmas." In striking confirmation of this, one often finds in early lectionaries Advent listed at the end of the "year," with Christmas as the starting point. This raises again the radically eschatological character of the church's definition of "time."

Even at the "beginning" of the church's "year" Advent introduces the particular and peculiar ways the Christian community thinks of Christ's time, and ours. To *begin* a year reflecting about the *end* of years is deeply expressive of the revolutionary attitude the church takes toward time and history, its own history as well.

The Advent-Christmas-Epiphany cycle, like the Lent-Easter-Pentecost cycle, is both historical and theological, commemorative and eschatological. It speaks of history and of hope. It has done so, and continues to do so, in a variety of ways. Certain variants need our attention. The season of "Kingdomtide" is widely used in the United Methodist Church to deal with the fact that the beginning of Advent is not the beginning of the congregation's year. Kingdomtide may be seen as theologically related to Advent's eschatological thrust and as historically an extension of Advent backward even beyond its early six-week length. In the end it may be best not to assign a season to the Kingdom, but rather to let the Second Coming lections provide their suggestive transition from "after Pentecost" to "before Christmas" as in the ecumenical lectionary.

Another designation that creates an ecumenical problem in coordinating use of the lectionary is the Roman Catholic Church's terminology for the Sundays after Epiphany and Pentecost as "Sundays of the Year" (*Dominicae per annum*). The intention was to suggest that Sunday is itself a worthy festival, whether or not it is part of an annual cycle. These "Sundays of the Year" together with the use of the First Sunday after Epiphany for lections concerning the Baptism of the Lord, and the Last Sunday after Epiphany for the Transfiguration, throw the Roman lections out of synchronization with the Presbyterian and Lutheran "after Pentecost" readings. The Consultation on Common Texts is seeking a method of resolving this situation.

Finally, a word about the Twelve Days of Christmas, from December 25 to January 6. Aside from the secular carol concerning the "partridge in the pear tree" a wealth of Christian symbolism associated with these days can enrich an evangelical celebration of this season. The Roman calendar, shared largely by the Episcopal and Lutheran churches, includes the following observances:

> December 26—St. Stephen, Deacon and Martyr
> December 27—St. John, Apostle and Martyr
> December 28—The Holy Innocents, Martyrs
> January 1　—Solemnity of Mary, Mother of God (Roman Catholic)
> 　　　　　　The Name of Jesus (Episcopal and Lutheran)

These feasts, though not traditionally part of Reformed consciousness, might function powerfully to preserve the evangelical integrity of what is clearly a popular and even secular folk festival, Christmas, and to illuminate what is at the same time a puzzling and obscure remnant of a festival, Epiphany.

The deepest significance of any of the church's annual festivals lies in the Biblical lections for which those festivals are the occasion. In the conjunction of calendar and lectionary lies the secret of the sanctification of time: the sanctification of our time by the "time of the church," between resurrection and return. So now we take up the lectionary.

IV. THE LECTIONARY

Calvin contends, "Wherever we see the word of God sincerely preached and heard . . . there we cannot have any doubt that the Church of God has some existence."[60] If this is so, a system of some sort for the choice of Scripture to be read and expounded would be essential. The church has produced such systems throughout its history. They are known as "lectionaries."

Lectionaries, as we have noted earlier, have been of two sorts: *lectio selecta*, wherein the readings were selected from all the books of the Bible according to thematic or calendar concerns, and *lectio continua*, wherein the readings follow one another, Sunday by Sunday, in continuous sequence through an entire book or books of the Bible. This latter system was clearly in force in the earliest centuries of the church as witnessed, for example, by Justin Martyr.

Quite clearly a different method finally prevailed in the Roman rite of the West: the *lectio selecta*. This became one of the points of divergence between the Reformed and other Reformation churches, such as the Lutheran, as well as with the Roman Church: "Zurich, Basel, Strasbourg, and Geneva all adopted the *lectio continua* at an early date in the Reformation and it is unquestionably one of the most clear restorations of the form of worship of the early Church."[61] In Scotland, "the practice was established of reading the Scriptures in course."[62] This was continued by the *Westminster Directory* (1644-45):

> How large a portion shall be read at once, is left to the wisdome of the Minister: But it is convenient that ordinarily one Chapter of each Testament bee read at every meeting; and sometimes more, where the Chapters be short, or the coherence of matter requireth it.
>
> It is requisite that all the Canonical books bee read over in order, that the people may be better acquainted with the whole Body of the Scriptures: And ordinarily, where the Reading in either Testament endeth on one Lords day, it is to begin the next.[63]

Although this implies that the number of lections has now reached a minimum of two, one from each of the Testaments, it does perpetuate the ancient practice of continuous reading. Even the discretion of the minister is not allowed to intrude upon that Biblical integrity.

Reformed churches today have largely abandoned anything like "in course" reading. By individual ministerial authority a succession of "selected" readings are chosen. Thus, the Roman *selecta* system is delivered into the hands of the preacher with little or no guidance from the church. Further, as expository preaching has given way to topical methods, and the number of readings has often fallen to one each Sunday, all pretense of a systematic reading of the Scriptures has disappeared from normative Lord's Day worship in Reformed churches.

One other aspect of this unfortunate process whereby the Bible has been almost lost to public worship has been the disuse of the Psalter. Authorities testify to the early and continuing use of sung psalmody as interventions in the succession of readings, Old and New Testament. The recovery of the Psalter as a corporate, sung experience was one of the great achievements of both the Reformed and the Lutheran churches. The Scottish metrical Psalter formed the core of praise for the early American Presbyterian church, before the controversial adoption of Watts's paraphrases. At that time (the middle of the eighteenth century) opponents warned that the introduction of "hymns of human composure" would ultimately displace the metrical Psalter. Only six strictly metrical psalms are included in *The Worshipbook* (1972). The absence of a printed Psalter in *The Worshipbook* would seem to signal the nadir of this development among us. *The Book of Common Prayer* of the Protestant Episcopal Church (1979), on the other hand, offers the Psalter in a new translation, also adopted by the *Lutheran Book of Worship*.

The *continua* system as well as sung psalmody having been lost, the use of the Scriptures in worship was entirely at the discretion of the minister and often limited to one lesson together with a responsive reading. This is not to say that guidance was totally unavailable: it was simply not used. All editions of the Presbyterian *Book of Common Worship* from 1932 on included both calendar and suggested lectionaries.

The intent of the Second Vatican Council in producing a lectionary, as stated in the Constitution on the Sacred Liturgy, applies in large measure to our own Reformed situation:

> The treasures of the Bible are to be opened up more lavishly so that a richer fare may be provided for the faithful at the table of God's word. In this way a more representative part of the sacred scriptures will be read to the people in the course of a prescribed number of years.[64]

The function of a weekly Sunday lectionary is to relate the "time of the church," between resurrection and return (spelled out in the annual cycles of Christmas and Easter), to the "time of salvation" (spelled out by the systematic reading and preaching of Holy Scripture). The question is: How does *this* lectionary serve that function? What are its controlling principles of selection and arrangement? Answers to these two questions will provide concrete guidance on how to use this lectionary as a fully evangelical source for preaching and instruction in the faith.

RATIONALE FOR THE READINGS

The lectionary provides three readings for every Sunday over a three-year period. The three readings are drawn respectively from the Old Testament, the Epistles (and Revelation), and the Gospels. This is to provide a witness to "the unity of the Old and New Testaments and the continuity of the work of salvation: it is announced and initiated in the Old Testament, it reaches its full realization in the paschal mystery of Christ, and through the apostolic preaching reaches all the generations of man."[65]

The main consideration in adopting a triennial cycle is the possibility of giving "in course" attention to each of the Synoptic Gospels:

> Thus Matthew is read in Year A, Mark in Year B and Luke in Year C. But this arrangement is not rigid: on the other hand, John's Gospel enjoys pride of place during the seasons of Christmas, Lent, and Easter; on the other hand, John, Chapter 6, takes up five Sundays in Year B, which gets over the problem of Mark being shorter.[66]

In like manner, the three-year cycle makes possible a semicontinuous reading of the Epistles (as with the Gospels, on the Sundays after Epiphany and Pentecost). This suggests an immediate caution about preaching from this lectionary. Its commitment to the *lectio continua* principle for Gospels and Epistles during the Sundays after Epiphany and Pentecost means that these two lessons on any of those Sundays will not necessarily be in thematic relationship with each other. The framers of the lectionary felt it more important that the Biblical books be heard in their literary integrity, week by week, than that every Sunday's lessons should form a thematic unity. The latter *is* the case, however, in the more intense seasons of Advent and Christmas, and Lent and Easter. Thus, this lectionary combines the two historic principles of *continua* (Epiphany and "after" Pentecost), and *selecta* (Advent, Christmas, Lent, and Easter).

A further principle is the practice of choosing the Old Testament lesson to coordinate with the Gospel. This "typological" arrangement has its weakness, but it does provide the preacher with a clear clue as to sermon preparation. One should always "start" with the Gospel and proceed to the Old Testament passage. Depending on the season then, the Epistle may or may not be thematically related.

Turning to specific seasons, the following particularities may be identified:

In Advent, Isaiah is the main source for the Old Testament lections.

On Advent's first two Sundays, the proper Synoptic Gospel is used

(for their eschatological passages), John and Luke becoming
predominant on the latter Sundays.

In Epiphany, the continua Gospel readings begin on the first
Sunday (the second Sunday being an interruption to include
Johannine material that was not found in the Synoptics and that
was prominent in Eastern lectionaries at Epiphany), and the
continua Epistle readings on the third Sunday.

In Lent, the Gospel lessons are predominantly Johannine and are
"prefigurations" of resurrection.

The Sunday before Easter (now known as "Passion (Palm)
Sunday") is exclusively devoted to the triumphal entry, although in
the Roman and other editions of the lectionary this is but the entry
rite, the Gospel reading being the Passion narrative of the year's
Gospel.

In the Season of Easter ("Eastertide" in The Worshipbook), John
predominates as the Gospel lesson; Acts replaces the Old
Testament (on the assumption that the apostolic church is itself the
primary witness to the resurrection, and to avoid imposing
resurrection typology on the Old Testament).

On Pentecost, Acts 2 naturally appears as the Epistle and John 14
and 16 as the Gospel.

On the Sunday after Pentecost, the traditional Trinity Sunday
lessons are retained.

On succeeding Sundays, the continua readings of Epistles and
Gospels pick up where they left off after Epiphany.

Such is the basic design of the three-year ecumenical lectionary as
found in The Worshipbook. It differs from its Roman "parent" only in
minor respects. Extracanonical lections in the Roman original were
replaced with canonical readings. Some readings were lengthened;
some "filled in" where the Roman editors had skipped verses or
portions of verses.

Since its publication in 1969 by the Roman Catholic Church and its
appearance in The Worshipbook—Services in 1970 this lectionary
has been adopted by several other denominations and interdenomina-
tional bodies: The Consultation on Church Union; The Armed Forces
Chaplains Board; The Inter-Lutheran Commission on Worship; The
Episcopal Church; and The United Methodist Church.

A measure of the ecumenical commitment of the Roman Catholic
Church with regard to the lectionary is given in a recent statement by
the International Commission on English in the Liturgy (A Joint
Commission of Catholic Bishops' Conferences):

The Roman lectionary, whatever its limitations, stands as one of the
principal achievements of the entire liturgical reform. The use of the

Sunday lectionary of the Roman liturgy, with minor adaptations, by major separated churches has given it unexpected and providential ecumenical dimension. Any eventual revision of the system of readings should be undertaken only in closest collaboration with the other interested churches and ecclesial communities.[67]

The ecumenical and liturgical assumptions underlying such a commitment and such widespread common use are surely occasions for rejoicing and hope throughout Western Christendom.

V. PROBLEMS AND POSSIBILITIES

A system as comprehensive as this lectionary is bound to present problems. Some have to do with lectionary itself; others with its use by preachers today. The latter is somewhat more easily dealt with than the former, so we will take it up first.

At first blush a lectionary seems to remove from the preacher all flexibility to deal with pastoral and contemporary concerns. Further, it seems to rule out the possibility of preaching series of sermons on doctrines, denominational emphases, social issues, and the like.

A number of responses can be made to this objection. The first is that in the Reformed church the Bible is the primary source for all preaching. Perhaps the lectionary will force upon us some prior questions about the nature of preaching within the community and the distinction between that action and strictly didactic or promotional efforts. The authoritative place of Scripture in the community of faith may become more obvious to both preacher and people under the impact of a commitment to use a lectionary.

It has also been noted that the calendar presupposed by the lectionary is essentially a six-month "year" (from 1st Advent to the Day of Pentecost). The other six months of summer and fall might be used for nonlectionary preaching. While this would interrupt the semicontinuous readings from Gospels and Epistles, it would open up time for other needs. Particularly in September and October the lectionary readings could be suspended with minimum loss.

Another option would be to suspend either the Gospel–Old Testament or the Epistle sequence in favor of another of the preacher's choosing. With proper introduction this should not be confusing to the people. The same could be done during Epiphany.

Concerning particular pastoral or parochial emergencies, it might be interesting to submit such moments to the larger witness of Scripture by sticking to the lectionary rather than searching for the passage that might more obviously speak.

At the outset we said the Reformed tradition of worship is a delicate but serious synthesis of freedom and form. This should be manifest in the manner of reading and preaching Holy Scripture.

Aside from its use, this lectionary has problems of its own which should not be overlooked. A full and fair analysis of many of them is to be found in an issue of the journal *Interpretation* (Vol. XXXI, No. 2, April 1977).[68]

Gerard Sloyan has identified the most widespread criticism of the ecumenical lectionary: its exclusively typological use of the Old Testament.[69] Almost by definition, the lectionary makes impossible the consecutive reading of the great narrative sagas such as the Joseph story, or even the exodus epic. Also missing is much of the ethical material of the prophets. Another author cites a different difficulty:

> In contrast to Gospel and Epistle, the Old Testament readings have little continuity from one Sunday to the next. Hence the congregation is not aided in acquiring a sense of the style, content, development, uniqueness, or theology of individual books.[70]

These criticisms and others have recently been assessed at a special consultation convened by the (North American) Consultation on Common Texts. It will address these problems over the next few years. Those who wish to use the lectionary but who feel the weight of these criticisms might drop the Old Testament lection or produce a more sequential, independent cycle. The usefulness of this particular lectionary, however, can better be measured against the prevailing Biblical poverty of both Protestant and Catholic worship of late than against the standard of an ideal but as yet nonexistent lectionary.

ADVANTAGES OF THE LECTIONARY

Use of the lectionary can free congregations from ministerial limitations in the choice of Biblical books and chapters. Stated in another way, the use of a lectionary puts the preacher in a slightly different relationship to Scripture than when he or she is choosing the texts. That difference may be evangelically appropriate since it moves in the direction of obedience and service, of the Word of God. One remembers Kierkegaard's "Short and Sharp" from *Attack Upon "Christendom"*:

> In the magnificent cathedral the Honorable and Right Reverend *Geheime-General-Ober-Hof-Praedikant*, the elect favorite of the fashionable world, appears before an elect company and preaches *with emotion* upon the text he himself elected: "God hath elected the base things of the world, and the things that are despised." And nobody laughs.[71]

A further possibility provided by the lectionary in a time of growing Biblical illiteracy is to acquaint congregations with books of the Bible in their literary and historical integrity. As liturgical reform revives the nurturing capabilities of worship this way of reading the Scripture will make increasing sense, to young and old alike. Such a scheme makes possible the study of Sunday's lections by all members of the congregation well in advance of the day on which they are read.

Preparation for worship which deliberately includes the laity provides learning opportunities for the whole congregation. Nor should the possibilities for growth in the preacher be ignored. There will be a new and important means of monitoring his or her own development as an exegete and preacher, as the same passages recur in the three-year cycle.

The lectionary and its wide acceptance has produced a vast volume of exegetical, liturgical, and homiletical literature. While not all of this material is of worthy quality, much of it is. And that provides resources for the preacher's continuing education.

Perhaps the most important possibility which the lectionary provides for Reformed worship is an integrative role. This integrative possibility has three principal thrusts. One is liturgical, another is educational, and the third is ecumenical.

Recent Protestant and Reformed worship has shown little serious integration of the various components of Sunday's service. Aside from the sometimes dubious connection even between Scripture and sermon, it has been virtually impossible for parish musicians to rehearse hymns or plan choral and instrumental music in relation to Scripture, if only because they must work on a longer "lead time" than the clergy usually do. This writer once attended Sunday worship in a sophisticated Presbyterian church wherein the musician was celebrating Memorial Day and the minister, Pentecost!

It would seem to be an axiom of Reformed worship that the Scriptural content of the Sunday service should function as the integrating center for everything else that is to happen. This can only occur if the Scripture readings can be identified well in advance. A vast body of hymns, anthems, organ, and other instrumental literature can be drawn upon. A lectionary makes possible that kind of thorough planning. Moreover, a common lectionary opens up resources being produced by many denominations and private publishers.

Use of the lectionary also opens up the process whereby Sunday's service is put together. It offers an accessible body of preplanned content, to which preacher, musician, and other artists might relate. An open process of planning, whereby all sit down together to work through the lessons well in advance, bears a significant relationship to our own Reformed doctrine of the ministry as servant both of the Word and of the community.

Another area of integration too long neglected is that between worship and education. Sunday Church School and Morning Worship have become almost alternate institutions (often meeting at the same time). Youth feel little relationship to the worshiping congregation, and the worshiping congregation has little interest in being a community of learners. The lectionary now provides a totally new opportunity to bring the two together. Conceivably the entire educational program of the church could be organized around it. This would open up new vistas for liturgical and musical integration which would in turn redeem the educational enterprise from its preoccupation with facts and its monogenerational character.

As Presbyterians become more conscious of the need for youth and children to feel at home with worship and the Sacraments, the continuity of the Gospel story or Epistle in the liturgy from week to week becomes a powerful teaching instrument. That same sort of teaching power resides in the cycle of seasons and symbols associated with the lectionary's calendar. But to celebrate that calendar without its lectionary is to indulge in symbolism without an adequate Biblical base. A full integration of symbol, season, and Scripture is good teaching.

A third area where the lectionary plays an interpretive role is the ecumenical. The three-year lectionary is a product of the profound liturgical reform now going on within the Roman Catholic Church. It has commended itself to a rich diversity of non-Catholic Western Christendom. A modality of ecumenical cooperation has appeared in the latter part of the twentieth century which was entirely unexpected. An expression of Christian unity which lies close to the source of all Christian unity has suddenly taken form. Even if we are not yet gathered around one Holy Table, we are now gathering around the word of God. Already across the length and breadth of our land Christians of many parishes and communions are becoming aware that up and down Main Street on Sunday morning the same Scripture lessons are being read. Groups of ministers, priests, pastors, and laity are gathering weekly to discuss those texts to prepare for the coming Sunday in their various houses of worship. In some places musicians are shuttling back and forth across the community to play the same organ music and hymns, and sing the same anthems. Common celebrations on great days are now far more easily planned, and become signs of far greater common faith than was thought possible even ten years ago.

"Separated" sisters and brothers are discovering a deep commonality around the Holy Scriptures. We Reformed Christians believe that those Holy Scriptures are the hidden bedrock beneath "one Lord, one faith, one baptism." An ecumenism that starts there will not end there.

NOTES

1. The Constitution of The United Presbyterian Church in the United States of America, Part II: Book of Order (New York: The Office of the General Assembly of The United Presbyterian Church in the United States of America, 1967), Form of Government, Ch. I, Sec. 1 (31.01).

2. The Book of Church Order of the Presbyterian Church in the United States (Richmond: The Office of the Stated Clerk of the General Assembly of the Presbyterian Church in the United States, 1965, 1972), The Form of Government, Preface, p. 20.

3. *The Book of Church Order* (Presbyterian Church U.S.), The Directory for the Worship and Work of the Church, Pt. I, Ch. 4 (204-1, 2), pp. 131-132.

4. *Book of Order* (The United Presbyterian Church U.S.A.), Form of Government, Ch. VIII, Sec. 4 (38.04).

5. *Book of Order* (The United Presbyterian Church U.S.A.), Directory for the Worship of God, Ch. IV, Sec. 6 (19.06).

6. *The Constitution on the Sacred Liturgy*, para. 51, in Austin Flannery, O.P., ed., *Vatican Council II: The Conciliar and Post-Conciliar Documents* (Liturgical Press, 1975), p. 17.

7. James F. White, *Christian Worship in Transition* (Abingdon Press, 1976), p. 139.

8. A. Allan McArthur, *The Christian Year and Lectionary Reform* (London: SCM Press, 1958), p. 35.

9. Hughes Oliphant Old, *The Patristic Roots of Reformed Worship* (Zurich: Theologischer Verlag Zurich, 1975), pp. 194-195.

10. William D. Maxwell, *The Liturgical Portions of the Genevan Service Book* (London: Faith Press, 1965), p. 184.

11. Ibid., p. 186.

12. *The Worshipbook—Services and Hymns* (Westminster Press, 1970, 1972), p. 479.

13. Karl Barth, *Church Dogmatics*, tr. G.W. Bromiley and ed. G.W. Bromiley and T.F. Torrance, IV/1, para. 62 (Edinburgh: T. & T. Clark, 1958), p. 725.

14. Ibid., p. 728.

15. James F. White, *New Forms of Worship* (Abingdon Press, 1971), p. 63.

16. Paul L. Lehmann, *The Transfiguration of Politics* (Harper & Row, 1975), p. 7.

17. Oscar Cullmann, *Christ and Time*, rev. ed. (Westminster Press, 1964), p. 52.

18. R. Le Déaut, A. Jaubert, and K. Hruby, *The Spirituality of Judaism* (Abbey Press, 1977), p. 35.

19. Peter G. Cobb, "The History of the Christian Year," in Cheslyn Jones, Geoffrey Wainwright, and E. Yarnold, eds., *The Study of Liturgy* (Oxford University Press, 1978), p. 404.

20. Barth, *Church Dogmatics*, III/1, para. 41, p. 228. In the English edition of Barth's *Church Dogmatics* this citation is incorrectly printed as Gen. 1:2. It should be Gen. 1-2, as on p. 258 of the German edition of III/1.

21. Cullmann, *Christ and Time*, p. 21.

22. Nahum N. Glatzer, ed., *The Passover Haggadah*, rev. ed. (Schocken Books, 1969), pp. 21, 85.

23. Cullmann, *Christ and Time*, p. 74.

24. Ibid., pp. 155-156.

25. Peter Selby, *Look for the Living: The Corporate Nature of Resurrection Faith* (Fortress Press, 1976), p. 125.

26. Ibid., pp. 119-120.

27. James Garcia, "Contributions and Challenges to the Theology of Sunday," *Worship*, Vol. 52, No. 4 (July 1978), p. 371.

28. *The Worshipbook—Services and Hymns*, pp. 167 and 174.

29. John Calvin, *Commentaries on the Epistles of Paul the Apostle to the Philippians, Colossians and Thessalonians*, tr. and ed. John Pringle (Wm. B. Eerdmans Publishing Co., 1948), p. 239.

30. *The Constitution on the Sacred Liturgy,* para. 106, in Flannery, ed., *Vatican II: The Conciliar and Post-Conciliar Documents,* p. 30.

31. Barth, *Church Dogmatics,* IV/2, para. 67, pp. 638 and 640.

32. *The Book of Church Order* (Presbyterian Church U.S.), Directory for Worship, Pt. I, Ch. 1 (201-1, 2, 3, and 4), p. 130.

33. *Book of Order* (The United Presbyterian Church U.S.A.), Directory for Worship, Ch. II, Sec. 4 (17.04).

34. A. Allan McArthur, *The Evolution of the Christian Year* (London: SCM Press, 1953), p. 13.

35. C. W. Dugmore, *The Influence of the Synagogue Upon the Divine Office* (London: Faith Press, 1964), p. 31.

36. Ibid., pp. 31-32.

37. McArthur, *The Evolution of the Christian Year,* p. 22.

38. Henry Bettenson, ed., *Documents of the Christian Church* (London: Oxford University Press, 1943), p. 93.

39. Willy Rordorf, *Sunday: The History of the Day of Rest and Worship in the Earliest Centuries of the Christian Church,* tr. A. A. K. Graham (Westminster Press, 1968), p. 234.

40. *The Worshipbook—Services and Hymns,* p. 34.

41. *The Book of Church Order* (Presbyterian Church U.S.), Directory for Worship, Pt. I, Ch. 1 (202-3), p. 131.

42. *Book of Order* (The United Presbyterian Church U.S.A.), Directory for Worship, Ch. IV, Sec. 4 (19.04).

43. *Lutheran Book of Worship* (Ministers Edition) (Minneapolis: Augsburg Publishing House; Philadelphia: Board of Publication, Lutheran Church in America, 1978), p. 13.

44. *The Worshipbook—Services and Hymns,* p. 134.

45. McArthur, *The Evolution of the Christian Year,* pp. 82-83.

46. Dom Gregory Dix, *The Shape of the Liturgy* (London: Dacre Press, 1945), pp. 338-339.

47. Peter G. Cobb, "The Calendar," in Jones, Wainwright, and Yarnold, eds., *The Study of Liturgy,* p. 407.

48. McArthur, *The Evolution of the Christian Year,* p. 125.

49. Ibid., p. 129.

50. *The Worshipbook—Services and Hymns,* p. 47.

51. Cobb, "The Calendar," p. 411.

52. McArthur, *The Evolution of the Christian Year,* p. 143.

53. Ibid., p. 148.

54. A. Allan McArthur, "Holy Week," in J. G. Davies, ed., *The Westminster Dictionary of Worship* (Philadelphia: Westminster Press, 1979), p. 193. (First published as *A Dictionary of Liturgy and Worship;* London: SCM Press, 1972.)

55. *Reformed Liturgy and Music,* published by the Joint Office of Worship of The United Presbyterian Church in the U.S.A. and the Presbyterian Church in the U.S. in cooperation with the Presbyterian Association of Musicians, 1044 Alta Vista Road, Louisville, Ky. 40205.

56. Cobb, "The Calendar," p. 414.

57. McArthur, *The Evolution of the Christian Year,* pp. 39-40.

58. Ibid., p. 69.

59. Cobb, "The Calendar," p. 415.

60. John Calvin, *Institutes of the Christian Religion*, tr. Henry Beveridge (Wm. B. Eerdmans Publishing Co., 1953), Vol. 2, p. 289.

61. Old, *The Patristic Roots of Reformed Worship*, pp. 194-195.

62. William D. Maxwell, *A History of Worship in the Church of Scotland* (London: Oxford University Press, 1955), p. 57.

63. Bard Thompson, ed., *Liturgies of the Western Church* (World Publishing Co., 1961), p. 358.

64. *The Constitution on the Sacred Liturgy*, para. 51, in Flannery, ed., *Vatican Council II: The Conciliar and Post-Conciliar Documents*, p. 17.

65. Unpublished article by Fr. Gaston Fontaine, C.R.I.C., Secretary to Coetus XI, Concilium for the Implementation of the Constitution on the Sacred Liturgy, pp. 5-6.

66. Ibid., p. 8

67. International Commission on English in the Liturgy, 1234 Massachusetts Avenue, N.W., Washington, D.C. 20005, Reference 2045.

68. *Interpretation*, published quarterly by Union Theological Seminary in Virginia, 3401 Brook Road, Richmond, Va. 23227.

69. Gerard S. Sloyan, "The Lectionary as a Context for Interpretation," *Interpretation*, Vol. XXXI, No. 2 (April 1977), p. 138.

70. Lloyd R. Bailey, "The Lectionary in Critical Perspective," *Interpretation*, Vol. XXXI, No. 2 (April 1977), pp. 151-152.

71. Søren Kierkegaard, *Attack Upon "Christendom,"* tr. Walter Lowrie (Princeton University Press, 1944), p. 181.

PART II

USING
THE LECTIONARY

INTRODUCTION TO PART II

Leaders of worship who desire to use the lectionary will find practical help for doing so in the pages that follow. Liturgical resources related to the readings for the day have been selected for all Sundays and certain other days in each year of the three-year cycle.

The liturgical year begins with the first Sunday in Advent. By ecumenical consent the readings and resources for year A will be used in the liturgical year beginning with Advent in 1980; year B in 1981; and year C in 1982. In 1983 the year A resources will be repeated and B and C will follow in order.

Resources for each day begin with a collect. These prayers are meant to be spoken by the leader of worship or by the congregation in unison, immediately before the reading of the lessons. The collects tend to anticipate the content of the readings; therefore those appropriate for one cycle of readings may not be appropriate for another. The collects have been selected from a number of sources identified by the symbols that follow: *The Worshipbook* (WB), pp. 135-157; the Roman Catholic *Sacramentary* (RC), p. 524; the Episcopal *Book of Common Prayer* (BCP), p. 213; and the *Lutheran Book of Worship* (LBW), pp. 121-170. Collects identified by the initials HTA were written by Horace T. Allen, author of Part I of this Handbook. None of these collects has the "Amen" printed, since it is not needed when the prayer is spoken by the congregation. If, however, the prayer is said by the leader of worship, the "Amen" should be used and spoken by all.

The Scripture readings for the day follow the collect. Brief notes have been provided for each reading. Their purpose is to help identify the content of the passage and serve as an aid in planning services of worship and courses of study.

A psalm or a portion of one is also suggested for each day. This selection has been borrowed with permission from a publication of the United Methodist Church, *Word and Table*. It is a refinement and correlation of lists used in several communions.

The readings are followed by a list of appropriate hymns. All are from Presbyterian hymnals, although most of them can be found in other hymnals as well. Horace T. Allen chose the hymns from *The Hymnal* (HL), *The Hymnbook* (HB), or *The Worshipbook* (WB). Whenever a hymn is followed by the symbol (Ps.), this hymn may be used for the Psalm of the day.

Perhaps most helpful for those who plan worship, particularly those with limited training in music, are the suggestions for anthems. Many of the selected anthems are evaluated in terms of performing difficulty: E (easy), M (medium), and D (difficult). Abbreviations CC I and CC II refer to *Carols for Choirs*, Books I and II, published by Oxford. I Mot refers to *A First Motet Book*; LH, *Lift Up Your Hearts*; and SAB, *The SAB Choral Book*, all published by Concordia. Fuller information is found in the resources listed at the end of this volume.

Most of the materials in this Handbook were first published in different forms in the quarterly journal *Reformed Liturgy and Music*. This journal is a publication of the Joint Office of Worship of the Presbyterian Church in the United States and The United Presbyterian Church in the United States of America, and of the Presbyterian Association of Musicians. The actual choosing of anthems that relate to the readings of the day, the evaluation of the musical selections, and the notations on the readings are the work of a number of persons. We hope our labors will provide strong encouragement to use the lectionary, and practical assistance as you do so. You can identify our respective contributions by the following initials:

HTA	Horace T. Allen, Jr.	JGK	James G. Kirk
HFA	Harold F. (Pete) Apple, Jr.	DL	David Lowry
LAB	Lewis A. Briner	PM	Paul Milio
DB	David Buttrick	RSM	Robert S. Moorhead
RD	Rosella Duerksen	JM	Jeannine Murphy
JTF	Jere T. Farrah, Jr.	DCR	Don C. Robinson
BH	Bess Hieronymous	JBR	John B. Rowland
HH	Hal Hopson	TPS	Thomas P. Stewart
LLH	Lucile L. Hudson (Hair)		

KEY TO ABBREVIATIONS

Collects

WB *The Worshipbook—Services and Hymns*
RC Roman Catholic *Sacramentary*
BCP Episcopal *Book of Common Prayer*
LBW *Lutheran Book of Worship*

Hymns

HL *The Hymnal*
HB *The Hymnbook*
WB *The Worshipbook*

Anthems

(E) Easy
(M) Medium
(D) Difficult

CC I *Carols for Choirs, Book I*
CC II *Carols for Choirs, Book II*
I Mot *A First Motet Book*
LH *Lift Up Your Hearts*
SAB *The SAB Choral Book*

COLLECT FOR THE DAY

O Lord: keep us awake and alert, watching for your kingdom. Make us strong in faith, so we may greet your Son when he comes, and joyfully give him praise, with you, and with the Holy Spirit. (WB)

READINGS

Isa. 2:1-5 A messianic expectation in which all nations shall flow to the mountain of the house of the Lord and be taught his ways; they shall beat their swords into plowshares and their spears into pruning hooks. The word of the Lord shall go forth from Jerusalem.

Rom. 13:11-14 The urgency of the advent expectation is expressed by Paul in terms of salvation being very near. Therefore, cast off the works of darkness and put on the armor of light. Put on the Lord Jesus Christ.

Matt. 24:36-44 Be ready. The Son of Man is coming at an hour you do not expect. HFA

PSALM FOR THE DAY: Psalm 122

HYMNS FOR THE DAY	HL	HB	WB
Watchman, Tell Us of the Night	109	149	617
Jesus Calls Us (for St. Andrew's Day, Nov. 30, see WB, stanza 2) (tune: Stuttgart or Charleston)	223	269	439
O God of Every Nation	—	—	498
O God of Earth and Altar	419	511	497
Wake, Awake, for Night Is Flying	—	—	614
Hark, What a Sound	110	150	—
Hark! the Glad Sound, the Savior Comes	—	—	410

ANTHEMS FOR THE DAY

Isa. 2:1-5 *Advent Matin Responsory* and/or *Come Thou Redeemer of Our Race* (see CC II, pp. 68, 71). SATB (MD)

Savior of the Nations, Come, Gerhard Krapf (Augsburg). SATB, optional congregation (M)

Rom. 13:11-14 *Lord of All Being, Throned Afar* (WB, p. 463). (E)

Matt. 24:36-44 *The Eyes of All Wait Upon Thee,* Jean Berger (Augsburg). SATB (MD) DL

COLLECT FOR THE DAY
God of prophets: in the wilderness of Jordan you sent a messenger to prepare our hearts for the coming of your Son. Help us to hear good news, to repent, and be ready to welcome the Lord, our Savior, Jesus Christ.   (WB)

READINGS
Isa. 11:1-10   There shall come forth a shoot from the stump of Jesse; the Spirit of the Lord shall rest upon him, the Spirit of wisdom and understanding, the Spirit of counsel and might, the Spirit of knowledge and the fear of the Lord.

Rom. 15:4-9   The servant Christ confirms God's promises to the patriarchs.

Matt. 3:1-12   John the Baptist baptizes with water for repentance, but He who is coming will baptize with the Holy Spirit and with fire.   HFA

PSALM FOR THE DAY: Psalm 72:1-19

HYMNS FOR THE DAY	HL	HB	WB
O Come, O Come, Emmanuel	108	147	489, 490
Come, Thou Long-expected Jesus	113	151	342
Comfort, Comfort You My People	—	—	347
O Word of God Incarnate	215	251	532
Descend, O Spirit, Purging Flame	—	—	353
Love Divine, All Loves Excelling	308	399	471

ANTHEMS FOR THE DAY

Isa. 11:1-10   *O Come, O Come, Emmanuel* (WB, p. 489 or p. 490). The new second tune at 490 can be effective

O Come, O Come, Emmanuel, arr. David Willcocks (see CC II, p. 120). Can be performed in unison, in four parts, or, for congregations that are used to the chant rhythm, SATB and congregation

Rom. 15:4-9   *The Linden Tree Carol,* arr. Reginald Jacques (CC I, p. 110)

Gabriel's Message, arr. Desmond Ratcliffe (Novello)

Gabriel's Message, arr. David Willcocks (CC II, p. 191)

Matt. 3:1-12   *Comfort Ye, Comfort Ye My People* (Recitative) and *Every Valley Shall Be Exalted* (Air), G. F. Handel (from *Messiah,* Novello, ed. Watkins Shaw). Tenor Solos   DL

COLLECT FOR THE DAY

Mighty God: you have made us and all things to serve you; now ready the world for your rule. Come quickly to save us, so that violence and crying shall end, and your children shall live in peace, honoring each other with justice and love; through Jesus Christ, who lives in power with you, and with the Holy Spirit, one God, forever.   (WB)

READINGS

Isa. 35:1-6, 10   At the coming of the Lord, all creation will rejoice, the blind will see, the deaf will hear, the lame will leap like a hart, and the dumb will sing for joy.

James 5:7-10   Be patient until the coming of the Lord after the example of the prophets' suffering and patience.

Matt. 11:2-11   Is Jesus, indeed, the expected one? The blind see, the lame walk, lepers are cleansed, the deaf hear, the dead are raised up, and good news is preached to the poor.   HFA

PSALM FOR THE DAY: Psalm 146

HYMNS FOR THE DAY

	HL	HB	WB
Hail to the Brightness	391	505	—
Break Forth, O Living Light of God	—	—	316
Come, You Thankful People, Come	460	525	346
Christ Is the World's True Light	—	492	326
The Morning Light Is Breaking	389	499	—
Thy Kingdom Come, O Lord	425	488	—
Jesus Shall Reign	377	496	443

ANTHEMS FOR THE DAY

Isa. 35:1-6, 10   *Like as the Hart Desireth the Waterbrooks,* Herbert Howells (Oxford). SATB, some divisi (D)

James 5:7-10   *Thou Knowest, Lord, the Secrets,* Henry Purcell (Novello). SATB (M)

Matt. 11:2-11   *This Is the Record of John,* Orlando Gibbons (Oxford). SAATB with Tenor or Soprano Solo (D)   DL

COLLECT FOR THE DAY
   Eternal God: through long generations you prepared a way in our world
   for the coming of your Son, and by your Spirit you are still bringing the
   light of the gospel to darkened lives. Renew us, so that we may welcome
   Jesus Christ to rule our thoughts and claim our love, as Lord of lords and
   King of kings, to whom be glory always.   (WB)

READINGS
   Isa. 7:10-15   The Lord will give you a sign. A young woman will conceive
   and bear a son, and shall call his name Immanuel.

   Rom. 1:1-7   You are called to belong to Christ, who is descended from
   David and designated Son of God. Let us then be about our task of bringing
   about the obedience of faith among all the nations for the sake of his name.

   Matt. 1:18-25   Matthew reports the birth of Jesus, the son of David, the son
   of Abraham, as fulfillment of Isaiah's prophecy. God is with us.   HFA

PSALM FOR THE DAY: Psalm 24

HYMNS FOR THE DAY

	HL	HB	WB
Lift Up Your Heads (Ps.)	114	152	454
Savior of the Nations, Come	—	—	565
O for a Thousand Tongues	199	141	493
God Himself Is with Us	51	13	384

ANTHEMS FOR THE DAY

   Isa. 7:10-15   *Audivi Vocem de Caelo*, Thomas Tallis (Oxford). SATB (D)

   Rom. 1:1-7   *Comfort, Comfort Ye My People*, Claude Goudimel (I Mot, p.
   23). SATB (MD)

   Comfort, Comfort Ye My People, Paul Bunjes (LH, p. 5). SATB (M)

   Matt. 1:18-25   *A White Dove Flew from Heaven*, Johannes Brahms
   (Belwin). SATB (MD)   DL

COLLECT FOR THE DAY
> Give us, O God, such love and wonder, that with shepherds, and wise men, and pilgrims unknown, we may come to adore the holy child, the promised King; and with our gifts worship him, our Lord and Savior Jesus Christ. (WB)

READINGS
> **Isa. 62:1-4** In the very midst of a forsaken and desolate land, God himself will come bringing salvation and hope. Jerusalem, who has carried the names Forsaken and Desolate, will be a crown of beauty in the hand of the Lord.

> **Col. 1:15-20** In Christ dwells the fullness of God. All things were created through him and for him. Through him all things are reconciled to God.

> **Luke 2:1-14** "Be not afraid; . . . to you is born this day in the city of David a Savior, who is Christ the Lord." HFA

PSALM FOR THE DAY: Psalm 96

HYMNS FOR THE DAY	HL	HB	WB
Angels, from the Realms of Glory	124	168	298
Angels We Have Heard on High	—	158	299
Of the Father's Love Begotten	—	7	534
The True Light That Enlightens Man	—	—	598
It Came Upon the Midnight Clear	127	160	438
Deck Yourself, My Soul (for Communion)	—	—	351
Silent Night (German words in WB)	132	154	567
Hark! the Herald Angels Sing	117	163	411

ANTHEMS FOR THE DAY

> **Isa. 62:1-4** *A Great and Mighty Wonder*, Michael Praetorius (CC I, p. 1). SATB (M)

> *A Babe Is Born I Wys*, F. Bainton (CC II, p. 6). SATB (MD)

> **Col. 1:15-20** *The Not-Yet Flower*, Richard Felciano (E. C. Schirmer). Unison voices and electronic prerecorded tape (E)

> *Of the Father's Love Begotten*, arr. David Willcocks (CC II, p. 128). SATB (MD)

> **Luke 2:1-14** *While Shepherds Watched*, arr. David Willcocks (CC II, p. 210). SATB (M)

> *The Sussex Carol*, arr. David Willcocks (CC I, p. 96). Can be performed SATB with alterations; works best with SSATB and added Children's Choir (D)

> *And There Were Shepherds* (Recitative). Tenor and/or Soprano Solos (M)

> *Break Forth* (Chorale), J. S. Bach (from *Christmas Oratorio*, in CC I, p. 10). SATB (M) DL

COLLECT FOR THE DAY

All glory to you, great God, for the gift of your Son, light in darkness and hope of the world, whom you sent to save us all. With singing angels, let us praise your name, and tell the earth his story, so everyone may believe, rejoice, and bow down, acknowledging your love; through Jesus Christ our Lord.   (WB)

READINGS

Isa. 9:2, 6-7 To us a child is born, to us a son is given. To those who dwell in a land of deep darkness, on them has light shined.

Titus 2:11-15 Jesus Christ has given himself to redeem us from all iniquity and to purify for himself a people of his own who are zealous of good deeds.

Luke 2:1-14 "Be not afraid; . . . to you is born this day in the city of David a Savior, who is Christ the Lord."   HFA

PSALM FOR THE DAY: Psalm 96

HYMNS FOR THE DAY	HL	HB	WB
Joy to the World!	122	161	444
Born in the Night, Mary's Child	—	—	312
O Sing a Song of Bethlehem	138	177	526
O Little Town of Bethlehem	121	171	511
Once in Royal David's City	454	462	539
On This Day Earth Shall Ring	—	—	538
O Come, All Ye Faithful	116	170	486

ANTHEMS FOR THE DAY

Isa. 9:2, 6-7 *For Unto Us* (Chorus), G. F. Handel (from *Messiah*, Novello, ed. Watkins Shaw). SATB (D)

In Dulci Jubilo, Robert Lucas de Pearsall (CC I, p. 42). For divisi SATB, needs at least two on a part. Macaronic text. (D)

Titus 2:11-15 *The Blessed Son of God*, R. Vaughan Williams (CC I, p. 112). SATB (MD)

Unto Us Is Born a Son, arr. David Willcocks (CC I, p. 154). SATB (M)

Luke 2:1-14 *The Shepherd's Pipe Carol*, John Rutter (CC II, p. 39). SATB (D)

God Rest You Merry, arr. David Willcocks (CC I, p. 29). SSATB (D)   DL

COLLECT FOR THE DAY

God our Father: your Son Jesus came to claim us as sisters and brothers in faith. Make us one with him, so that we may enjoy your love, and live to serve you as he did, who rules with you and with the Holy Spirit, one God, forever.   (WB)

READINGS

Eccl. 3:1-9, 14-17   God has appointed a time for everything. Indeed, God has made all life beautiful when it is lived in harmony with his will. How desperately do we yearn for his relationship to us and our world to be clearly visible!

Col. 3:12-17   We in the church, the Christian community, are to exercise compassion, kindness, lowliness, meekness, and patience, forbearing and forgiving each other. Above all else, love binds everything together in perfect harmony. Be what you are called to be: the Christian community—the body of Christ.

Matt. 2:13-15, 19-23   Joseph and Mary flee to Egypt with Jesus to escape Herod. Following Herod's death, Joseph, Mary, and Jesus return to Nazareth. The words of the prophets are fulfilled: "Out of Egypt have I called my son" and "he shall be called a Nazarene."   HFA

PSALM FOR THE DAY: Psalm 111

HYMNS FOR THE DAY	HL	HB	WB
All Beautiful the March of Days	471	96	281
Ancient of Days	58	246	297
Open Now the Gates of Beauty	—	40	544
O What Their Joy	430	424	—
Lord God of Hosts, Whose Purpose	368	288	460
Son of God, Eternal Savior	—	—	573

ANTHEMS FOR THE DAY

Eccl. 3:1-9, 14-17   *O Little One Sweet*, J. S. Bach (CC I, p. 87). SATB (M)

Col. 3:12-17   *Torches*, John Joubert (CC I, p. 150). Unison or SATB (M)

Harvest Time of Love, Wilma Jensen (Choristers Guild). Unison, voice part, flute, handbells, organ, guitar, finger cymbals (ME). Text by Helen Keller

Matt. 2:13-15, 19-23   *Coventry Carol* (CC I, pp. 82, 83). Two versions: SAB original and SATB arr. Martin Shaw. (ME)

The Bells of Paradise, arr. David S. Walker (Concordia). Unison or 3-voice, 2 flutes, small bell instrument (ME)   DL

THE SECOND SUNDAY AFTER CHRISTMAS (A)

COLLECT FOR THE DAY

Eternal God: to you a thousand years go by as quickly as an evening. You have led us in days past; guide us now and always, that our hearts may turn to choose your will, and new resolves be strengthened; through Jesus Christ our Lord.   (WB)

READINGS

Prov. 8:22-31   The ancient proverbs declare wisdom as the first of God's creations.

Eph. 1:15-23   Paul prays for wisdom for the church at Ephesus that will give them hope through the power of God revealed in Christ's resurrection and ascension.

John 1:1-5, 9-14   John declares the Christ as the eternal Word of God, with him at creation and now appearing in the flesh as the light of life.   PM

PSALM FOR THE DAY: Psalm 147:12-20

HYMNS FOR THE DAY	HL	HB	WB
O Worship the King	2	26	533
Praise Ye the Lord, for It Is Good (Ps.)	—	36	—
At the Name of Jesus	—	143	303
Light of the World	422	138	—
He Did Not Want to Be Far	—	—	412
Light of Light, Enlighten Me	21	73	—

ANTHEMS FOR THE DAY

Prov. 8:22-31   *Lord of the Dance* (WB, p. 426). (E)

The Twelve Days of Christmas, arr. John Rutter (CC II, p. 134). SATB (MD)

Eph. 1:15-23   *How Excellent Is Thy Name,* Howard Hanson (C. Fischer). SSAATTB (D)

Born in the Night, Mary's Child (WB, p. 312). (E)

John 1: 1-5, 9-14   *The Not-Yet Flower,* Richard Felciano (E. C. Schirmer). Unison voices and electronic prerecorded tape (E)

The True Light That Enlightens Man (WB, p. 598). (E)

Let All Mortal Flesh Keep Silence, Gustav Holst (Galaxy). SATB (M)   DL

EPIPHANY (A)

COLLECT FOR THE DAY

God of light, who by a star led wise men from far away to see the child Jesus: draw us to him, so that, praising you now, we may in life to come meet you face to face; through Christ our Lord.   (WB)

READINGS

Isa. 60:1-6 Keys to the attractive force of God are light and glory. We respond to him and are in turn made radiant and wealthy. Gold and frankincense are symbols of response to God in praise and rejoicing.

Eph. 3:1-6 The apostle is in a favored position as a steward of God's grace. Apostles and prophets by the Spirit know what was not revealed in other generations. Gentiles are fellow heirs, members of the same body, and partakers of the promises in Christ.

Matt. 2:1-12 Familiar is the story of the nativity as it recalls the prophecy concerning the Messiah. The Wise Men fulfill prophecy (Isaiah) in the giving of gifts of gold, frankincense, and myrrh. What is in the dream that warns them to return home another way?   RSM

PSALM FOR THE DAY: Psalm 72:1-19

HYMNS FOR THE DAY

	HL	HB	WB
Brightest and Best	136	175	318
The Morning Light Is Breaking	389	499	—
Jesus Shall Reign (Ps.)	377	496	443
O Morning Star, How Fair and Bright	321	415	521
We Three Kings	—	176	—

ANTHEMS FOR THE DAY

Isa. 60:1-6 *Arise, Shine, for Thy Light Has Come*, Kenneth Jennings (Augsburg). SATB (M)

For Your Light Has Come, Ronald A. Nelson (Augsburg). SATB, trumpets (E)

Eph. 3:1-6 *Arise, O God, and Shine*, arr. S. Drummond Wolff (Concordia). SATB, trumpet (ME)

Matt. 2:1-12 *To Jesus from the Ends of the Earth* (Huron Indian carol), arr. Kenneth Jewell (Concordia). SATB or SSA (E)

Epiphany Alleluias, John Weaver (Boosey & Hawkes). SATB (ME)   RD

COLLECT FOR THE DAY

Holy God: you sent your Son to be baptized among sinners, to seek and save the lost. May we, who have been baptized in his name, never turn away from the world, but reach out in love to rescue the wayward; by the mercy of Christ our Lord. (WB)

READINGS

Isa. 42:1-7 The Lord's servant is the one who will bring forth justice, open the eyes of the blind, and release the prisoners from the dungeon.

Acts 10:34-43 Jesus is the promised one who went about doing good and healing the oppressed. It is Jesus, who rose from the dead, who is the judge of the living and the dead. Everyone who believes in him receives forgiveness of sins through his name.

Matt. 3:13-17 Jesus is baptized by John, a baptism with water for repentance. Jesus is like us in every respect. HFA

PSALM FOR THE DAY: Psalm 29: 1-4, 9-10

HYMNS FOR THE DAY

	HL	HB	WB
As with Gladness Men of Old	135	174	302
Christ Shall Have Dominion	—	502	—
O God, Who by a Star Did Guide	—	—	502
What Star Is This	—	—	632
Light of the World (tune: Salve Domine)	422	138	—
Brightest and Best	136	175	318

ANTHEMS FOR THE DAY

Isa. 42:1-7 *I Will Lift Up Mine Eyes*, Leo Sowerby (Boston Music). SATB with Alto Solo (MD)

Acts 10:34-43 *God Has Spoken—by His Prophets* (WB, p. 382). (E)

Matt. 3:13-17 *The Lone, Wild Bird* (WB, p. 591). Unison (ME) DL

COLLECT FOR THE DAY
Father in heaven, at the baptism of Jesus in the River Jordan you proclaimed him your beloved Son and anointed him with the Holy Spirit. Make all who are baptized into Christ faithful in their calling to be your children and inheritors with him of everlasting life; through your Son, Jesus Christ our Lord. (LBW)

READINGS
Isa. 49:3-6 The Lord's servant is a light to the nations.

I Cor. 1:1-9 Through Jesus Christ we know God's grace, receive all spiritual gifts, and we are sustained to the end, when we will be found guiltless. All this belongs to us as we await his revealing.

John 1:29-34 Jesus is revealed as the Lamb of God who takes away the sin of the world. He baptizes with the Holy Spirit. HFA

PSALM FOR THE DAY: Psalm 40:1-11

HYMNS FOR THE DAY	HL	HB	WB
Christ, Whose Glory Fills the Skies	26	47	332
O Morning Star, How Fair and Bright	321	415	521
O Love, How Deep, How Broad, How High!	139	—	518
He Did Not Want to Be Far	—	—	412
Spirit of God, Descend Upon My Heart (tune: Toulon)	204	236	575

ANTHEMS FOR THE DAY

Isa. 49:3-6 *Adam Lay Ybounden*, Boris Ord (CC II, p. 10). SATB (MD)

Adam Lay Ybounden, Peter Warlock (Oxford). Unison (ME)

I Cor. 1:1-9 *Almighty and Everlasting God*, Orlando Gibbons (Oxford). SATB (MD)

John 1:29-34 *Dawn Carol*, Malcolm Williamson (Chappell). SA(A)TB (MD) DL

COLLECT FOR THE DAY
> Almighty God: your Son our Lord called disciples to serve him. May we who have also heard his call rise up to follow where he leads, obedient to your perfect will; through Jesus Christ our Lord.   (WB)

READINGS

Isa. 9:1-4   The people who walked in darkness have seen a great light.

I Cor. 1:10-17   Allegiance to any particular church leader is inappropriate behavior for the Christian. The only appropriate allegiance is to Christ himself. Furthermore, preaching that is eloquent can only rob the cross of Christ of its power.

Matt. 4:12-23   Jesus begins to fulfill Isaiah's prophecy: "the people who sat in darkness have seen a great light," as he calls Peter and Andrew, James and John, to be his disciples.   HFA

PSALM FOR THE DAY: Psalm 27: 1, 4, 13-14

HYMNS FOR THE DAY	HL	HB	WB
O Morning Star, How Fair and Bright	321	415	521
God Is Our Strong Salvation (Ps.)	92	347	388
We Are One in the Spirit	—	—	619
Through the Night of Doubt and Sorrow (tune: Ebenezer)	345	475	—
He Who Would Valiant Be	276	345	414

ANTHEMS FOR THE DAY

Isa. 9:1-4   *Creator of the Stars of Night* (WB, p. 348). (E)

I Cor. 1:10-17   *Blessed Jesus, at Thy Word*, arr. Theophil Rothenberg (SAB, p. 8). (M)

Matt. 4:12-23   *Brightest and Best*, John Gardner (No. 1 of *Five Hymns in Popular Style*, Oxford). Also in SSA, using accompaniment from SATB score (MD)
                                                                            DL

THE FOURTH SUNDAY AFTER EPIPHANY (A)

COLLECT FOR THE DAY

Give us, O God, patience to speak good news to those who oppose us, and to help those who may rage against us, so that, following in the way of your Son, we may rejoice even when rejected, trusting in your perfect love which never fails; through Jesus Christ our Lord.   (WB)

READINGS

Zeph. 2:3; 3:11-13   Seek the Lord, seek righteousness; seek humility.

I Cor. 1:26-31   Our life is in Christ. We have no need to achieve and boast of high standards according to the world; we boast only in the Lord.

Matt. 5:1-12   Jesus begins the Sermon on the Mount with the Beatitudes. "Rewards" are, indeed, demonstrations of God's free gift of grace to us. Our obedience in living the type of life commended by Jesus is a response to his grace.   HFA

PSALM FOR THE DAY: Psalm 1

HYMNS FOR THE DAY

	HL	HB	WB
All Hail the Power of Jesus' Name!	192	132	285,286
So Lowly Does the Savior Ride	—	—	571
O Master, Let Me Walk with Thee	364	304	520
All Poor Men and Humble	—	—	289
Be Thou My Vision	325	303	304

ANTHEMS FOR THE DAY

Zeph. 2:3; 3:11-13   *O Lord, Support Us*, Samuel Walter (Belwin). SATB (MD)

St. Teresa's Bookmark, Louis White (Belwin). SATB (D)

Matt. 5:1-12   *Blest Are the Pure in Heart*, Eric Thiman (Novello). SATB (M)   DL

COLLECT FOR THE DAY

God our Father: you have appointed us witnesses, to be a light that shines in the world. Let us not hide the bright hope you have given us, but tell everyone your love, revealed in Jesus Christ the Lord. (WB)

READINGS

Isa. 58:7-10   Your light shall break forth like the dawn; it shall rise in the darkness when you share your bread with the hungry, bring the homeless poor into your house, and satisfy the desire of the afflicted.

I Cor. 2:1-5   Paul advises us not to rely on the wisdom of people but on the power of God.

Matt. 5:13-16   You are the salt of the earth and the light of the world. Let your light shine.   HFA

PSALM FOR THE DAY: Psalm 112:4-9

HYMNS FOR THE DAY	HL	HB	WB
Hope of the World	—	291	423
When I Survey the Wondrous Cross	152	198	635
O Brothers, Lift Your Voices	372	333	—
O Lord of Life	—	256	—
Come, Labor On	366	287	—
Spread, O Spread the Mighty Word	—	—	577

ANTHEMS FOR THE DAY

Isa. 58:7-10   *Surge, Illuminare*, Ned Rorem (Boosey & Hawkes). SATB (D)

I Cor. 2:1-5   *How Excellent Is Thy Name*, Howard Hanson (C. Fischer). SATB, optional divisi (MD)

Matt. 5:13-16   *O Morning Star, How Fair and Bright* (WB, p. 521). (E)

                                                                    DL

COLLECT FOR THE DAY
Almighty God: you gave the law as a good guide for our lives. May we never shrink from your commandments, but, as we are taught by your Son Jesus, fulfill the law in perfect love; through Christ our Lord and Master.   (WB)

READINGS
Deut. 30:15-20   Moses puts obedience to the law of the Lord in ultimate terms: life or death. Prosperity and the Promised Land are to be the signs of life, and the whole of Old Testament history is commentary on this covenant of obedience and promise, beginning with Moses himself, who is not permitted to cross the Jordan.

I Cor. 2:6-10   Christian truth is not primarily philosophy, but the power of Christ's cross. It is hidden only to those who look everywhere else but there.

Matt. 5:27-37   Jesus, at the outset of his ministry, assumes a Moses-like stance ("on the mount") to call his followers to an obedience which goes far deeper than external keeping of commandments, to an integrity whose "Yes" or "No" is final.   HTA

PSALM FOR THE DAY: Psalm 119:1-16

HYMNS FOR THE DAY	HL	HB	WB
Praise to the Lord, the Almighty	6	1	557
How I Love Thy Law (Ps.)	—	253	—
In the Cross of Christ I Glory	154	195	437
O Master Workman of the Race	140	178	—
O Master, Let Me Walk with Thee	364	304	520

ANTHEMS FOR THE DAY

God Be in My Head, A. Eugene Ellsworth (Abingdon). SATB (M)

Blessed Is the Man, Corelli-Stone (Boston Music). SAB (ME)

Create in Me a Clean Heart, O God, Paul Bouman (Concordia). SA (E)

Create in Me, O God, a Clean Heart, Johannes Brahms (G. Schirmer). SATBB (M)

Cause Us, O Lord, Ron Nelson (Boosey & Hawkes). SATB (M)   LLH

COLLECT FOR THE DAY

Almighty God: you have commanded us to love our enemies, and to do good to those who hate us. May we never be content with affection for our friends, but reach out in love to all your children; through Jesus Christ our Lord.   (WB)

READINGS

Lev. 19:1-2, 17-18 Holiness and perfection are not far away: they are as near as neighbor and one's regard for oneself.

I Cor. 3:16-23 The Christian community of neighbor-love is God's new holy temple, God's dwelling place. Here the ancient law comes to life and makes everything and everybody fresh and new.

Matt. 5:38-48 Giving to the needy and going the second mile are given by Christ as signs of perfection. They will soon be seen concretely enough in his own life and death, our only boast.   HTA

PSALM FOR THE DAY: Psalm 103:1-13

HYMNS FOR THE DAY

	HL	HB	WB
Praise, My Soul, the King of Heaven (Ps.)	14	31	551
O Thou My Soul, Bless God (Ps.)	16	121	—
Where High the Heavenly Temple Stands	—	389	—
We Dedicate This Temple	—	519	—
O Love, How Deep, How Broad, How High!	139	—	518
Walk Tall, Christian	—	—	616

ANTHEMS FOR THE DAY

Temples of God, Ronald A. Nelson (Augsburg). 2-Part Mixed (E)

Help Us to Help Each Other, Lord, S. Drummond Wolff (Concordia). SATB (ME)

Christians and Pagans, Vulpius-Young (Agape). 2-Part Mixed (E). Text by Bonhoeffer

Prayer, Lloyd Pfautsch (Lawson-Gould). SATB (M). Text by Dag Hammarskjöld

The Bethlehem Boy, Robert Leaf (Art Masters). SATB (ME)

Three Peace and Brotherhood Canons (Choristers Guild). (E)

O Love, How Deep, How Broad, How High, Schütz-Dietterich (Abingdon). SA/SATB (E)

Bless the Lord, O My Soul, Ippolitoff-Ivanoff (Boston Music). SATB (M)

LLH

THE EIGHTH SUNDAY AFTER EPIPHANY (A)

COLLECT FOR THE DAY

Gracious God: you know that we are apt to bring back the troubles of yesterday, and to forecast the cares of tomorrow. Give us grace to throw off fears and anxieties, as our Lord commanded, so that today and every day we may live in peace; through Jesus Christ our Lord.   (WB)

READINGS

Isa. 49:14-18 Return and rebuilding of ruins are among the Old Testament's most powerful symbols of hope in the midst of defeat and exile. The Lord's people are his children, whom he never forgets (v. 15).

I Cor. 4:1-5 Members of Christ's community are never one another's judges, but servants one of another. Only at the return of Christ will all accounts be settled.

Matt. 6:24-34 Followers of Christ are free to serve. They know that the future is his just as the world is his Father's. His kingdom overshadows the evil of today or tomorrow.   HTA

PSALM FOR THE DAY: Psalm 62

HYMNS FOR THE DAY	HL	HB	WB
This Is My Father's World	70	101	602
My Soul with Expectation (Ps.)	86	113	—
The Lord Will Come and Not Be Slow	185	230	—
Give to the Winds Your Fears	294	364	377
If You Will Only Let God Guide You	105	344	431
All Things Bright and Beautiful	—	456	—

ANTHEMS FOR THE DAY

This Is the Day, Daniel Moe (in *Ecumenical Praise*, No. 109, Hope)

A Blessing, Martin Shaw (G. Schirmer). SATB (ME)

Strengthen for Service, Lord, Austin Lovelace (Canyon). Unison (E)

Behold, God Is My Salvation, Leo Sowerby (H. W. Gray). SA (E)

By Gracious Powers, Gelineau-Routley (Hinshaw). SATB (M)   LLH

COLLECT FOR THE DAY
Almighty God: you love all your children, and do not hate them for their sins. Help us to face up to ourselves, admit we are in the wrong, and reach with confidence for your mercy; in Jesus Christ the Lord.

(WB)

READINGS

Joel 2:12-18   The prophet Joel interprets a plague of locusts as the judgment of God upon his disobedient people. Joel calls the people to a repentance deeper than external expressions of contrition, with the assurance that God will respond favorably.

II Cor. 5:20 to 6:2   The apostle Paul entreats his hearers to accept reconciliation with God immediately. Delay might make their acceptance of God's grace meaningless.

Matt. 6:1-6, 16-18   In the Sermon on the Mount, Jesus teaches that inner attitudes of worship are more effective in the worshiper's communion with God than external displays of religiosity.   JBR

PSALM FOR THE DAY: Psalm 51:1-17

HYMNS FOR THE DAY	HL	HB	WB
God of Compassion, in Mercy Befriend Us	290	122	392
Lord, from the Depths to You I Cry	240	277	459
I'm So Glad Troubles Don't Last Always	—	—	432
The Church's One Foundation	333	437	582
Lord, Who Throughout These Forty Days	144	181	470

ANTHEMS FOR THE DAY

Joel 2:12-18   *Ye People, Rend Your Hearts* and *If with All Your Hearts,* Mendelssohn (from *Elijah,* any edition). Tenor Solo

O My God, Bestow Thy Tender Mercy, Pergolesi-Hopson (C. Fischer). 2-Part (E)

II Cor. 5:20 to 6:2   *Grant Us Thy Peace,* Mendelssohn (Boosey & Hawkes). SATB (E)

Matt. 6:1-6, 16-18   *When Thou Prayest,* Carl F. Mueller (C. Fischer). SATB (M)

Psalm 51:1-17   *Create in Me a Clean Heart, O God,* Paul Bouman (Concordia). 2-Part (E)

Create in Me, O God, Johannes Brahms (G. Schirmer). SATBB (M)   LLH

COLLECT FOR THE DAY

O Lord God, you led your ancient people through the wilderness and brought them to the promised land. Guide now the people of your Church, that, following our Savior, we may walk through the wilderness of this world toward the glory of the world to come; through your Son, Jesus Christ our Lord, who lives and reigns with you and the Holy Spirit, one God, now and forever. (LBW)

READINGS

Gen. 2:7-9; 3:1-7 God creates man and woman out of the dust of the earth as the crown of his creation, but they sin by disobeying God's command not to eat of the tree of the knowledge of good and evil.

Rom. 5:12-19 As we share in the sin of disobedience which Adam committed, so we may share in the redemption achieved by Christ's self-sacrificing act of obedience.

Matt. 4:1-11 After receiving God's commendation at his baptism and pondering his mission for forty days in the wilderness, Jesus is tempted to use questionable means for accomplishing the objectives of his mission.

JBR

PSALM FOR THE DAY: Psalm 130

HYMNS FOR THE DAY	HL	HB	WB
O Worship the King	2	26	533
The Man Who Once Has Found Abode	—	—	594
Cast Your Burden on the Lord	288	—	323
Lord, Who Throughout These Forty Days	144	181	470
When We Are Tempted to Deny Your Son	—	—	640
Call Jehovah Your Salvation (tune: Hyfrydol)	292	123	322

ANTHEMS FOR THE DAY

Gen. 2:7-9; 3:1-7 *The Tree of Life* (in *Westminster Praise*, Hinshaw). SATB, Unison

In Adam We Have All Been One (in *Westminster Praise*, Hinshaw). SATB

O God, Be Merciful, Christopher Tye (Oxford). SATB (M)

Rom. 5:12-19 *Since by Man Came Death*, G. F. Handel (from *Messiah*, any edition)

Matt. 4:1-11 *Man Shall Not Live by Bread Alone*, Rudolf Moser (Concordia). Unison or Mixed (E)

Father, with All Your Gospel's Power, harm. J. S. Bach (in *Westminster Praise*, Hinshaw)

Psalm 130 *Out of the Deep*, Croft-Lovelace (Abingdon). SATB (ME)

Psalm 130, Paul Manz (Summy-Birchard). SATB (E)

LLH

COLLECT FOR THE DAY

O God, who revealed glory in Jesus Christ to disciples: help us to listen to your word, so that, seeing the wonders of Christ's love, we may descend with him to a sick and wanting world, and minister as he ministered with compassion for all; for the sake of Jesus, your Son, our Lord.   (WB)

READINGS

Gen. 12:1-7 God selects Abraham to be the father of his covenant people, commanding him to leave Haran, where he had been living, and to begin his pilgrimage.

II Tim. 1:8-14 Paul admonishes his spiritual son, Timothy, to hold fast to the call of God which he received through Christ.

Matt. 17:1-9 Jesus passes the tests of the scribes and the Pharisees and reveals himself as Christ to the disciples at Caesarea Philippi. The Father reveals his pleasure in Jesus through the transfiguration.   JBR

PSALM FOR THE DAY: Psalm 33:12-22

HYMNS FOR THE DAY	HL	HB	WB
The God of Abraham Praise	8	89	587
He Who Would Valiant Be	276	345	414
I'm Not Ashamed to Own My Lord	—	292	—
O Wondrous Type, O Vision Fair	142	182	531
Where Cross the Crowded Ways of Life	410	507	642
Strong Son of God, Immortal Love	175	228	578

ANTHEMS FOR THE DAY

Gen. 12:1-7 *If Thou but Suffer God to Guide Thee,* Jody Lindh (Concordia). SATB (E)

To Abraham the Promise Came (American folk tune) (WB, p. 608)

II Tim. 1:8-14 *Sing, My Soul, His Wondrous Love,* Ned Rorem (Peters). SATB (MD)

Matt. 17:1-9 *Transfiguration,* Peter Cutts (in *Westminster Praise,* Hinshaw)

We Saw His Glory, Erhard Mauersberger (Concordia). 2-Part Mixed, Unison (E)

This Is My Beloved Son, Knut Nystedt (Concordia). SAB (E)   LLH

COLLECT FOR THE DAY

God of holy love: you have poured out living water in the gift of your Son Jesus. Keep us close to him, and loyal to his leading, so that we may never thirst for righteousness, but live eternal life; through our Savior, Christ the Lord. (WB)

READINGS

Ex. 24:12-18 God affirms his covenant with his people by giving Moses the commandments on Mt. Sinai.

Rom. 5:1-5 Paul tells his hearers that since they believe in God they are at peace with him and may rejoice in the hope of sharing his glory. Even suffering cannot destroy their joy.

John 4:5-15, 19-26 The human Jesus, who asks water of a Samaritan woman, offers her the living water of the Spirit when he addresses her as the divine Christ. JBR

PSALM FOR THE DAY: Psalm 95:1-2, 6-11

HYMNS FOR THE DAY	HL	HB	WB
God Himself Is with Us	51	13	384
I to the Hills Will Lift My Eyes	—	377	430
Descend, O Spirit, Purging Flame	—	—	353
I'm So Glad Troubles Don't Last Always	—	—	432
If You Will Only Let God Guide You	—	—	431
Guide Me, O Thou Great Jehovah	104	339	409
God of Grace and God of Glory	—	358	393

ANTHEMS FOR THE DAY

Rom. 5:1-5 *O Jesus, Grant Me Hope and Comfort,* Franck-Stein (Schmitt, Hall & McCreary). SATB (ME)

John 4:5-15, 19-26 *By the Springs of Water,* Cecil Effinger (Augsburg). SATB (MD)

Jesus, Thou Joy of Loving Hearts (HB, No. 215)

I Am the Bread of Life, Sven-Erik Bäck (Walton). SATB (MD)

First Song of Isaiah, Jack Noble White (H. W. Gray). SATB with congregational response (ME)

Psalm 95:1-2, 6-11 *O Come Let Us Sing Unto the Lord,* Donald Swann (G. Schirmer). 2-Part Mixed (E)

O Come Let Us Worship, Mendelssohn (G. Schirmer). SATB with Tenor Solo (MD) LLH

COLLECT FOR THE DAY
God of all mercy, by your power to heal and to forgive, graciously cleanse us from all sin and make us strong; through your Son, Jesus Christ our Lord, who lives and reigns with you and the Holy Spirit, one God, now and forever.   (LBW)

READINGS
II Sam. 5:1-5   Recognizing that God has selected David to be the leader of his people, the elders of the Children of Israel make a covenant with him and anoint him king.

Eph. 5:8-14   The author admonishes his readers whom Christ has brought out of darkness to walk as children of light.

John 9:1-11   Jesus shows himself to be the light of the world through his power to restore vision to a man born blind.   JBR

PSALM FOR THE DAY: Psalm 23

HYMNS FOR THE DAY	HL	HB	WB
The King of Love My Shepherd Is (Ps.)	99	106	590
Hail to the Lord's Anointed	111	146	—
Wake, Awake, for Night Is Flying	—	—	614
The True Light That Enlightens Man	—	—	598
Light of Light, Enlighten Me	21	73	—
Light of the World	422	138	—
Christ Is the World's True Light	—	492	326
Work, for the Night Is Coming	—	297	—
Amazing Grace! How Sweet the Sound	—	—	296

ANTHEMS FOR THE DAY

Eph. 5:8-14   *Walk in the Light*, Sven Lekberg (G. Schirmer). SSATB (MD)

Be Filled with the Spirit, Ronald A. Nelson (Augsburg). 2-Part (E)

O Mighty God, Our Lord, Heinrich Schütz (Mercury). 2-Part (M)

The Eyes of All Hope in Thee, Richard Felciano (E. C. Schirmer). SATB (D)

John 9:1-11   *Christ Is the World's Light* (in *Westminster Praise*, Hinshaw). Unison

Jesus! Name of Wondrous Love, Robert J. Powell (Abingdon). SATB (E)

The Lord, My God, Be Praised, Bach-Lundquist (E. C. Schirmer). Solo or Unison (E)

Psalm 23   *Psalm 23*, Heinz Werner Zimmermann (Augsburg). SATB (ME)   LLH

COLLECT FOR THE DAY

O God: your Son Jesus set his face toward Jerusalem, and did not turn from the cross. Save us from timid minds that shrink from duty, and prepare us to take up our cross, and to follow in the way of Jesus Christ our Lord. (WB)

READINGS

Ezek. 37:11-14 The prophet declares that God can restore the spiritual life of his people even as he had seen him bring life in his vision of the valley of dry bones.

Rom. 8:6-11 Paul tells his hearers that those who have received the Spirit of Christ live a new life in the spirit even though they may die in the flesh.

John 11:1-4, 17, 34-44 Moved by the sorrow of Mary and Martha, Jesus restores their brother Lazarus to life, an act which the Gospel writer interprets as illustrative of his power to give spiritual life, even to the dead. JBR

PSALM FOR THE DAY: Psalm 116:1-9

HYMNS FOR THE DAY	HL	HB	WB
Spirit Divine, Attend Our Prayers	212	243	574
God Has Spoken—by His Prophets	—	—	382
Hope of the World	—	291	423
When Jesus Wept	—	—	636
All Praise Be Yours	—	—	290
The Son of God Goes Forth to War	271	354	—
O Jesus Christ, to You May Hymns Be Rising	—	—	509

ANTHEMS FOR THE DAY

Ezek. 37:11-14 *O God, Our Help in Ages Past*, Leo Sowerby (H. W. Gray). SATB with optional brass (E)

Restore Unto Me, Lully-Nelson (Augsburg). SS with 2 violins (M)

Rom. 8:6-11 *My Song Is Love Unknown*, Carl Schalk (Concordia). 2-Part Mixed (E)

The Fruit of the Spirit Is Love, J. C. Geisler (Boosey & Hawkes). SATB, flute (MD). Moravian Anthem

John 11:1-4, 17, 34-44 *Jesus, Priceless Treasure*, harm. J. S. Bach (WB, p. 442). SATB

If a Man Die, Jean Berger (C. Fischer). SATB (M)

When Jesus Wept, William Billings, arr. Shaw-Parker (Lawson-Gould). SATB (E) LLH

COLLECT FOR THE DAY

Almighty God: you gave your Son to be the leader of us all. As he entered Jerusalem, may we enter our world to follow him, obeying you and trusting your power, willing to suffer or die; through Jesus Christ the Lord.
(WB)

READINGS

Isa. 50:4-7 The prophet tells of his function as minister to his people, for which he suffers, but in which he is sustained by God. The church reads this as a prophecy of the suffering of the Messiah.

Phil. 2:5-11 The humility of Christ as shown in his incarnation, ministry, and death receives the approval of God in his exaltation. Christ's humility is to be a model for the life of the Christian believer.

Matt. 21:1-11 Jesus enters Jerusalem, fulfilling prophecy, proclaiming himself the Messiah, and accepting the praise of the crowd.
JBR

PSALM FOR THE DAY: Psalm 22:1-11

HYMNS FOR THE DAY	HL	HB	WB
All Glory, Laud, and Honor	146	187	284
At the Name of Jesus	—	143	303
When Jesus Wept	—	—	636
All Praise Be Yours	—	—	290
The Son of God Goes Forth to War	271	354	—
O Jesus Christ, to You May Hymns Be Rising	—	—	509

ANTHEMS FOR THE DAY

Isa. 50:4-7 *He Was Despised*, G. F. Handel (from *Messiah*, any edition)

Let This Mind Be in You, Lee Hoiby (Presser). SATB (M)

Phil. 2: 5-11 *Jesus! Name of Wondrous Love*, Robert J. Powell (Abingdon). SATB (E)

Matt. 21:1-11 *Dawn Carol*, Malcolm Williamson (Marks). SATB (MD)

Shout, Shout Hosanna, Scott Wilkinson (Byron-Douglas). Youth and Adult Choirs (M)

Procession of Palms, Malcolm Williamson (G. Schirmer). SATB (ME)

Hosanna to the Son of David, Daniel Moe (Mercury). SATB (MD)   LLH

MAUNDY THURSDAY (A)

COLLECT FOR THE DAY

O God: your love lived in Jesus Christ, who washed disciples' feet on the night of his betrayal. Wash from us the stain of sin, so that, in hours of danger, we may not fail, but follow your Son through every trial, and praise him to the world as Lord and Christ, to whom be glory now and forever. (WB)

READINGS

Ex. 12:1-8, 11-14 God speaks through Moses and Aaron to instruct the people for their liberation from Egypt.

I Cor. 11:23-32 Paul recounts Jesus' institution of the Lord's Supper in order to correct the manner in which it was being observed in the Corinthian church.

John 13:1-15 Jesus dramatically presents himself to the disciples at the Last Supper as one who serves. JBR

PSALM FOR THE DAY: Psalm 116:12-19

HYMNS FOR THE DAY	HL	HB	WB
O God of Bethel, by Whose Hand	98	342	496
Ancient of Days	58	246	297
'Twas on That Night (as Epistle Lection)	360	448	—
O Love, How Deep, How Broad, How High!	139	—	518
Deck Yourself, My Soul	—	—	351
One Table Spread	—	—	541

ANTHEMS FOR THE DAY

I Cor. 11:23-32 This Do in Remembrance of Me, Austin Lovelace (Agape). SATB (E)

Psalm 116:12-19 What Shall I Render to My God, Austin Lovelace (Canyon). 2-Part Mixed (E)

John 13:1-15 Love Consecrates the Humblest Act (LWB, No. 122). (E) LLH

GOOD FRIDAY (A)

COLLECT FOR THE DAY
Merciful Father: you gave your Son to suffer the shame of the cross. Save
us from hardness of heart, so that, seeing him who died for us, we may
repent, confess our sins, and receive your overflowing love, in Jesus
Christ our Lord.
(WB)

READINGS
Isa. 52:13 to 53:12   The Suffering Servant of the prophet's vision is thought
to have been a prophet, or the nation of Judah, but it has been read most
generally as descriptive of Jesus' sacrifice.

Heb. 4:14-16; 5:7-9   Jesus' humanity and perfect submission to the will of
God make him an effective priest to represent us before God.

John 19:17-30   The author gives the account of the crucifixion of Jesus.
Although Jesus is described as king of the Jews, his humanity is
emphasized.
JBR

PSALM FOR THE DAY: Psalm 22:1-18

HYMNS FOR THE DAY

	HL	HB	WB
Throned Upon the Awful Tree	—	197	605
The Son of God Goes Forth to War	271	354	—
There Is a Green Hill Far Away	157	202	—
When Christ Comes to Die	—	—	634
O Sacred Head	151	194	524
Ah, Holy Jesus	158	191	280
Go to Dark Gethsemane	—	193	—
Were You There When They Crucified My Lord?	—	201	—

ANTHEMS FOR THE DAY

Heb. 4:14-16; 5:7-9   *God So Loved the World*, Jan Bender (Concordia).
SATB (M)

God So Loved the World, Hugo Distler (Concordia). SAB (M)

John 19:17-30   *Ah, Holy Jesus*, Robert J. Powell (Choristers Guild). SAB (E)

Seven Words from the Cross, Knut Nystedt (Augsburg). SATB (M). Duration:
17 minutes

'Tis Finished, Shaw-Parker (G. Schirmer). SATB (E)

Crucifixus, Antonio Lotti (G. Schirmer). SATB (D)

Darkness Was Over All, Francis Poulenc (Salabert). *Tenebrae factae sunt*
(from *Sept Répons des Ténèbres*). Latin and English texts (D)   LLH

EASTER DAY (A)

COLLECT FOR THE DAY

Almighty God: through the rising of Jesus Christ from the dead you have given us a living hope. Keep us joyful in all our trials, and guard faith, so we may receive the wonderful inheritance of life eternal, which you have prepared for us; through Jesus Christ the Lord. (WB)

READINGS

Acts 10:34-43 Peter presents the ministry, death, and resurrection of Jesus as they were preached in the New Testament church, with the result that those who believe receive forgiveness of their sins.

Col. 3:1-11 The resurrection of Christ gives assurance that those who believe in him rise also. In that new life which they now experience, they must live by new standards.

John 20:1-9 The empty tomb which the women had discovered became proof of the resurrection to the disciples. JBR

PSALM FOR THE DAY: Psalm 118:1-2, 14-24

HYMNS FOR THE DAY	HL	HB	WB
Jesus Christ Is Risen Today	163	204	440
Christ Jesus Lay in Death's Strong Bands (for Holy Communion)	—	—	327
Come, Risen Lord (for Holy Communion)	—	—	340
O Splendor of God's Glory Bright (for Baptism)	—	—	529
Come, You Faithful, Raise the Strain	168	205	344
The Head That Once Was Crowned with Thorns	195	211	589

ANTHEMS FOR THE DAY

Acts 10:34-43 *Today Is Risen Christ the Lord*, Melchior Vulpius (Concordia). SATB, brass (M)

Jesus Christ, the Lord of Joy, Paul Bouman (Concordia). SATB, brass (E)

Col. 3:1-11 *He Is Risen*, Kenneth Jennings (Augsburg). 2-Part (E)

Jesus Christ Is Risen Today, Alan Hovhaness (AMP). SATB (ME)

John 20:1-9 *Christ Lay by Death Enshrouded*, Johann Hermann Schein (A. Broude). Two high voices, one low, chorus or solo (M)

His Spirit Leads On, Lloyd Pfautsch (Lawson-Gould). SATB (M)

Christ the Lord Is Risen Again, John Rutter (Oxford). SATB (ME)

Christ the Lord Is Risen Again, Walter Pelz (Augsburg). (M)

Alleluia! For Christ the Lord Is Risen, J. S. Bach (Concordia). (ME)

An Easter Processional, Gerald Near (H. W. Gray). 2-Part Mixed (E)

Fanfare and Alleluias, Paul Lindsley Thomas (H. W. Gray). SATB and 3 trumpets (M)

Easter Carol, Charles Ives (AMP). Solo Quartet, SATB (D) LLH

THE SECOND SUNDAY OF EASTER (A)

COLLECT FOR THE DAY

Mighty God, whose Son Jesus broke bonds of death and scattered the powers of darkness: arm us with such faith in him that, facing evil and death, we may overcome as he overcame, Jesus Christ, our hope and our redeemer.

(WB)

READINGS

Acts 2:42-47 The worship, activity, way of life, and growth of the New Testament church are described.

I Peter 1:3-9 Through the resurrection of Jesus Christ, the Christian has a living hope of an ultimate salvation which sustains in times of trial.

John 20:19-31 Jesus' appearance to the disciples after the resurrection confirms their faith which had begun at the empty tomb. He gives them the Holy Spirit.

JBR

PSALM FOR THE DAY: Psalm 105:1-7

HYMNS FOR THE DAY

	HL	HB	WB
The Day of Resurrection!	166	208	584
He Did Not Want to Be Far	—	—	412
All Who Love and Serve Your City	—	—	293
O Sons and Daughters	167	206	527
Thine Is the Glory	—	209	—
Fairest Lord Jesus	194	135	360

ANTHEMS FOR THE DAY

Acts 2:42-47 *Here, O Lord, Thy Servants Gather*, Japanese Mode, arr. Richard Peek (Choristers Guild). SATB (E)

As the Disciples, Lee Hastings Bristol (Presser). SATB (E)

I Peter 1:3-9 *Lord All Glorious, Lord Victorious*, K. K. Davis (Galaxy). Mixed voices with Junior Choir or Soprano Soloist (ME)

John 20:19-31 *Peace Be with You*, Jan Bender (Concordia). 2 equal voices (ME)

Strengthen for Service, Lord, Austin Lovelace (Canyon). Unison (E) LLH

COLLECT FOR THE DAY

Tell us, O God, the mystery of your plans for the world, and show us the power of our risen Lord, so that day by day obeying you, we may look forward to a feast with him within your promised kingdom; by the grace of our Lord Jesus Christ. (WB)

READINGS

Acts 2:22-28 Peter testifies to the resurrection publicly and for the first time in his sermon at Pentecost.

I Peter 1:17-21 Through Christ's sacrificial death, the Christian has a better way to achieve atonement.

Luke 24:13-35 Jesus appears to the travelers to Emmaus, explains to them how his life, death, and resurrection fulfilled the Scriptures, and reveals himself to them as he acts the part of the host in the breaking of bread.

JBR

PSALM FOR THE DAY: Psalm 16

HYMNS FOR THE DAY	HL	HB	WB
"Christ the Lord Is Risen Today"	165	—	330
Behold the Lamb of God!	153	—	307
He Did Not Want to Be Far	—	—	412
That Easter Day with Joy Was Bright	—	—	581
O Sons and Daughters	167	206	527
Come, Christians, Join to Sing	191	131	333

ANTHEMS FOR THE DAY

Acts 2:22-28 *Worthy Is the Lamb*, Malcolm Williamson (Marks). SATB with Soprano Solo

I Peter 1:17-21 *Out of the Depths*, Walther-Erickson (Hinshaw). 2-Part Mixed (E)

O Jesus, Thou Son of God, Heinrich Schütz (Capella). 2-Part Mixed (ME)

Luke 24:13-35 *He Comes to Us*, Jane Marshall (C. Fischer). SATB (ME)

Psalm 16 *Preserve Me, God, I Take Refuge in You*, Joseph Gelineau (in *The Grail Gelineau Psalter*, G.I.A.)

LLH

COLLECT FOR THE DAY

Almighty God, who sent Jesus, the good shepherd, to gather us together: may we not wander from his flock, but follow where he leads us, knowing his voice and staying near him, until we are safely in your fold, to live with you forever; through Jesus Christ our Lord. (WB)

READINGS

Acts 2:36-41 The proclamation of the resurrection and exaltation of the crucified Christ moves to repentance.

I Peter 2:19-25 Jesus' acceptance of suffering becomes the example for the Christian who must also endure suffering.

John 10:1-10 Jesus, the good shepherd, provides abundant life for his followers.

JBR

PSALM FOR THE DAY: Psalm 23

HYMNS FOR THE DAY	HL	HB	WB
You Servants of God	198	27	645
There's a Wideness in God's Mercy	93	110	601
God, Be Merciful to Me	—	282	—
Saviour, like a Shepherd Lead Us	458	380	—
Saviour, Who Thy Flock Art Feeding (for Baptism)	348	—	—
The King of Love My Shepherd Is	99	106	590

ANTHEMS FOR THE DAY

Acts 2:36-41 *Brethren, We Have Met to Worship,* arr. Randolph Currie (Choristers Guild). 2-Part Mixed (E)

I Peter 2:19-25 *Greater Love Hath No Man,* John Ireland (Galaxy). SATB (M)

John 10:1-10 *I Am the Good Shepherd,* Thomas Matthews (Presser). 2-Part, Treble (E)

My Jesus Is My Lasting Joy, Buxtehude-Bitgood (H. W. Gray). Unison (E)

Psalm 23 *Psalm 23,* Philip Dietterich (Agape). Choir and Congregation (E)

The Lord to Me a Shepherd Is, Jean Berger (Kjos). SATB (M) LLH

COLLECT FOR THE DAY
God of hope: you promise many homes within your house where Christ
now lives in glory. Help us to take you at your word, so our hearts may
not be troubled or afraid, but trust your fatherly love, for this life, and
the life to come; through Jesus Christ our Lord.   (WB)

READINGS
Acts 6:1-7 Recognizing that the church has diverse tasks to perform, the
disciples ask for officers to accept responsibility for these tasks.

I Peter 2:4-10 The church, built like stones upon the cornerstone of Christ,
fulfills the function of the chosen people of God.

John 14:1-12 The church will do the work of Christ after his return to the
Father.   JBR

PSALM FOR THE DAY: Psalm 33:1-11

HYMNS FOR THE DAY	HL	HB	WB
Sing Praise to God	—	15	568
Christ Is Made the Sure Foundation	336	433	325
Built on the Rock	—	—	320
He Is the Way	—	—	413
Thou Art the Way	254	221	—
Blessing and Honor and Glory and Power	196	137	311

ANTHEMS FOR THE DAY

Acts 6:1-7 *Forth in Thy Name, O Lord, My Daily Labor to Pursue*, David H.
Williams (Shawnee). SATB (E)

I Peter 2:4-10 *Sacrifices Acceptable to God*, Gerhard Krapf (*Six Scriptural
Affirmations*, Sacred Music). 2-Part Mixed (ME)

You That Know the Lord Is Gracious, Cyril V. Taylor (in *Westminster Praise*,
Hinshaw). SATB; preferable unison

Christ: Foundation, Head and Cornerstone, Lloyd Pfautsch (Lawson-
Gould). SATB (M)

Christ Is Our Cornerstone, Edgar Aufdemberge (Concordia). SATB (E)

Christ Is Made the Sure Foundation, Dale Wood (Schmitt, Hall & McCreary).
(E)

John 14:1-12 *Thy Hand, O God, Has Guided*, David S. York (in
Westminster Praise, Hinshaw). Unison

Come, My Way, My Truth, My Life, Philip Dietterich (H. W. Gray). SATB
(ME)   LLH

COLLECT FOR THE DAY

O God: your Son Jesus prayed for his disciples, and sent them into the world to preach good news. Hold the church in unity by your Holy Spirit, and keep the church close to your word, so that, breaking bread together, disciples may be one with Christ in faith and love and service. (WB)

READINGS

Acts 8:4-8, 14-17 The persecution of the early church led to the dispersion of the disciples, who preach and found churches in other cities.

I Peter 3:13-18 The author admonishes his readers to prepare to give a reasonable argument for their faith, even though their testimony may mean suffering.

John 14:15-21 Jesus promises the disciples that he will continue with them in the person of the Holy Spirit. JBR

PSALM FOR THE DAY: Psalm 66:1-7, 16-20

HYMNS FOR THE DAY	HL	HB	WB
Rejoice, the Lord Is King	193	140	562
I Sing as I Arise Today	—	—	428
Holy Spirit, Truth Divine	208	240	422
Come Down, O Love Divine	—	—	334
O Spirit of the Living God	207	242	528

ANTHEMS FOR THE DAY

Acts 8:4-8, 14-17 *Send Forth Thy Spirit*, Franz Joseph Schuetky (Summy-Birchard). SSATTBB (M)

O Come, Holy Spirit, Telemann-Nelson (Augsburg). Unison with violin and continuo (ME)

I Peter 3:13-18 *When Christ Calls*, Avery and Marsh (Proclamation). Combining "A Mighty Fortress" with text by Dietrich Bonhoeffer. (E)

John 14:15-21 *If Ye Love Me, Keep My Commandments*, Thomas Tallis (G. Schirmer). SATB (M)

I Will Not Leave You Comfortless, William Byrd (E. C. Schirmer, Concord Series). (MD)

I Will Not Leave You Comfortless, Ronald A. Nelson (in *Four Anthems for Young Choirs*, Boosey & Hawkes). Unison (E) LLH

COLLECT FOR THE DAY
Almighty God: your Son Jesus promised that if he was lifted up, he would draw all to himself. Draw us to him by faith, so that we may live to serve you, and look toward life eternal; through Jesus Christ the Lord.   (WB)

READINGS
Acts 1:1-11 Having promised the apostles that "before many days you shall be baptized with the Holy Spirit," Jesus "was lifted up, and a cloud took him out of their sight."

Eph. 1:16-23 God has made Christ to "sit at his right hand" and "has put all things under his feet and has made him the head over all things for the church."

Luke 24:44-53 (Continues the Gospel pericope of Easter 3.) Jesus led the disciples out to Bethany, where he blessed them, and "while he blessed them, he parted from them."   LAB

PSALM FOR THE DAY: Psalm 110

HYMNS FOR THE DAY	HL	HB	WB
Come, Christians, Join to Sing (Ps.)	191	131	333
The Lord Ascendeth Up on High	172	212	—
Light of Light, Enlighten Me	21	73	—
Christ, Whose Glory Fills the Skies	26	47	332
Crown Him with Many Crowns	190	213	349

ANTHEMS FOR THE DAY

Acts 1:1-11 *Come Away to the Skies*, arr. Parker (G. Schirmer). SATB (M)

At the Name of Jesus, R. Vaughan Williams (Oxford). SATB (M)

Eph. 1:16-23 *Alleluia! Sing to Jesus*, Hal Hopson (Augsburg). 2-Part (E)

My Jesus Is My Lasting Joy, Buxtehude-Bitgood (H. W. Gray). Unison (E). Children's Choir

Luke 24:44-53 *The Praises of a King*, Austin Lovelace (Augsburg). 2-Part Mixed (E)   HH

COLLECT FOR THE DAY

Lord of all times and places: your thoughts are not our thoughts, your ways are not our ways, and you are lifted high above our little lives. Rule our minds, and renew our ways, so that, in mercy, we may be drawn near you; through Jesus Christ our Lord and Master.   (WB)

READINGS

Acts 1:12-14 Luke, author of Acts, turns our attention from Jesus' local ministry among his followers to his universal lordship of the whole world through the witness and mission of those followers as the church.

I Peter 4:12-19 This letter, written much later than Acts, reflects the fiery trials through which Christians were going as part of their Spirit-given mission to the whole world, which was given with tongues of flame.

John 17:1-11 Jesus joins himself to his church which will proclaim God's glory just as he did in his "hour" of trial and suffering. He prays that the unity of the blessed Trinity be given to the church in the world.   HTA

PSALM FOR THE DAY: Psalm 47

HYMNS FOR THE DAY	HL	HB	WB
All Hail the Power of Jesus' Name!	192	132	285
Glory Be to God the Father	60	—	—
Glorious Is Your Name, Most Holy	—	—	378
Christ, Whose Glory Fills the Skies	26	47	332
The Lord Ascendeth Up on High	172	212	—
The Friends of Christ Together	—	—	586
Jesus Shall Reign	377	496	443

ANTHEMS FOR THE DAY

I Peter 4:12-19 *God Is Ever Sun and Shield*, J. S. Bach (in *Third Morning Star Book*, Concordia). Unison with oboe or flute (M)

God Is Our Strength and Refuge, Philip Landgrave (Hope). Unison with Narration (E)

John 17:1-11 *Come, Holy Ghost, God and Lord*, Johann Hermann Schein (in *Third Morning Star Book*, Concordia). SAB (ME)

Psalm 47 *God Has Gone Up*, Jack Goode (H. W. Gray). SATB (ME) LLH

COLLECT FOR THE DAY

O God: you sent the promised fire of your Spirit to make saints of common folk. Once more, as we are waiting and together, may we be enflamed with such love for you that we may speak boldly in your name, and show your wonderful power to the world; through Jesus Christ our Lord.   (WB)

READINGS

I Cor. 12:4-13   Through the one Holy Spirit, God gives different gifts and abilities to different people for the welfare of the church.

Acts 2:1-13   This account tells of the coming of the Holy Spirit to the church on Pentecost.

John 14:15-26   The author recounts Jesus' promise of the Holy Spirit. This promise is fulfilled when Jesus gives them the Spirit in his first appearance to them after the resurrection.   JBR

PSALM FOR THE DAY: Psalm 104: 1-4, 24-33

HYMNS FOR THE DAY	HL	HB	WB
God Has Spoken—by His Prophets	—	—	382
Spirit Divine, Attend Our Prayers	212	243	574
Upon Your Great Church Universal	—	—	611
Come, Holy Ghost, Our Souls Inspire	—	237	335
The Day of Pentecost Arrived	—	—	583
O Spirit of the Living God	207	242	528

ANTHEMS FOR THE DAY

I Cor. 12:4-13   *The Fruit of the Spirit Is Love,* J. C. Geisler (Boosey & Hawkes). SATB, flute (MD). Moravian Anthem

Come, Holy Ghost, Orlando Gibbons (A. Broude). SATB (ME)

Acts 2:1-13   *Carol for Pentecost,* Judy Hunnicutt (Augsburg). Unison Narrative (E)

Speak to One Another of Psalms, Jean Berger (Augsburg). SATB (M)

Hail Thee, Spirit, Lord Eternal, Robert Wetzler (Augsburg). 2-Part Mixed (E)

Two for Pentecost, Erik Routley (Hinshaw). SATB (ME)

John 14:15-26   *Peace I Leave with You,* David Eddleman (C. Fischer). SATB (ME)   LLH

COLLECT FOR THE DAY
Almighty God, Father of our Lord Jesus Christ and giver of the Holy
Spirit: keep our minds searching your mystery, and our faith strong to
declare that you are one eternal God and Father, revealed by the Spirit,
through our Lord Jesus Christ.   (WB)

READINGS
Ezek. 37:1-4 The prophet recognizes the work of the Spirit of God in the
vision of the valley of dry bones.

II Cor. 13:5-13 Paul describes the Spirit in the life of the individual
Christian as "Jesus Christ in you." He calls upon his readers to accept
Christ's authority.

Matt. 28:16-20 This passage is the clearest expression concerning the
Trinity in the Gospels, setting forth the existence of the Holy Spirit with the
Father and the Son.   JBR

PSALM FOR THE DAY: Psalm 150

HYMNS FOR THE DAY	HL	HB	WB
God Has Spoken	—	—	382
O Word of God Incarnate	215	251	532
Jesus, Stand Among Us	—	222	—
Jesus, Lead the Way	—	334	441
Go, Labor On	376	283	—
Father, We Greet Thee (for Holy Communion)	—	285	—
Come, Labor On	366	287	—
How Firm a Foundation	283	369	425

(In addition, it should be noted that all of the following hymns from *The
Worshipbook*, many of which will be found in the other two books, have as
their last stanzas Trinitarian doxologies which commend them for use at the
Offering, or as Trinitarian hymns: pp. 273, 279, 282, 283, 292, 297, 307, 320,
324, 325, 335, 339, 343, 344, 345, 348, 356, 365, 369, 382, 399, 420, 421, 428,
440, 481, 494, 504, 534, 541, 546, 581, 619, 622, 632.)

ANTHEMS FOR THE DAY

II Cor. 13:5-13 *Thy Truth Is Great*, Ron Nelson (Boosey & Hawkes). SATB
(MD)

I Sing as I Arise Today, Joseph Clokey (Concordia). SATB (or setting found
in WB, pp. 428-9) (E)

Matt. 28:16-20 *Come, Ye Servant People*, Charlotte Garden (H. W. Gray).
SATB with brass and tympani (ME)

Psalm 150 *Psalm 150*, César Franck (Summy-Birchard). SATB (M) LLH

THE SECOND SUNDAY AFTER PENTECOST (A)

COLLECT FOR THE DAY

Almighty God: you have commanded us to rise up and walk in righteousness. Help us not only to hear you, but to do what you require; through Jesus Christ, our rock and our redeemer. (WB)

READINGS

Deut. 11:18-21 God promises the Children of Israel that if they keep and teach the law, they will enjoy long life and possession of their homeland.

Rom. 3:21-28 The righteousness of God which he showed in the law is demonstrated clearly in Christ's sacrifice. Through God's grace, we become participants in that righteousness by faith.

Matt. 7:21-29 Obedience to the will of God rather than wordy creeds is necessary for citizenship in the kingdom of heaven. JBR

PSALM FOR THE DAY: Psalm 31:1-5,19-24

HYMNS FOR THE DAY	HL	HB	WB
From All That Dwell Below the Skies	388	33	373
We Come Unto Our Fathers' God	342	16	623
Built on the Rock	—	—	320
The Lord Will Come and Not Be Slow	185	230	—
O Day of God, Draw Nigh	—	—	492
For All the Saints	429	425	369

ANTHEMS FOR THE DAY

Deut. 11:18-21 *Hear, O Israel*, Ron Nelson (Boosey & Hawkes). SATB (ME)

Rom. 3:21-28 *O Lord, Increase My Faith*, Orlando Gibbons (H. W. Gray). SATB (M)

Matt. 7:21-29 *Christ Is Made the Sure Foundation*, Dale Wood (Schmitt, Hall & McCreary). SATB (E)

Sing Praises, John Horman (Hinshaw). SATB (E) LLH

COLLECT FOR THE DAY

God of power: you work for good in the world, and you want us to work with you. Keep us from being divided, so that when you call, we may follow single-mindedly in the way of Jesus Christ, our Lord and Master.   (WB)

READINGS

Hos. 6:1-6   The prophet stresses God's desire for love rather than ritual observances.

Rom. 4:13-25   The promises of God made to Abraham and his descendants were fulfilled for those who believed in them. By faith, the Christian is also a descendant of Abraham and a recipient of the promises available through the death and resurrection of Christ.

Matt. 9:9-13   In the life and teachings of Jesus, love for the sinner and outcast is justified by God's expressed preference for mercy rather than sacrifice.   JBR

PSALM FOR THE DAY: Psalm 50:1-15

HYMNS FOR THE DAY	HL	HB	WB
Heaven and Earth, and Sea and Air	27	6	415
Come, Let Us to the Lord	—	125	—
O Brother Man, Fold to Your Heart	403	474	484
Go to Dark Gethsemane	—	193	—
Jesus Calls Us	223	269	439
Sinners Jesus Will Receive	227	—	—
Somebody's Knocking at Your Door	—	—	572

ANTHEMS FOR THE DAY

Hos. 6:1-6   *A Psalm of Praise*, Hal Hopson (Presser). SATB, 2-Part (E)

Rom. 4:13-25   *O Lord, Increase My Faith*, Orlando Gibbons (H. W. Gray). SATB (M)

Matt. 9:9-13   *Jesu, Friend of Sinners*, Edvard Grieg (H. W. Gray). SATB (MD)

We Hurry with Tired, Unfaltering Footsteps, J. S. Bach (Galaxy). SA (M)   LLH

THE FOURTH SUNDAY AFTER PENTECOST (A)

COLLECT FOR THE DAY
Mighty God: your kingdom has come in Jesus of Nazareth, and grows among us day by day. Send us out to preach good news, so that the world may believe, be rescued from sin, and become your faithful people; through Jesus Christ our Savior. (WB)

READINGS
Ex. 19:2-6 In the wilderness, God renews his covenant with the Children of Israel, calling them to be a kingdom of priests and a holy nation.

Rom. 5:6-11 Reconciled with God by the death of Christ, Paul assures us that we may rejoice in the new life which is ours because Christ lives.

Matt. 9:36 to 10:8 Jesus extends his mission through the commissioning of the disciples to preach and heal. JBR

PSALM FOR THE DAY: Psalm 100

HYMNS FOR THE DAY	HL	HB	WB
All People That on Earth Do Dwell (Ps.)	1	24	288
Guide Me, O Thou Great Jehovah (Ps.)	104	339	409
Through the Night of Doubt and Sorrow (tune: Ebenezer)	345	475	—
Sinner, Please Don't Let This Harvest Pass	—	—	570
Sinners Jesus Will Receive	227	—	—
God of Compassion, in Mercy Befriend Us	290	122	392
Come, Labor On	366	287	—
Turn Back, O Man	424	490	—

ANTHEMS FOR THE DAY

Rom. 5:6-11 *God of Mercy*, J. S. Bach (Boosey & Hawkes). SATB

Wondrous Love, J. J. Niles-Sheppard (G. Schirmer). SATB (E)

God So Loved the World, Jan Bender (Concordia). SATB (M)

God So Loved the World, Hugo Distler (Concordia). SAB (M)

Psalm 100 *Make a Joyful Noise Unto the Lord*, François Couperin (Concordia). SAB (ME)

Make a Joyful Voice Unto the Lord, William Mathias (Oxford). SATB (M)

Psalm 100, Charles Ives (Presser). SA, SATB, and bells (D) LLH

COLLECT FOR THE DAY

Great God: you guard our lives, and put down powers that could overturn us. Help us to trust you, to acknowledge you, and to live for Jesus Christ, the Lord of all.   (WB)

READINGS

Jer. 20:10-13 The unwilling prophet, ridiculed for prophetic denunciation of his people, expresses his confidence in God.

Rom. 5:12-15 Paul sees all people, although sinners and mortal because of Adam's sin, now able to free themselves of sin and to walk in new life through the grace of God made available through Jesus Christ.

Matt. 10:26-33 Jesus warns his disciples that the dangers that temptation brings are even greater than the external dangers from which God protects them.

JBR

PSALM FOR THE DAY: Psalm 69:1-18, 34-36

HYMNS FOR THE DAY	HL	HB	WB
Praise, My Soul, the King of Heaven	14	31	551
Who Trusts in God (tune: Ebenezer)	—	375	—
Come, Thou Fount of Every Blessing	235	379	341
Go, Tell It on the Mountain	—	—	380
A Mighty Fortress	266	91	274, 276
I'm Not Ashamed to Own My Lord	—	292	—

ANTHEMS FOR THE DAY

Jer. 20:10-13 *Behold, God Is My Salvation*, Leo Sowerby (H. W. Gray). SA or 2-Part Mixed (ME)

Rom. 5:12-15 *To Thee We Turn Our Eyes*, Heinrich Schütz (Concordia). SATB (ME)

Grant Us Grace, Lord, Alfred Whitehead (Curwen). SSATB (M)

Matt. 10:26-33 *Prayer*, Lloyd Pfautsch (Lawson-Gould). 2-Part Mixed (E).Text by Dag Hammarskjöld

LLH

COLLECT FOR THE DAY

Holy God: your Son demands complete devotion. Give us courage to take up our cross, and, without turning back, to follow where he leads us, Christ our Lord and Master.   (WB)

READINGS

II Kings 4:8-16 In this tale, the prophet Elisha rewards the Shunammite woman for her hospitality by granting her the son she desired.

Rom. 6:1-11 Christians who enjoy the new life in Christ would not sin even though they believe the grace of God will pardon any new sin.

Matt. 10:37-42 For the disciple, Christ must have first priority. Anyone who serves as a disciple will receive a special reward.   JBR

PSALM FOR THE DAY: Psalm 89:1-4, 15-18

HYMNS FOR THE DAY	HL	HB	WB
Heaven and Earth, and Sea and Air	27	6	415
God of the Prophets!	481	520	398
Christ Is the World's True Light	—	492	326
The Day of Resurrection!	166	208	584
"Take Up Thy Cross"	—	293	—
Be Thou My Vision	325	303	304

ANTHEMS FOR THE DAY

II Kings 4:8-16 *O Christ Whose Love Has Sought Us Out*, Lee Hastings Bristol (in *Westminster Praise*, Hinshaw)

Rom. 6:1-11 *Father, with All Your Gospel's Power*, harm. J. S. Bach (in *Westminster Praise*, Hinshaw)

Matt. 10:37-42 *They Cast Their Nets in Galilee*, Michael McCabe (C. Fischer). 2 equal voices (E)

I Saw a Stranger Yestreen, L. Stanley Glarum (G. Schirmer). 2-Part Mixed (ME)   LLH

COLLECT FOR THE DAY

Almighty God: you have disclosed your purpose in Jesus of Nazareth. May we never reject him, but, hearing his message with childlike faith, praise him, our Lord and Master.   (WB)

READINGS

Zech. 9:9-13 The author of these words lived during the Greek invasion of Palestine under Alexander the Great. In his vision he looked beyond the military emperor to a messianic king who would establish peace.

Rom. 8:6-11 Paul says that although the physical body dies because of sin, the person who possesses the Holy Spirit will live eternally.

Matt. 11:25-30 In these words Jesus discloses that the childlike heart is necessary to understand spiritual truth, and offers such understanding and rest to those who come to him.   JBR

PSALM FOR THE DAY: Psalm 145

HYMNS FOR THE DAY

	HL	HB	WB
Rejoice, O Pure in Heart	297	407	561
Come, Holy Spirit, God and Lord!	—	—	336
I Heard the Voice of Jesus Say	236	280	—
"Come Unto Me, Ye Weary"	222	268	—
Once in Royal David's City	454	462	539
God of Our Life (tune: Sandon)	88	108	395

ANTHEMS FOR THE DAY

Zech. 9:9-13 *Rejoice Greatly*, G. F. Handel (from *Messiah*, any edition)

Rom. 8:6-11 *Cause Us, O Lord*, Ron Nelson (Boosey & Hawkes). SATB (M)

Matt. 11:25-30 *Come Unto Me* and *His Yoke Is Easy*, G. F. Handel (from *Messiah*, any edition)

Thy Kingdom Come on Earth, Paul Christiansen (Augsburg). SATB and Narrators (M)

Psalm 145 *The Eyes of All*, Geoffrey Schroth (J. Fischer). SATB (D)

The Eyes of All Wait Upon Thee, Jean Berger (Augsburg). SATB (M) LLH

THE EIGHTH SUNDAY AFTER PENTECOST (A)

COLLECT FOR THE DAY
> Great God: your word is seed from which faith grows. As we receive good news, may your love take root in our lives, and bear fruit of compassion; through Jesus Christ our Lord. (WB)

READINGS
> **Isa. 55:10-13** The prophet foretells the joyous return of the exiles to Jerusalem, for God's promises are as certain as the dependable cycles of the seasons and the rebirth of nature.

> **Rom. 8:12-17** If as spiritual beings we receive the Spirit of God, we become children of God and heirs with Christ of all the blessings of God.

> **Matt. 13:1-17** Jesus tells the parable of the seed and the soil as a means of teaching truths about the kingdom of heaven which only these with spiritual understanding can understand. JBR

PSALM FOR THE DAY: Psalm 65

HYMNS FOR THE DAY	HL	HB	WB
Comfort, Comfort You My People	—	—	347
Let Us with a Gladsome Mind	64	28	453
Father, We Greet You	—	285	364
Sing to the Lord of Harvest	—	—	569
Come, You Thankful People, Come	460	525	346
Thy Might Sets Fast the Mountains	—	99	—

ANTHEMS FOR THE DAY

Rom. 8:12-17 *By Gracious Powers*, Gelineau-Routley (Hinshaw). SATB (ME)

Time (Behold the Sower of the Seed), Benjamin Britten (Boosey & Hawkes). SATB (D)

Matt. 13:1-17 *The Lord Is Rich and Merciful*, Austin Lovelace (Canyon). SA, TB, or 2-Part Mixed

Psalm 65 *Thou Visitest the Earth*, Maurice Greene (Concordia). 2-Part Mixed (E) LLH

COLLECT FOR THE DAY

God of compassion: you are patient with evil, and you care for lost sheep. Teach us to obey you, and to live our lives following the good shepherd, Jesus Christ our Lord.   (WB)

READINGS

II Sam. 7:18-22 David's prayer is his response to God's promise to him concerning the future of his family line.

Rom. 8:18-25 The children of God who have received his Spirit can look forward to a glorious fulfillment of God's promises after the suffering of the present time.

Matt. 13:24-35 Jesus tells parables of the kingdom which explain the presence of sinful members in the present kingdom.   JBR

PSALM FOR THE DAY: Psalm 86:11-17

HYMNS FOR THE DAY

	HL	HB	WB
Immortal, Invisible, God Only Wise	66	85	433
Praise We Our Maker	—	—	558
Come, Lord, and Tarry Not	188	233	—
Come, You Thankful People, Come	460	525	346
Father Eternal, Ruler of Creation	—	486	362
Lord, Bless and Pity Us	—	493	456

ANTHEMS FOR THE DAY

Rom. 8:18-25 *Sing, My Soul, His Wondrous Love*, Ned Rorem (Peters). SATB (M)

Matt. 13:24-35 *Lord, Keep Us Steadfast*, Hugo Distler (Augsburg). SAB (ME)

                                                                      LLH

COLLECT FOR THE DAY

Help us to seek you, God of our lives, so that in seeking, we may find the hidden treasure of your love, and rejoice in serving you; through Jesus Christ our Lord.   (WB)

READINGS

I Kings 3:5-12 God found Solomon humble and teachable when Solomon prayed for an understanding heart after he was declared king, so God renews to Solomon the promises he had made to his father David.

Rom. 8:26-30 The Spirit sustains us in the weakness of our spiritual life in order that we may participate in the good life which God ordains for those who love him.

Matt. 13:44-52 Jesus describes the supreme value of the kingdom as an inner possession.   JBR

PSALM FOR THE DAY: Psalm 119:129-136

HYMNS FOR THE DAY	HL	HB	WB
We Sing the Mighty Power of God	65	84	628
I Bind My Heart This Tide	243	286	—
Come, O Come, Great Quickening Spirit	—	—	338
When I Survey the Wondrous Cross	152	198	635
Come, You Thankful People, Come	460	525	346
We Love Your Kingdom, Lord	337	435	626

ANTHEMS FOR THE DAY

I Kings 3:5-12 *Teach Me, O Lord*, Rogers-Wienandt (Flammer). SATB (ME)

Holy, Loving Father, Palestrina (E. C. Schirmer). SATB (MD)

Rom. 8:26-30 *Thou, Lord, the Refuge of the Meek*, Josquin Desprez (J. Fischer). SAB (M)

Matt. 13:44-52 *The King Shall Come*, Ludwig Lenel (in *Morning Star Book II*, Concordia). 2-Part Mixed (E)

Arise, the Kingdom Is at Hand, Gilbert Martin (Flammer). SATB (E) LLH

COLLECT FOR THE DAY

God of grace: your Son fed the hungry crowd with loaves of borrowed
bread. May we never hoard what we have, but gratefully share with
others good things you provide; through Jesus Christ, the bread of
life. (WB)

READINGS

Isa. 55:1-3 Here is an invitation to come to real satisfaction and
nourishment, which is available without money. Listen and your soul will
live.

Rom. 8:31-39 A hymn of God's love, significant in the life of the church,
which gives a clear statement of the source of our security. If God is for us,
who is against us? Who indeed! If Christ is our judge, and Christ died for
us—the case is stacked in our favor. It is like going to court and finding the
judge is your closest friend. So, what can possibly separate us from the love
of Christ? After a consideration of every possible dimension, the conclusion
is that nothing exists that can separate us.

Matt. 14:13-21 Jesus sought a retreat in which to grieve the loss of John the
Baptist, but the people crowded in. His heart went out to them, and he asked
the disciples to share their food with the crowd. The 5,000 were fed, with
food left over. JM

PSALM FOR THE DAY: Psalm 78:14-20, 23-29

HYMNS FOR THE DAY

	HL	HB	WB
Let Us with a Gladsome Mind	64	28	453
Cast Your Burden on the Lord	288	—	323
Lord, by Whose Breath	—	—	457
Father, We Thank You that You Planted	—	—	366
The Great Creator of the Worlds	—	—	588
We Plow the Fields	464	524	—

ANTHEMS FOR THE DAY

Isa. 55:1-3 *Ho! Everyone That Thirsteth,* B. C. Pulkingham (G.I.A.). SATB
(E)

Comfort All Ye My People (Seek Ye the Lord), Fauré-Hopson (C. Fischer).
SATB (ME)

Rom. 8:31-39 *Who Shall Separate Us,* Heinrich Schütz (Chantry). SATB
(M)

Who Shall Separate Us, John Ness Beck (Art Masters). SATB (ME) LLH

COLLECT FOR THE DAY
> Mighty God: your Son Jesus came to comfort the fearful. May we never be afraid, but, knowing you are with us, take heart, and faithfully serve Christ the Lord.   (WB)

READINGS
> **I Kings 19:9-16**   Elijah is running for his life. He is filled with despair, and, perhaps, self-pity: "I am zealous!" "I alone am left!" Does he want God to flex his celestial muscles? Instead of earthquake or fire, God speaks in a small voice telling Elijah to provide for political and prophetic continuities. God's purposes are masked in history.

> **Rom. 9:1-5**   Think of Paul willing to give up his own salvation ("Oh, that will be glory for me!") for the sake of his Jewish brothers and sisters. Paul knows that the Jews are God's people, chosen in covenant love, recipients of the Law and the Promises. From them, Christ has come and in him their salvation is assured.

> **Matt. 14:22-33**   Here is Christ saying to a scared, storm-tossed huddle of disciples, "Courage! I AM!" But Peter's faith slips away when he catches sight of the waves. He is rescued by a Lord whom the disciples confess to be the strong "Son of God."   DB

PSALM FOR THE DAY: Psalm 85:8-13

HYMNS FOR THE DAY

	HL	HB	WB
The God of Abraham Praise	8	89	587
Ancient of Days	58	246	297
How Firm a Foundation	283	369	425
Eternal Father, Strong to Save	492	521	356
Give to the Winds Your Fears	294	364	377
O Come and Sing Unto the Lord	49	29	488
Lead On, O King Eternal	371	332	448

ANTHEMS FOR THE DAY

> **I Kings 19:9-16**   *God Is My Strong Salvation*, Austin Lovelace (Canyon). SATB (M)

> *What God Ordains Is Always Good*, Johann Pachelbel (Concordia). SATB (M)

> *Fret Not Thyself*, Gordon Young (Flammer). SATB (M)

> **Rom. 9:1-5**   *Salvation Is Created*, Paul Tschesnokoff (Bourne). SATB (M)

> **Matt. 14:22-33**   *The God of Glory Thundereth*, Alan Hovhaness (Peters). SATB (M)

> *O Lord of Hosts*, Alan Hovhaness (Peters). SATB (M)   BH

COLLECT FOR THE DAY

> Holy God: we do not deserve crumbs from your table, for we are sinful and dying. May we have grace to praise you for the bread of life you give in Jesus Christ, the Lord of love, and the Savior of us all.　(WB)

READINGS

Isa. 56:1-7　Though eunuchs and "foreigners" were excluded from the worshiping congregation and therefore felt estranged from God, here is Yahweh promising to gather them in along with Israel. They are not to be banished, because Yahweh's house shall be a "house of prayer for all."

Rom. 11:13-16, 29-32　Think of it, if Jews had not refused faith in Christ, we might never have heard the gospel message. If their rejection of Christ resulted in our liberation, how much more wonderful will be the reconciliation of us all! Jews were a holy people, are a holy people, and will be fulfilled as a holy people through their own child, Jesus the Christ.

Matt. 15:21-28　Yes, Jesus' ministry was to a lost Israel and then through them to other lands. But Jesus scolds his disciples for their rigid protocol in sending away a non-Israelite. Instead, Jesus responds to the woman's faith, "Lord, help me!" and to her wit, "Even puppies get leftovers!"　DB

PSALM FOR THE DAY: Psalm 67

HYMNS FOR THE DAY

	HL	HB	WB
Father, We Praise You	24	43	365
Before the Lord Jehovah's Throne	63	81	306
God of Mercy, God of Grace (Ps.)	465	—	—
Lord, Bless and Pity Us (Ps.)	—	493	456
The King of Love My Shepherd Is	99	106	590
At Even, When the Sun Was Set	43	55	—
O for a Thousand Tongues	199	141	493

ANTHEMS FOR THE DAY

Isa. 56:1-7　*Lord, I Love the Habitation of Thy House,* Graun-Wienandt (Gamut). SATB (E)

This Is the Covenant, Jean Berger (Augsburg). SATB (E)

Rom. 11:13-16, 29-32　*Sighing, Sorrow, and Need* (from Cantata No. 21, J. S. Bach, in *Anthology of Sacred Solos,* Vol. I, G. Schirmer). Soprano Solo (D)

If Thou but Suffer God to Guide Thee, Jody Lindh (Concordia). SATB (E)

The Lord Will Suffer God to Guide Thee, J. S. Bach (Fischer). SATB (M)

Matt. 15:21-28　*Great and Glorious,* F. J. Haydn (B. F. Wood). SATB (M)

BH

COLLECT FOR THE DAY
God our Father: you sent your Son to be our Savior. Help us to confess his name, to serve him without getting in the way, and to hear words of eternal life through him, Jesus Christ our Lord.   (WB)

READINGS
Isa. 22:19-23 Yahweh appoints a deputy and turns over to him a key to the royal palace in Jerusalem as a sign of authority. The deputy is to rule enthroned in Yahweh's name, and he will be kept firm in his position.

Rom. 11:33-36 When you trace God's mysterious purpose through all generations, through Jews and Gentiles, black and white, east and west, all you can do is to shout out a hymn of praise. How deep are God's ways; how wise his plans—glory, glory, glory!

Matt. 16:13-20 (The lectionary has split the story of Peter's confession between consecutive Gospel lections; they might be preached as a two-part sermon series.) Peter confesses that Jesus is the Christ, contra pop piety which supposed he might be one of the prophets *redivivus*. Upon the "Rock," Peter, a fallible disciple who obviously doesn't understand his own confession, Christ promises to found a congregation. Then he announces that his apostolic people will have authority (the keys) "to bind and to free," perhaps by their bold preaching of the gospel.   DB

PSALM FOR THE DAY: Psalm 138

HYMNS FOR THE DAY	HL	HB	WB
Immortal, Invisible, God Only Wise	66	85	433
Open Now the Gates of Beauty	—	40	544
There's a Wideness in God's Mercy	93	110	601
Built on the Rock	—	432	320
A Mighty Fortress	266	91	274
At the Name of Jesus	—	143	303

ANTHEMS FOR THE DAY

Rom. 11:33-36 *Blessed Be Thou, Lord God of Israel*, H. A. Matthews (G. Schirmer). SATB (D)

Alleluia, All the Earth Doth Worship Thee, Everett Titcomb (B. F. Wood). SATB (M)

Let All Nations Shout and Sing, Theron Kirk (C. Fischer). SATB (M)

Matt. 16:13-20 *Built on a Rock*, Lindeman-Brandon (Augsburg). SATB (M)

At the Name of Jesus, R. Vaughan Williams (Oxford). SATB (E)   BH

COLLECT FOR THE DAY
Holy God: you welcome those who are modest and loving. Help us to give up pride, serve neighbors, and humbly walk with your Son, our Lord, Jesus Christ.   (WB)

READINGS
Jer. 20:7-9 Wouldn't you want to give up preaching God's word if every time you opened your mouth you were greeted by hoots of derision, if not outright abuse? Jeremiah is angry with God for making him a laughingstock. So, why not give up preaching? Jeremiah can't: God's word is like a blazing fire in him which he cannot suppress. And it is, isn't it?

Rom. 12:1-7 Let pagans boast that their worship is "spirrrrrritual"; we must avoid such high-minded nonsense. Christ gave himself bodily. In turn, we must "present our bodies" to work as members of the body of Christ. So, if you can teach, teach; if you can preach, preach; if you can care, care; if you have money, give it cheerfully—all ways of presenting ourselves bodily!

Matt. 16:21-28 Well, Peter doesn't understand his own words, "You are the Christ!" He looks for a triumphant Messiah, and so rebukes Jesus for suggesting suffering and death. Peter, the Rock, has become a stumbling block tempting Jesus to turn from filial obedience. The church is always tempted to dream of triumph, to "win the world," when instead Christ offers those who follow him a cross on which to die!   DB

PSALM FOR THE DAY:Psalm 26

HYMNS FOR THE DAY	HL	HB	WB
God's Word Is like a Flaming Sword	—	—	405
As Men of Old Their Firstfruits Brought	—	—	301
Onward, Christian Soldiers	365	350	542
The Son of God Goes Forth to War	271	354	—
Alone You Journey Forth, O Lord	—	—	294
"Take Up Thy Cross"	—	293	—
When I Survey the Wondrous Cross	152	198	635

ANTHEMS FOR THE DAY

Jer. 20:7-9 *From the End of the Earth*, Alan Hovhaness (Peters). SATB (M)

Rom. 12:1-7 *Though I Speak with the Tongues of Men*, Felton Rapley (Boosey & Hawkes). SATB (D)

Beloved, Let Us Love One Another, Gerhard Schroth (Kjos). SATB (E)

Matt. 16:21-28 *If a Man Die*, Jean Berger (C. Fischer). SATB (M)   BH

COLLECT FOR THE DAY

God our Father: you have promised the Holy Spirit whenever we gather in the name of your Son. Be with us now, so we may hear your word, and believe in Christ, our Lord and Savior. (WB)

READINGS

Ezek. 33:7-9 The prophet is appointed a "watchman," charged with warning Israel of God's impending judgment. Ezekiel is to speak the word to the wicked, and to those who may fall away from God's will. Should he fail to speak, the blood of Israel will be on him. A formidable commission!

Rom. 13:8-10 Just as God fulfills his covenant by loving all no matter who, what, or how we are; so we fulfill his will in the same extravagant love. All the "shall nots" written to protect us from each other are positively carried out when we deliberately love neighbors.

Matt. 18:15-20 Most scholars see this passage as the product of an early church polity. It does stand over against our too casual church discipline, and loveless lack of concern for each other's Christian formation. We are the body of Christ with his Spirit among us. If we are to serve him, we shall have to exercise mutual discipline in love, for one member's lapse will weaken all. DB

PSALM FOR THE DAY: Psalm 119:33-40

HYMNS FOR THE DAY	HL	HB	WB
God Himself Is with Us	51	13	384
Lord, from the Depths to You I Cry	240	277	459
O Brother Man, Fold to Your Heart	403	474	484
Where Charity and Love Prevail	—	—	641
Lord, We Thank You for Our Brothers	—	—	468
He Did Not Want to Be Far	—	—	412
Jesus, Stand Among Us	—	222	—
O Son of Man	182	—	—

ANTHEMS FOR THE DAY

Ezek. 33:7-9 *God, Bring Thy Sword*, Ron Nelson (Boosey & Hawkes). SATB (M)

Rom. 13:8-10 *If Ye Love Me, Keep My Commandments*, Thomas Tallis (Choral Art). SATB (E)

Teach Me, O Lord, the Way of Thy Statutes, Thomas Attwood (E. C. Schirmer). SATB (E)

Matt. 18:15-20 *Cause Us, O Lord*, Ron Nelson (Boosey & Hawkes). SATB (D) BH

COLLECT FOR THE DAY

Loving Father: whenever we wander, in mercy you find us. Help us to forgive without pride or ill will, as you forgive us, so that your joy may be ours; through Jesus Christ the Lord.　　　　　　　　　　　　(WB)

READINGS

Gen. 4:13-16　Cain, who has killed his brother, is condemned to be a fugitive on an inhospitable earth. He is horrified and frightened: "Whoever finds me will slay me!" But Cain has forgotten The Mercy. God, the same God who judged, puts a protective "brand" on Cain as a sign of his unswerving love. We forget God *is* Mercy.

Rom. 14:5-9　Perhaps the lectionary has combined two separate sayings, vs. 5-6 and vs. 7-9. However, we can sense the logic that combined them. There are different Christian life-styles—e.g., with regard to religious observance and food and drink—but all can be done with thanksgiving. After all, Christ died and is risen: he is the one Lord in whom and for whom all Christians live.

Matt. 18:21-35　Are there limits to forgiveness? (Peter is still trying to handle mercy with a calculator!) In the parable, one man is forgiven a billion dollars, but then tries to wring out every cent from a small-change borrower. Well, Christians who live in startled gratitude for the immense mercy of God can only forgive and forgive and forgive ad infinitum.　　　　　DB

PSALM FOR THE DAY: Psalm 103:1-13

HYMNS FOR THE DAY

	HL	HB	WB
Praise, My Soul, the King of Heaven	14	31	551
Bless, O My Soul! (Ps.)	—	8	—
O My Soul, Bless God, the Father (Ps.)	—	—	523
Majestic Sweetness Sits Enthroned	197	142	—
O Lord of Life, Where'er They Be	—	—	513
Praise We Our Maker	—	—	558
Pardoned Through Redeeming Grace	—	—	550
God of Compassion, in Mercy Befriend Us	290	122	392

ANTHEMS FOR THE DAY

Gen. 4:13-16　*See What Love,* Mendelssohn (Augsburg). SATB (M)

Have Mercy, Lord, C. Morales (Concordia). SATB (M)

Matt. 18:21-35　*Turn Thy Face from My Sins,* Thomas Attwood (in *The Church Anthem Book,* Oxford). SATB (E)

Thou Knowest, Lord, the Secrets of Our Hearts, Henry Purcell (Kjos). SATB (E)　　　　　　　　　　　　　　　　　　　　　　　　　　BH

THE EIGHTEENTH SUNDAY AFTER PENTECOST (A)

COLLECT FOR THE DAY
> Almighty God: you call us to serve you, and count desire more than
> deeds. Keep us from measuring ourselves against neighbors who are
> slow to serve you; and make us glad whenever people turn to you in
> faith; through Jesus Christ our Lord. (WB)

READINGS
> **Isa. 55:6-11** God's wish to forgive is a mark of his freedom: he needn't but
> he may . . . his "thoughts are not our thoughts." God's power to forgive
> follows from his freedom just as the fruit of the earth is the project of his
> "rain and snow" . . . his "word," his "will." HTA

> **Phil. 1:21-27** For Christians, united to Christ by faith, death can only mean
> a nearer, dearer union. So, like Paul, we can be torn between wanting to live
> and, though it may seem odd, longing to die. However, we choose life
> because Christ has set us in the world with neighbors to love and serve.

> **Matt. 20:1-16** Maybe there are two ways to live: we can turn faith into a
> legal contract—"I do and I deserve"—or we can rejoice in a world where
> everything is undeserved, free grace. If you try to live a "bargain" in the
> kingdom (where all is grace), you can end up with a hard word, "Take your
> pay and go!" Good heavens, we've got to change! DB

PSALM FOR THE DAY: Psalm 27:1-9

HYMNS FOR THE DAY	HL	HB	WB
Thanks to God, Whose Word Was Spoken	—	—	580
A Hymn of Glory Let Us Sing	—	—	273
God Is Our Strong Salvation (Ps.)	92	347	388
Work, for the Night Is Coming	—	297	—
God Is Working His Purpose Out	—	500	389
Sinner, Please Don't Let This Harvest Pass	—	—	570
Come, You Thankful People, Come			
(begin with stanza 2)	460	525	346

ANTHEMS FOR THE DAY

> **Isa. 55:6-11** *Comfort All Ye My People*, Gabriel Fauré (C. Fischer). Use the
> General text. SATB (M)

> **Phil. 1:21-27** *Lord, Let Me Know Mine End*, Maurice Greene (Oxford). SA
> (M)

> *O Lord, Thou Art My God and King*, arr. Leland Sateren (Augsburg). SATB
> (M)

> **Matt. 20:1-16** *The Prayer of St. Francis*, Searle Wright (Warner). SATB (D)

> *Man Born to Toil*, Gustav Holst (G. Schirmer). SATB (M) BH

COLLECT FOR THE DAY
Great God, Father of us all: you send us into the world to do your work. May we not only promise to serve you, but do what you command, loving neighbors, and telling the good news of Jesus Christ our Lord.   (WB)

READINGS
Ezek. 18:25-29 We complain of Yahweh's ways, but they are just. In his world, wickedness is self-destructive, whereas repentance leads to life. So Yahweh's judgments are fair. Perhaps the problem is our ways, not his!

Phil. 2:1-11 In the church, we must never be divided by rivalry, prides, or personal ambitions. Paul quotes a familiar hymn (vs. 6-11) urging Christians to humble themselves as did Christ, who set aside his glory and came among us as a slave!

Matt. 21:28-32 Odd how sometimes those who have no interest in God will serve him faithfully, whereas we who have pledged our faith may not. Look out, remodeled B-girls and racketeers are entering the kingdom now, and we . . . ? Lord, in Christ we know your will; help us to repent!   DB

PSALM FOR THE DAY: Psalm 25:1-10

HYMNS FOR THE DAY

	HL	HB	WB
Grace and Truth Shall Mark the Way (Ps.)	—	372	—
All Hail the Power of Jesus' Name!	192	132	285
Oh, Freedom!	—	—	535
Ah, Holy Jesus	158	191	280
O Love, How Deep, How Broad, How High!	139	—	518
Let All Together Praise Our God	—	—	450
Sinners Jesus Will Receive	227	—	—

ANTHEMS FOR THE DAY
Ezek. 18:25–29 *Psalm 67*, Regina Holmen Fryxell (H. W. Gray). SATB (D)

The Last Words of David, Randall Thompson (E. C. Schirmer). SATB (D)

Phil. 2:1-11 *Praise Ye the Lord*, W. A. Mozart (Presser). SATB (M)

How Excellent Is Thy Name, Howard Hanson (C. Fischer). SATB (D)

I Will Magnify Thee, O Lord, Joseph Corfe (Novello). SA (M)

Matt. 21:28-32 *Call to Remembrance*, Richard Farrant (Mills). SATB (E)   BH

COLLECT FOR THE DAY

Great God: you have put us to work in the world, reaping the harvest of your word. May we be modest servants, who follow orders willingly, in the name of Jesus Christ, your faithful Son, our Lord.　　　　(WB)

READINGS

Isa. 5:1-7　Israel is a vineyard which Yahweh has tended with care, and from which he expects a fine yield—justice and righteousness. Unfortunately, the vineyard is unproductive. So Yahweh, though he loves Israel, may let her go to ruin . . . unless?

Phil. 4:4-9　"Whatever is true, honorable, just, pure, lovely . . ." These are not abstract virtues, for we have seen them alive in Jesus Christ. We can live them too, when we are joined to Christ by thoughtful prayer and thanksgiving.

Matt. 21:33-43　Well, the human world has knocked off its share of prophets—even in our generation. Certainly, we once made short work of God's own son! We know what we deserve. Yet, because of Jesus Christ, we live in the second chance of God's mercy, so we can still turn, obey, and acknowledge that "the earth is the Lord's."　　　　DB

PSALM FOR THE DAY: Psalm 80:7-15, 18-19

HYMNS FOR THE DAY

	HL	HB	WB
We Sing the Mighty Power of God	65	84	628
Lord, Bless and Pity Us	—	493	456
Rejoice, O Pure in Heart	297	407	561
Come, We That Love the Lord	—	408	—
Father, We Thank You that You Planted	—	—	366
Christ Is Made the Sure Foundation	336	433	325

ANTHEMS FOR THE DAY

Come, Ye Servant People, Charlotte Garden (H. W. Gray). SATB with brass and tympani (ME)

Seek Ye His Countenance in All Places, Johannes Herbst (C. Fischer Moravian Series). SATB (M)

Psalm 80 (79), Joseph Gelineau (in *Thirty Psalms and Two Canticles,* Gregorian Institute). (E)

Rejoice, Ye Pure in Heart, Richard Dirksen (in *Ecumenical Praise,* No. 48, Hope; also published in octavo by Harold Flammer). SATB (M)　　　　LLH

COLLECT FOR THE DAY

Gracious God: you have invited us to feast in your promised kingdom. May we never be so busy taking care of things that we cannot turn to you, and thankfully celebrate the power of your Son, our Lord, Jesus Christ.   (WB)

READINGS

Isa. 25:6-9 Here is a vision of a great feast in which all nations celebrate with Yahweh the end of trouble and grief. A later editor has added the destruction of death to the list of promises. No wonder the feasting will be glad. Remember the old hymn, "The song of them that triumph, The shout of them that feast."

Phil. 4:12-20 Paul has received a generous gift from the Christians in Philippi, whom he regards as partners in his ministry. Though he has learned to get by, no matter what he has—wealth or poverty, food or hunger—he is grateful for their sacrificial love.

Matt. 22:1-14 Wow, we've an invitation to the joy of the kingdom: R.S.V.P. at once, unless your own affairs are too important. Maybe those who know they don't deserve an invitation come quickly. Of course, it's appropriate to arrive dressed for the occasion. Check your wardrobe, and put on the new life in Christ!   DB

PSALM FOR THE DAY: Psalm 23

HYMNS FOR THE DAY

	HL	HB	WB
Glory Be to God the Father	60	—	—
All Glory Be to God on High	—	—	283
The Lord's My Shepherd (Ps.)	97	104	592,593
O Jesus, Joy of Loving Hearts	354	215	510
O How Shall We Receive You	—	—	506
O Holy City, Seen of John	409	508	505

ANTHEMS FOR THE DAY

Isa. 25:6-9 *All for Love*, Robert Young (C. Fischer). SATB (E)

Evening Song to God, F. J. Haydn (Mercury). SATB (M)

Phil. 4:12-20 *O Lord, Increase My Faith*, Orlando Gibbons (H. W. Gray). SATB (E)

Jesus, Sun of Life, My Splendor, G. F. Handel (Concordia). SATB (E)

Matt. 22:1-14 *Go Not Far from Me, O God*, Niccolo Zingarelli (Belwin). SATB (E)

Bow Down Thine Ear, César Franck (Fitzsimons). SA (M)   BH

THE TWENTY-SECOND SUNDAY AFTER PENTECOST (A)

COLLECT FOR THE DAY

Almighty God: in your kingdom the last shall be first, and the least shall be honored. Help us to live with courtesy and love, trusting the wisdom of your rewards, made known in Jesus Christ our Lord.　　(WB)

READINGS

Isa. 45:1-6　There is no God beside Yahweh! He's in charge of the world. He chooses and uses the powers of this world, whether they know him or not, to bring about his purposes. Yahweh displays his sovereignty over the daily headlines.

I Thess. 1:1-5　Paul is ever thankful for the faith of the Thessalonians. In spite of persecution they have been patient. Surely they are "chosen," for they display both the strength and the fervor of the Holy Spirit.

Matt. 22:15-22　When we show Christ our "coins" he can see that we've already sold out to the powers of this world. (How do you make a buck?) So he says, "Give back to Caesar what you got from him!" "Now then, about the things of God!" What doesn't belong to God? What?　　DB

PSALM FOR THE DAY: Psalm 96

HYMNS FOR THE DAY

	HL	HB	WB
Sing Praise to God	—	15	568
God Moves in a Mysterious Way	103	112	391
O Sing a New Song (Ps.)	68	37	525
Holy Spirit, Truth Divine	208	240	422
O God of Every Nation	—	—	498

ANTHEMS FOR THE DAY

Isa. 45:1-6　*Let All the World in Every Corner Sing*, Don McAfee (Hope). SATB (M)

Glory to God, J. S. Bach (Colombo). SATB (M)

Song of Exultation, John Ness Beck (G. Schirmer). SATB (D)

I Thess. 1:1-5　*All Ye Saints Be Joyful*, K. K. Davis (Warner). SATB (E)

Thanksgiving We Give to God, Schütz-Ehret (Colombo). SATB (E)　　BH

COLLECT FOR THE DAY

Eternal God: you taught us that we shall live, if we love you and our neighbor. Help us to know who our neighbors are, and to serve them, so that we may truly love you; through Jesus Christ our Lord.   (WB)

READINGS

Ex. 22:21-27   How do we love neighbors? We love strangers as if they were kinfolk, take care of the unprotected, widow or orphan, lend money without interest, and restore collateral when it is needed: love is a deed. Why should we love neighbors? Because, says Yahweh, "I am compassionate!" Reason enough.

I Thess. 1:2-10   Though their faith has gotten them into trouble, the Thessalonians are joyful. Thus, they have spread the good news, and are a "model" community for other Christians to follow. Obviously they have turned from idle idol worship (idols will never get you in trouble!) to the real God, who is alive in Jesus Christ the Lord.

Matt. 22:34-40   We're still trying to trap Jesus into pushing piety to the neglect of neighbors, or neighbors to the neglect of piety (check the polarities in your parish!). No, to him love of God and love of neighbor are *one* commandment. Note: Some scholars argue that "as yourself" could better be translated "as your own"—i.e., your own kin.   DB

PSALM FOR THE DAY: Psalm 18:1-3, 46, 50

HYMNS FOR THE DAY	HL	HB	WB
Before the Lord Jehovah's Throne	63	81	306
The Lord Will Come and Not Be Slow	185	230	—
Come Down, O Love Divine	—	—	334
Come, Holy Ghost, Our Souls Inspire	—	237	335
Love Divine, All Loves Excelling	308	399	471

ANTHEMS FOR THE DAY

Ex. 22:21-27   *Great and Glorious*, F. J. Haydn (Belwin). SATB (M)

God Is My Guide, Franz Schubert (G. Schirmer). SATB (E)

Jesus, Refuge of the Weary, von Rosenroth (in *The Morning Star Choir Book*, Concordia). SA (E)

I Thess. 1:2-10   *Sing, Pray and Keep His Ways*, Glenn Darst (C. Fischer). SATB (M)

He Who Would Valiant Be, arr. Gerald Near (Augsburg). SATB (M)

Matt. 22:34-40   *The Great Commandment*, Carl Mueller (C. Fischer). SATB (M)   BH

THE TWENTY-FOURTH SUNDAY AFTER PENTECOST
(A)

COLLECT FOR THE DAY

Lord God: open our eyes to see wonderful things in your law, and open our hearts to receive the gift of your saving love; through Jesus Christ the Lord. (WB)

READINGS

Mal. 2:1-10 Priests of Israel are condemned for laziness, arrogance, and lack of concern. A true priest ("Levi") is a devout teacher of the law, a messenger of the Lord, and is concerned for God's loved people. Above all, a true priest is faithful.

I Thess. 2:7-13 Some have accused Paul of self-seeking, "showboating," and of running a religious con game. He answers that he has paid his own way so as to offer the good news freely. Like a loving Father, he pleaded with his "children" in faith, for their own good, urging them to live the gospel.

Matt. 23:1-12 When you're living under a weight of law, it's easy to overload others with your own "oughts," or to swagger about clothed in your knowledge of morality. Among Christians there is no moral status gained by imposing on others. Instead, all that matters is a willingness to serve neighbors in the freedom of love. DB

PSALM FOR THE DAY: Psalm 131

HYMNS FOR THE DAY	HL	HB	WB
Father, in Your Mysterious Presence	256	384	363
Father, We Praise You	24	43	365
God Has Spoken—by His Prophets	—	—	382
God of the Prophets!	481	520	398
We Are One in the Spirit	—	—	619

ANTHEMS FOR THE DAY

Mal. 2:1-10 *Thou Knowest, Lord, the Secrets of Our Hearts*, Henry Purcell (E. C. Schirmer). SATB (E)

The Highway of the Upright, Jean Berger (Kjos). SATB (M)

I Thess. 2:7-13 *Blessed Is the Man*, Arcangelo Corelli (Boston Music). SATB (M)

Psalm 23, Heinz Werner Zimmermann (Augsburg). SATB (M)

Psalm 23, Jean Berger (in *Bay Psalm Book*, Shawnee). SATB (M)

Matt. 23:1-12 *Father, in Thy Mysterious Presence Kneeling*, David Wehr (J. Fischer). SATB (E) BH

COLLECT FOR THE DAY

Eternal God: help us to watch and wait for the coming of your Son, so that when he comes, we may be found living in light, ready to celebrate the victory of Jesus Christ the Lord.   (WB)

READINGS

S. of Sol. 3:1-5   Here is a woman dreaming the meaning of her life. She longs for a lover from whom she is separated, and wanders day after day seeking him, night after night through dark streets asking, "Have you seen him?" When she finds him, she vows never to let him go.

I Thess. 4:13-18   God has promised to bring a kingdom of justice, peace, and love. But what of Christians who die before the kingdom comes? Christ has been raised by God. Surely those who are joined to him by faith, living or dead, will share his triumph. We need not grieve the dead: in Christ we have more than hope!

Matt. 25:1-13   In a world where God's promised kingdom is not yet fulfilled (check the headlines in your local paper!), it's easy for Christian commitment to "burn out." So, again and again, crises have caught the church unprepared. We must trust the promises—Christ's work will joyfully be fulfilled—and stay ready to "shine" when called on.   DB

PSALM FOR THE DAY: Psalm 63:1-7

HYMNS FOR THE DAY

	HL	HB	WB
Comfort, Comfort You My People	—	—	347
O Lord, Our God, Most Earnestly (Ps.)	—	—	514
Jesus, the Very Thought of Thee	309	401	—
Jesus, Priceless Treasure	—	414	442
Wake, Awake, for Night Is Flying	—	—	614
The Church's One Foundation	333	437	582

ANTHEMS FOR THE DAY

S. of Sol. 3:1-5   *Awake, My Heart*, Jane Marshall (H. W. Gray). SATB (E)

Jesu, Joy of Man's Desiring, J. S. Bach (H. W. Gray). SATB (E)

I Thess. 4:13-18   *Canticle of Praise*, John Ness Beck (Presser). SATB (D)

Song of Hope, John Ness Beck (Hinshaw). SATB (D)

Matt. 25:1-13   *Be Merciful, Lord*, Daniel Sternberg (Word). SATB (M)

Turn Ye, Turn Ye, Charles Ives (Mercury). SATB (M)

The Eyes of All Wait Upon Thee, Jean Berger (Augsburg). SATB (M)   BH

COLLECT FOR THE DAY

God our Father: you have given us a measure of faith, and told us to be good investors. Keep us busy, brave, and unashamed, ever ready to greet your Son Jesus Christ, our judge and our redeemer. (WB)

READINGS

Prov. 31:10-13, 19-20, 30-31 Here are portions of an acrostic poem celebrating the virtues of a capable woman. She carries out responsibilities by working hard, giving generously, and loving. Of course, she deserves not only reward but praise.

I Thess. 5:1-6 God's judgment of the world should never catch us napping. By faith we have seen the light, and are children of light. We are already wide awake to God's love in Christ, so let's live accordingly.

Matt. 25:14-30 What a miscalculation! The servant not only thought his master was cruel but (a double miscalculation) he played it safe. The parable is not about "talents," i.e., natural abilities, but rather about risking oneself in the outgoing freedom of the gospel, instead of preserving self-righteous "purity" or identity. DB

PSALM FOR THE DAY: Psalm 128

HYMNS FOR THE DAY	HL	HB	WB
When I Survey the Wondrous Cross	152	198	635
As with Gladness Men of Old	135	174	302
We Thank You, Lord	—	—	629
Son of God, Eternal Savior	393	—	573
We Praise You, O God, Our Redeemer	461	17	627

ANTHEMS FOR THE DAY

I Thess. 5:1-6 *Lord, Thou Hast Been Our Refuge*, R. Vaughan Williams (G. Schirmer). SATB (D)

Stir Up, O Lord, W. A. Goldsworthy (H. W. Gray). SATB (M)

Matt. 25:14-30 *Create in Me, O God*, Johannes Brahms (G. Schirmer). SATBB (E)

O Savior of the World, John Goss (G. Schirmer). SATB (E) BH

COLLECT FOR THE DAY

Eternal God: in Jesus Christ you judge the nations. Give us a heart to love the loveless, the lonely, the hungry, and the hurt, without pride or a calculating spirit, so that at last we may bow before you, and be welcomed into joy; through Jesus Christ, King of ages and Lord of all creation.   (WB)

READINGS

Ezek. 34:11-17 The religious leaders of Israel have been bad shepherds and, as a result, their sheep are scattered and lost. So Yahweh announces that he himself will shepherd Israel, rescue the straying, and gather his flock in fine pastureland. He will watch over his people with faithful love.

I Cor. 15:20-28 In our world, sinful humanity self-destructs: death is fact. But Christ is risen, and all those who are his will rise. Just as in Christ God's power overthrew death, so all dark forces, including death, shall ultimately be conquered. God is life, and the risen Christ is his lifegiver!

Matt. 25:31-46 We will not be judged by an account book kept in heaven, but by the Christ who gave himself for us. Nations will not be rewarded for prosperity or military spending, but for their care of the poor, the hungry, the jailed, the homeless. (Will the United States make it?) Note: The righteous were not religious, they did not spot Christ in their neighbors, they fed the hungry merely because they were hungry!   DB

PSALM FOR THE DAY: Psalm 105:1-7

HYMNS FOR THE DAY

	HL	HB	WB
Mine Eyes Have Seen the Glory	—	—	474
My Shepherd Will Supply My Need	—	—	477
Sinner, Please Don't Let This Harvest Pass	—	—	570
Where Cross the Crowded Ways of Life	410	507	642

ANTHEMS FOR THE DAY

Ezek. 34:11-17 *Jubilate Deo,* Laszlo Halmos (Hinshaw). SATB (M)

How Beautiful Upon the Mountains, Daniel Moe (Presser). SATB (M)

I Was Glad, Daniel Pinkham (AMP). SATB (D)

I Cor. 15:20-28 *Forth the Conqueror Has Gone,* Dale Wood (Art Masters). SATB (M)

Let All Mortal Flesh, Glenn Darst (H. W. Gray). SATB (M)

Matt. 25:31-46 *If I Can Stop One Heart from Breaking,* Jean Berger (Kjos). SATB (E)

The Lady with the Lamp, Max Helfman (Transcontinental). SATB (M)

Prayer of Dedication, Max Helfman (Transcontinental). SATB (D)   BH

WORLD COMMUNION SUNDAY (A)

COLLECT FOR THE DAY

O God: your Son prayed for his disciples; that they might be one. Draw us to you, so that we may be united in communion with your Spirit, loving one another as in Jesus Christ you have loved us. (WB)

READINGS

Isa. 49:18-23 Here is Israel desolate, her land barren, her children scattered. But Yahweh says, "Look up and see," and he spreads a vision of restoration. Israel, now left alone, shall see all her children returning, filling her borders with the joy of reunion. Those who rely on me, says Yahweh, will never be embarrassed. What Yahweh promises, he will do.

Rev. 3:17-22 The church in Laodicea was well-to-do and carefully moderate. Christ's word to them is, "Repent!" He is banging on their church door, trying to get in. If they will welcome Christ as word and sacrament, and be faithful, they may share his triumph. Laodiceans, you have ears, hear!

John 10:11-18 "I am the good shepherd," says Christ; and he is. Has he not given his life for wayward sheep (read: us)? No hired hand would love a flock so fiercely. But Christ is a good shepherd who, in love, knows his sheep. Christians may rejoice in such love as long as they remember he has many flocks. (Guess what, there are Catholic sheep as well as Presbyterian sheep as well as . . .) DB

PSALM FOR THE DAY: Psalm 34

HYMNS FOR THE DAY

	HL	HB	WB
In Christ There Is No East or West	341	479	435
If You Will Only Let God Guide You	105	344	431
O God, Whose Will Is Life and Peace			
(as anthem)	—	—	503
Bread of the World	353	445	—
Bread of Heaven, on Thee We Feed	—	—	313
All Glory, Laud, and Honor	146	187	284

ANTHEMS FOR THE DAY

Isa. 49:18-23 *O Lord God, Unto Whom Vengeance Belongeth*, Robert Baker (H. W. Gray). SATB (M)

Incline Thine Ear, O Lord, G. Arkhangelsky (Warner). SATB (M)

Behold, the Lord Hath Proclaimed, Jean Berger (Kjos). SATB (M)

Rev. 3:17-22 *Rejoice in the Lord*, Henry Purcell (B. F. Wood). SATB (E)

Praise the Lord, Jane Marshall (C. Fischer). SATB (M)

John 10:11-18 *Show Me the Way to Thee*, A. Eugene Ellsworth (Abingdon). SATB (M) BH

COLLECT FOR THE DAY
> Stir up your power, O Lord, and come. Protect us by your strength and save us from the threatening dangers of our sins, for you live and reign with the Father and the Holy Spirit, one God, now and forever.
>
> (LBW)

READINGS

Isa. 63:16 to 64:4   The people of Israel pray to God: Why have their hearts been hardened? Why have they turned from God's way? They act as if they were not chosen people. Come down, they cry, help us; overthrow enemies and turn us to you! You, Yahweh, are the Father and Redeemer of Israel.

I Cor. 1:3-9   God has called us together by his Son, Jesus Christ, and has provided gifts for our task—eloquence, knowledge, everything needed. We can trust God to perfect us so that we may stand approved on the Day of Judgment.

Mark 13:32-37   We have work to do for Christ in the world. So, we should live as good servants every day, as if it were the day of our master's joyful return. Let us be on guard then against any letting down of our commitment.
                                                                    DB

PSALM FOR THE DAY: Psalm 80:1-7

HYMNS FOR THE DAY	HL	HB	WB
Wake, Awake, for Night Is Flying	—	—	614
The King Shall Come	187	232	—
Break Forth, O Living Light of God	—	—	316
O Day of God, Draw Nigh	—	—	492
Come, Lord, and Tarry Not	188	233	—
O How Shall We Receive You			
(for Holy Communion)	—	—	506
Watchman, Tell Us of the Night	109	149	617

ANTHEMS FOR THE DAY

Isa. 63:16 to 64:4   *Wash Me Thoroughly from My Wickedness*, Samuel Wesley (in *The Church Anthem Book*, Oxford). SATB (E)

Daughters of Jerusalem, F. J. Haydn (from *The Seven Words of Christ*, H. W. Gray). SATB (D)

I Cor. 1:3-9   *Praise Be to Thee*, Palestrina (Willis). SATB (E)

Mark 13:32-37   *Sound the Trumpet*, Henry Purcell (Elkan-Vogel). SATB (M)

O Clap Your Hands, R. Vaughan Williams (Galaxy). SATB (D)

O Clap Your Hands, John Rutter (Oxford). SATB (M)   BH

COLLECT FOR THE DAY

Stir up our hearts, O Lord, to prepare the way for your only Son. By his coming give us strength in our conflicts and shed light on our path through the darkness of this world; through your Son, Jesus Christ our Lord, who lives and reigns with you and the Holy Spirit, one God, now and forever. (LBW)

READINGS

Isa. 40:1-5, 9-11   Yahweh, like a contractor, gives orders to have a highway built so that his exiled people may return to Zion. Though they haven't heard the news yet, their time of penal servitude is over. The prophet is told to announce that God is coming to release his people, coming over the great highway, to lead his people, tenderly but triumphantly, home.

II Peter 3:8-14   God doesn't arrive when we schedule his arrival: he comes when he will! But we can trust his patience and, in the time he generously gives us, we can repent and be renewed, ready for his coming.

Mark 1:1-8   John's message demanding a right-about-face in view of the coming judgment is now changed. Christ has come. His love judges us, yes, but his Spirit enables. Christ is the highway of God's salvation to and for us. DB

PSALM FOR THE DAY: Psalm 85

HYMNS FOR THE DAY	HL	HB	WB
Heralds of Christ	379	498	416
Comfort, Comfort You My People	—	—	347
Go, Tell It on the Mountain	—	—	380
Hail to the Brightness	391	505	—
The Lord Will Come and Not Be Slow (Ps.)	185	230	—
Our God, Our Help in Ages Past	77	111	549
O Love, How Deep, How Broad, How High!	139	—	518

ANTHEMS FOR THE DAY

Isa. 40:1-5, 9-11   *The Advent of Our God*, Eugene Butler (Hope). SATB (D)

Messiah, G. F. Handel (several editions available). SATB (MD)

Comfort All Ye My People, Gabriel Fauré (C. Fischer). Use the Advent text. SATB (M)

II Peter 3:8-14   *At the Name of Jesus*, R. Vaughan Williams (Oxford). SATB (E)

E'en So, Lord Jesus, Quickly Come, Paul Manz (Concordia). SATB (M)

Mark 1:1-8   *The Lord's Prayer*, Flor Peeters (Peters). SATB (M)   BH

COLLECT FOR THE DAY

Almighty God, you once called John the Baptist to give witness to the coming of your Son and to prepare his way. Grant us, your people, the wisdom to see your purpose today and the openness to hear your will, that we may witness to Christ's coming and so prepare his way; through Jesus Christ our Lord, who lives and reigns with you and the Holy Spirit, one God, now and forever. (LBW)

READINGS

Isa. 61:1-4, 8-11   Two poems have been combined in Isaiah. In vs. 1-3, the prophet senses his calling: the spirit is upon him to announce liberation to the poor, the captives, and the oppressed. In turn (vs. 8-11), God himself, who hates injustice, will liberate his people so that nations will see their deliverance and acknowledge them to be "seed which Yahweh has blessed."

I Thess. 5:16-24   How can we be "blameless" at the coming of the Lord? We can let the Spirit of God make us holy, so that we never return evil for evil, but do good gratefully, prayerfully, and joyfully, no matter what.

John 1:6-8, 19-28   "Who are you?" they asked John the Baptist. He answered, "A voice crying . . . prepare the way of the Lord!" So he called folk to repent and make ready for the one who was to come. He came: the light of God's presence shone in Christ. Like John, we acknowledge him and know we are scarcely worthy to serve him.   DB

PSALM FOR THE DAY: Luke 1:46b-55

HYMNS FOR THE DAY	HL	HB	WB
Come, Thou Long-expected Jesus	113	151	342
Let All Mortal Flesh (Luke 1)	112	148	449
Christ Is the World's True Light	—	492	326
He Did Not Want to Be Far	—	—	412
Rejoice, Rejoice, Believers	115	231	—

ANTHEMS FOR THE DAY

Isa. 61:1-4, 8-11   *This Is the Covenant*, Jean Berger (Augsburg). SATB (E)

I Thess. 5:16-24   *Go Forth Into the World in Peace*, Martin Shaw (G. Schirmer). SATB (E)

O Be Joyful in the Lord, Charles Wood (Summy-Birchard). SATB (E)

John 1:6-8, 19-28   *This Is the Record of John*, Orlando Gibbons (H. W. Gray). SATB (D)   BH

COLLECT FOR THE DAY

Stir up your power, O Lord, and come. Take away the hindrance of our sins and make us ready for the celebration of your birth, that we may receive you in joy and serve you always; for you live and reign with the Father and the Holy Spirit, now and forever. (LBW)

READINGS

II Sam. 7:8-16 A message from the Lord is delivered to David by the prophet Nathan. Look, says God, I picked you out when you were chasing sheep, and raised you up to be a prince. When you are gone, I will raise up your son and establish his kingdom. I will fix his throne forever. "I will be his father, and he shall be my son."

Rom. 16:25-27 Here is an outburst of praise which was probably added to Paul's letter by a later editor. "To God be glory forever." Why? Because in the mystery of God's eternal purpose we have been given the gospel of Jesus Christ, by whom we are made strong in faith. To God be glory forever.

Luke 1:26-38 Well, who wouldn't be startled by an angel announcing, "The Lord is with you!" More startling still is the angel's message: Mary will give birth to a son, the promised Davidic Messiah. "How can this be?" Mary blurts out. When told of the Spirit's power, she admits, "Nothing is impossible with God," and then, in magnificent obedience, bows before God's mysterious will: "Let it be according to your word." DB

PSALM FOR THE DAY: Psalm 89:1-4, 14-18

HYMNS FOR THE DAY	HL	HB	WB
O Come, O Come, Emmanuel			
(see Episcopal *Hymnal* 1940 for all stanzas)	108	147	489, 490
Hail to the Lord's Anointed	111	146	—
Glory Be to God the Father	60	—	—
This Is the Good News	—	—	263
Son of God, Eternal Saviour	393	—	—
At the Name of Jesus	—	143	303

ANTHEMS FOR THE DAY

II Sam. 7:8-16 *Behold the Star of Jacob Rising*, Mendelssohn (E. C. Schirmer). SATB (M)

Rom. 16:25-27 *How Lovely Are the Messengers*, Mendelssohn (from *St. Paul*, G. Schirmer). SATB (M)

Alleluia! Sing Praise, J. S. Bach, arr. Hirt (C. Fischer). SATB (E)

Luke 1:26-38 *The Annunciation*, Randall Thompson (from the *Nativity According to Saint Luke*, E. C. Schirmer). Requires tenor and lyric soprano soloists. (D) BH

COLLECT FOR THE DAY

Almighty God, you made this holy night shine with the brightness of the true Light. Grant that here on earth we may walk in the light of Jesus' presence and in the last day wake to the brightness of his glory; through your only Son, Jesus Christ our Lord, who lives and reigns with you and the Holy Spirit, one God, now and forever.   (LBW)

READINGS

Isa. 52:7-10   What a glad song! Deutero-Isaiah pictures the moment when a messenger arrives to tell exiles of their liberation. When Israel's watchmen hear the message, "Your God is King!" they break into joyful song. All Jerusalem joins the song of celebration. Yahweh has rescued his people, and the whole world can see his saving power.

Heb. 1:1-9   God, who of old spoke through the prophets, has spoken his word to us through Jesus Christ, his own Son. Christ is greater than any gleaming angel. Enthroned in glory, Christ is the true image of God, the purpose of creation. He is God's faithful love in flesh.

John 1:1-14   God's word, all he planned from the beginning, *is* Jesus Christ, light of the world. The dark world rejected Christ, but to us he has given power to become God's faithful children. Of course, no darkness can ever overcome Christ, for he is the light of God's love with us, full of grace and truth, the only Son of the Father!   DB

PSALM FOR THE DAY: Psalm 96

HYMNS FOR THE DAY

	HL	HB	WB
Angels, from the Realms of Glory	124	168	298
Angels We Have Heard on High	—	158	299
O Sing a New Song (Ps.)	68	37	525
O Word of God Incarnate	215	251	532
Silent Night	132	154	567
Hark! the Herald Angels Sing	117	163	411

ANTHEMS FOR THE DAY

Isa. 52:7-10   *O Sing Unto the Lord*, Hans Leo Hassler (E. C. Schirmer). SATB (E)

How Beautiful Upon the Mountains, Jean Berger (Sheppard). SATB (M)

Heb. 1:1-9   *Ye Shall Go Out with Joy*, John Ness Beck (Kjos). SATB (M)

Praise God in His Holiness, Geoffrey Shaw (G. Schirmer). SATB (E)

John 1:1-14   *Of the Father's Love Begotten*, Malcolm Williamson (in *Six Christmas Songs*, Weinberger). SATB (M)

I Love Thee, My Lord, Dale Wood (Art Masters). SATB (E)

And the Word Was Made Flesh, Hans Leo Hassler (Chappell). SSATBB (MD)   BH

CHRISTMAS DAY (B)

COLLECT FOR THE DAY
    Almighty God, you have made yourself known in your Son, Jesus, redeemer of the world. We pray that his birth as a human child will set us free from the old slavery of our sin; through Jesus Christ our Lord, who lives and reigns with you and the Holy Spirit, one God, now and forever.   (LBW)

READINGS
    Isa. 62:6-12   The people of Israel are told to keep after Yahweh to fulfill his promises. Has he not promised peace and freedom to his people? Because Yahweh always keeps his word, we can celebrate now. So, "Build a highway for Yahweh!" Say, "Salvation comes!" for Yahweh will gather his exiled people and bring them triumphantly home.

    Col. 1:15-20   These verses are two stanzas of an early Christian hymn. The first stanza celebrates Christ as the *raison d'être* of creation. The second stanza praises the reconciliation he has brought about, namely peace among all and reunion with God. So Christ is what the human world was created to be, and also the "new man" of God's new creation. He is, in himself, the communion of God and humanity.

    Matt. 1:18-25   Jesus, a child of Israel, is welcomed by his father, Joseph, as a son of David. But he is Son of God as well, born by the power of the Holy Spirit. No wonder he is named Immanuel, which means "God with us"!   DB

PSALM FOR THE DAY: Psalm 98

HYMNS FOR THE DAY	HL	HB	WB
O Come, All Ye Faithful	116	170	486
Joy to the World! (Ps.)	122	161	444
Ah, Dearest Jesus	118	173	279
O Sing a Song of Bethlehem	138	177	526
Away in a Manger	126	157	—
Let All Mortal Flesh	112	148	449

ANTHEMS FOR THE DAY

    The Best of Rooms, Randall Thompson (E. C. Schirmer). SATB (MD)

    The Coming Child, Max Sinzheimer (Concordia). 2-Part Mixed (E)

    Hodie! Emmanuel! Gloria! Milburn Price (Hinshaw). SATB (E)

    Infant Holy, Infant Lowly, Gerre Hancock (H. W. Gray). SATB (M)

    If You Would Hear the Angels Sing, David H. Williams (H. W. Gray). (ME)

    Gentle Mary, John Fenstermaker (H. W. Gray). SSS (ME)   LLH

COLLECT FOR THE DAY

Almighty God, you wonderfully created and yet more wonderfully restored the dignity of human nature. In your mercy, let us share the divine life of Jesus Christ who came to share our humanity, and who now lives and reigns with you and the Holy Spirit, one God, now and forever.   (LBW)

READINGS

Jer. 31:10-13   God promises to be like a shepherd to Israel, gathering in the displaced flock and watching over them forever. They shall be radiant, young and strong, pastured in a pleasant land. Then shall sadness turn to celebration, for Israel shall "never want again"!

Heb. 2:10-18   Since we are flesh and blood and die, Jesus Christ, God's own saving purpose, shared our flesh and blood, suffered perfectly, and died. Thus, he is "high priest," humanly tempted and fragile as we, yet from God. By his faith, he sets us free from faithlessness and dying.

Luke 2:25-35   Old man Simeon longs for the renewal of Israel. He has been told that he will not die until he has seen the mighty, promised Messiah. He catches sight of Jesus and, embracing the child, breaks into song: God has kept his promise, for Simeon's old eyes have seen Messiah. The child will be savior of Jew and Gentile alike. At last Simeon, his eyes splintered by glints of glory, is free to go in peace.   DB

PSALM FOR THE DAY: Psalm 111

HYMNS FOR THE DAY

	HL	HB	WB
As with Gladness Men of Old	135	174	302
To Abraham the Promise Came	—	—	608
Lo, How a Rose E'er Blooming	—	162	455
God's Word Is like a Flaming Sword	—	—	405
Lord, Now Lettest Thou Thy Servant Depart	59(back)	597-600	—
Great God, We Sing That Mighty Hand	470	527	408

ANTHEMS FOR THE DAY

Jer. 31:10-13   *Make a Joyful Noise Unto the Lord*, William Mathias (Oxford). SATB (D)

Jubilate Deo, Dale Wood (Augsburg). SATB (M)

O All Ye Nations, Heinrich Schütz (Oliver Ditson). SATB (E)

Psalm 100, David Williams (Summy-Birchard). SATB (M)

O Be Joyful in the Lord, R. Vaughan Williams (Galaxy). SATB (M)

Heb. 2:10-18   *O Divine Redeemer*, Charles Gounod (G. Schirmer). SATB (M)

Luke 2:25-35   *Nunc Dimittis*. Settings such as R. Vaughan Williams'. SATB (M)   BH

COLLECT FOR THE DAY

Eternal Father, you gave to your incarnate Son the holy name of Jesus to be the sign of our salvation: Plant in every heart, we pray, the love of him who is the Savior of the world, our Lord Jesus Christ; who lives and reigns with you and the Holy Spirit, one God, in glory everlasting.

(BCP)

READINGS

Isa. 60:1-5 We have, at this season of the year, some sense for the festivity with which friends and family come from afar, bearing treasures and gifts. That is Isaiah's vision of the kingdom of God.

Rev. 21:22 to 22:2 The New Testament's ultimate picture of the kingdom of God finds even the Temple, the sun, and the moon to be pale substitutes for the glory of God and the Lamb who provide a river of life for all the nations.

Luke 2:21-24 The infant Jesus is portrayed by Luke as the turning point between Old and New Testament visions. At Israel's center, the Temple, he is greeted as a "light to the Gentiles" and the "glory of your people Israel" (Luke 2:32). HTA

PSALM FOR THE DAY: Psalm 84

HYMNS FOR THE DAY	HL	HB	WB
Lord of the Worlds Above (Ps.)	50	14	—
Let All Together Praise Our God	—	—	450
How Dear to Me, O Lord of Hosts (Ps.)	—	440	—
O What Their Joy	430	424	—
O for a Thousand Tongues	199	141	493
How Sweet the Name of Jesus Sounds	310	130	—
At the Name of Jesus	—	143	303

ANTHEMS FOR THE DAY

Isa. 60:1-5 *For, Behold, Darkness Shall Cover the Earth*, G. F. Handel (from *Messiah*). Bass Solo (D)

Rev. 21:22 to 22:2 *The Lord Is My Light*, Emma Lou Diemer (Centenary College). SATB (D) BH

EPIPHANY (B)

COLLECT FOR THE DAY

    Lord God, on this day you revealed your Son to the nations by the leading of a star. Lead us now by faith to know your presence in our lives, and bring us at last to the full vision of your glory, through your Son, Jesus Christ our Lord, who lives and reigns with you and the Holy Spirit, one God, now and forever.   (LBW)

READINGS

    Isa. 60:1-6 Israel is to rise, beaming with joy, to greet the dawning of her redeemer, Yahweh. The scattered Children of Israel shall come streaming back to Zion. Along with them will come the nations of the world, bringing treasures and proclaiming Yahweh's wonderful deeds.

    Eph. 3:1-6 Jesus came to the Jews by birth; to the Gentiles he comes as a gospel message. The mystery of God's love, hidden in the past, is now revealed to apostles as a message to speak: Jesus, Messiah, is savior of both Jew and Gentile, for all share his promises and all may receive his Spirit.

    Matt. 2:1-12 Here come the kings! They are wise Gentiles who see in a star's rising promise of a world-changing king, a king who may tumble empires. (No wonder Herod is threatened!) They find Jesus and worship him joyfully, just as in years to come other Gentiles will seek and find their Savior.   DB

PSALM FOR THE DAY: Psalm 72:1-19

HYMNS FOR THE DAY

	HL	HB	WB
Brightest and Best	136	175	318
O One with God the Father (tune: Ellacombe)	137	—	—
We Three Kings	—	176	—
Savior of the Nations, Come	—	—	565
What Star Is This	—	—	632
O Morning Star, How Fair and Bright	321	415	521

ANTHEMS FOR THE DAY

    Isa. 60:1-6 *Arise, Shine, for Thy Light Has Come,* Kenneth Jennings (Augsburg). SATB (M)

    For Your Light Has Come, Ronald A. Nelson (Augsburg). SATB, trumpets (E)

    All from Saba Shall Come, Robert J. Powell (Concordia). SATB/SATB (double chorus) (D)

    Eph. 3:1-6 *Arise, O God, and Shine,* arr. S. Drummond Wolff (Concordia). SATB, trumpet (ME)

    Matt. 2:1-12 *To Jesus from the Ends of Earth* (Huron Indian carol), arr. Kenneth Jewell (Concordia). SATB or SSA (E)   RD

COLLECT FOR THE DAY
> Father in heaven, at the baptism of Jesus in the River Jordan you proclaimed him your beloved Son and anointed him with the Holy Spirit. Make all who are baptized into Christ faithful in their calling to be your children and inheritors with him of everlasting life; through your Son, Jesus Christ our Lord, who lives and reigns with you and the Holy Spirit, one God, now and forever.   (LBW)

READINGS

Isa. 61:1-4   Yahweh has commissioned a prophet (Trito-Isaiah?), and given him the Spirit. He is to proclaim good news to the poor, bind up the brokenhearted, and tell imprisoned debtors that they are free. Actually, he is announcing the advent of a new era, a true Jubilee!

Acts 11:4-18   Peter, who held back his ministry to "unclean" Gentiles, has baptized Cornelius and friends. As he preached to them, they received Christ's own baptism, the Holy Spirit. "Could I withstand God?" asks Peter in explaining his sudden Gentile ministry. To the Gentiles, God had granted repentance unto life!

Mark 1:4-11   Jesus appeared and, expressing his solidarity with sinful humanity, was baptized in the muddy Jordan. He begins his messianic ministry, is endowed wth the Spirit, and is confirmed by God's own word, "This is my Son!"   DB

PSALM FOR THE DAY: Psalm 29:1-4, 9-10

HYMNS FOR THE DAY	HL	HB	WB
Brightest and Best	136	175	318
The Morning Light Is Breaking	389	499	—
Hark! the Glad Sound, the Savior Comes	—	—	410
Hills of the North, Rejoice (Ps.)	—	478	—
O Love, How Deep, How Broad, How High!	139	—	518
Guide Me, O Thou Great Jehovah	104	339	409

ANTHEMS FOR THE DAY

Acts 11:4-18   *Epiphany Alleluias,* John Weaver (Boosey & Hawkes). SATB (D)

What Shall I Render to My God, Austin Lovelace (Canyon). SATB (M)

How Beautiful Upon the Mountains, Daniel Moe (Presser). SATB (M) BH

THE SECOND SUNDAY AFTER EPIPHANY (B)

COLLECT FOR THE DAY

Lord God, you showed your glory and led many to faith by the works of your Son. As he brought gladness and healing to his people, grant us these same gifts and lead us also to perfect faith in him, Jesus Christ our Lord.

(LBW)

READINGS

I Sam. 3:1-10   What a time to be called by Yahweh! In Samuel's time, the Temple was stagnate, the word of God was rare, and visions few. No wonder Samuel couldn't guess who addressed him. Persistent Yahweh calls him three times, but does not speak freely until Samuel is ready to hear. Samuel says, "Speak! your servant hears." We are surely a called people. Question: Are we ready to hear?

I Cor. 6:12-20   We are free, because we have been ransomed by Christ. Nevertheless, our freedom is for God and neighbors. Because we are one body with Christ, and his Spirit is among us, we are not our own. We must never involve ourselves in immorality lest, unavoidably, we involve the Christ whose Spirit we have been given.

John 1:35-42   News of Christ comes to us secondhand, "Look, there's the Lamb of God!" Tentatively, we follow him, wanting to find out more. "Come and see," says Christ to us. When we truly see that he is God's own Son, then, like Peter, we can announce, "We have found the Savior!"   DB

PSALM FOR THE DAY: Psalm 67

HYMNS FOR THE DAY

	HL	HB	WB
Christ, Whose Glory Fills the Skies	26	47	332
Lord, Bless and Pity Us (Ps.)	—	493	456
God of Mercy, God of Grace (Ps.)	465	—	—
Behold the Lamb of God!	—	—	307
O Lamb of God	75(back)	585	—
Jesus Calls Us (include stanza 2 from WB for St. Andrew's Day)	223	269	439
Come, Labor On	366	287	—

ANTHEMS FOR THE DAY

I Sam. 3:1-10   *Bless the Lord, O My Soul*, Ippolitoff-Ivanoff (Boston Music). SATB (M)

I Cor. 6:12-20   *Jesu, Grant Me This, I Pray*, Charles H. Kitson (Oxford). SATB (M)

Prayer to Jesus, George Oldroyd (Oxford). SATB (E)

Jesu, the Very Thought of Thee, Dale Wood (Sacred Songs). SATB (M)

John 1:35-42   *Behold the Lamb of God*, G. F. Handel (from *Messiah*). SATB (M)

BH

COLLECT FOR THE DAY

Almighty God, you sent your Son to proclaim your kingdom and to teach with authority. Anoint us with the power of your Spirit, that we, too, may bring good news to the afflicted, bind up the brokenhearted, and proclaim liberty to the captive; through your Son, Jesus Christ our Lord.   (LBW)

READINGS

Jonah 3:1-5, 10   Think of God "repenting"! Here was Nineveh, a big, thoroughly corrupt city that Yahweh was fed up with. So Jonah is sent to preach. All day long he stalks city streets handing out a warning from Yahweh. Well, Nineveh believed and donned sackcloth. So God saw and he "repented"; he changed his mind and the city was spared.

I Cor. 7:29-31   Here Paul urges us to "sit loose" toward the world we live in. We are not to get caught up in either the moods of the world or the stuff of the world. After all, the kingdom of God is coming and therefore the world is going.

Mark 1:14-22   Almost indiscriminately, Jesus calls his disciples (notice, no vocational testing!), and with authority he commands their lives. As disciples we are told to "catch" people by preaching good news of the kingdom. We say, "The kingdom is near, repent!"   DB

PSALM FOR THE DAY: Psalm 62:5-12

HYMNS FOR THE DAY	HL	HB	WB
You Servants of God	198	27	645
Lord, from the Depths to You I Cry	240	277	459
My Soul with Expectation (Ps.)	86	113	—
"Thy Kingdom Come"	363	484	—
They Cast Their Nets	—	421	—
The Light of God Is Falling	400	482	—
Once to Every Man and Nation	373	361	540

ANTHEMS FOR THE DAY

Jonah 3:1-5, 10   *From the End of the Earth,* Alan Hovhaness (Peters). SATB (M)

I Cor. 7:29-31   *Blessed Jesu,* Glenn Darst (H. W. Gray). SATB (E)

Lord, Thou Hast Been Our Refuge, R. Vaughan Williams (G. Schirmer). SATB (D)

Mark 1:14-22   *With Jesus I Will Go,* George Heussenstamm (Concordia). SATB (M)   BH

COLLECT FOR THE DAY

O God, you know that we cannot withstand the dangers which surround us. Strengthen us in body and spirit so that, with your help, we may be able to overcome the weakness that our sin has brought upon us; through Jesus Christ, your Son our Lord. (LBW)

READINGS

Deut. 18:15-22   Here is a promise and a test. God has promised that he will raise a true prophet out of Israel, a prophet like Moses who will mediate God's word and be backed up with God's power. How will we know the Prophet when he comes? Easy, his words will come true!

I Cor. 7:32-35   Of course marriage can lead to divided loyalty, particularly if marriage becomes an ingrown mutual admiration society (often called a "meaningful relationship" nowadays!). Rightly, husband and wife should each put obedience to Christ above personal satisfactions. Married or single, every one of us should seek to serve the Lord.

Mark 1:21-28   Think of a teacher whose lessons have power to demolish the forces of evil. Such a teacher would be a true prophet. God's good word liberates and, in so doing, shatters every evil bondage. No wonder news of Jesus Christ spreads. DB

PSALM FOR THE DAY: Psalm 1

HYMNS FOR THE DAY

	HL	HB	WB
All Beautiful the March of Days	—	—	281
God Himself Is with Us	51	13	384
Cast Your Burden on the Lord	288	—	323
Make Me a Captive, Lord	247	308	—
All Hail the Power of Jesus' Name!	192	132	285,286

ANTHEMS FOR THE DAY

Deut. 18:15-22   *Glorify the Lord with Me,* Jean Berger (Sheppard). SATB (M)

I Cor. 7:32-35   *Commitment,* Lloyd Pfautsch (Augsburg). SATB (M)   BH

THE FIFTH SUNDAY AFTER EPIPHANY (B)

COLLECT FOR THE DAY

Almighty God, you sent your only Son as the Word of life for our eyes to see and our ears to hear. Help us to believe with joy what the Scriptures proclaim, through Jesus Christ our Lord.   (LBW)

READINGS

Job 7:1-7   Poor old Job, his life is harsh. He is depressed, in pain, and he tosses through night hours sleeplessly. His days are drear and, like wind, will soon be blown away. "We live like slaves," he snarls, hoping God will also hear!

I Cor. 9:16-19, 22-23   Who can boast of preaching the gospel? Usually, as with Paul, it is a terrible compulsion: "Woe is me if I do not preach!" So, a preacher expects no gain from preaching, except the inexplicable joy of announcing God's free grace in Jesus Christ.

Mark 1:29-39   Think of Jesus: when the sick and troubled are hounding him, he turns away from them and begins a journey that will end on a cross. Perhaps he did not wish to be tagged as a miracle-working Messiah (don't take your pastoral counseling courses too seriously!). So, in prayer, he bent himself to God's will and went on his way, preaching the kingdom come!   DB

PSALM FOR THE DAY: Psalm 147:1-12

HYMNS FOR THE DAY

	HL	HB	WB
We Sing the Mighty Power of God	65	84	628
Praise Ye the Lord, for It Is Good (Ps.) (tune: Forest Green)	—	36	—
Whate'er Our God Ordains Is Right	291	366	633
At Even, When the Sun Was Set	43	55	—
O Holy City, Seen of John	409	508	505

ANTHEMS FOR THE DAY

Job 7:1-7   *Lord, I Flee to Thee for Refuge*, Mendelssohn (in *The Church Anthem Book*, Oxford). SATB (M)

Let My Prayer Come Up, Henry Purcell (H. W. Gray). SATB (E)

Hear My Prayer, O God, Jacob Arcadelt (E. C. Schirmer). SATB (E)

I Cor. 9:16-19, 22-23   *How Lovely Are the Messengers*, Mendelssohn (from *St. Paul*, E. C. Schirmer). SATB (E)

Mark 1:29-39   *Jesus Said to the Blind Man*, Vulpius-Eggebrecht (Concordia). SATB (M)   BH

COLLECT FOR THE DAY

Lord God, mercifully receive the prayers of your people. Help us to see and understand the things we ought to do, and give us grace and power to do them; through your Son, Jesus Christ our Lord.　　(LBW)

READINGS

Lev. 13:1-2, 44-46　Here is a description of the terrors of leprosy. Actually the term "leper" in the Bible does not always indicate our Hansen's disease, which was relatively rare in those days. But whatever skin eruption it was, it was disfiguring and highly contagious. So lepers, after an examination by priests, were condemned to live in disarray, exiled from community crying, "Unclean! Unclean!" as a warning to all.

I Cor. 10:31 to 11:1　Though we are free in Christ to enjoy the good stuff of creation, we do not seek to exploit our freedom or to impose on others. So, let us use all things for the glory of God, with a loving regard for uptight neighbors, all of whom are nifty people in the Lord.

Mark 1:40-45　Oh, see the love of God in Christ! Christ is angry at the deforming power of evil that diseases folks' lives. He seeks to liberate. Yet, when he heals, he hushes people up lest his ministry be misunderstood (everyone looks for cheap medical services nowadays!). Nevertheless, how can those whom Christ saves be silent? Still, still we speak.　　DB

PSALM FOR THE DAY: Psalm 32

HYMNS FOR THE DAY

	HL	HB	WB
Heaven and Earth, and Sea and Air	27	6	415
All Glory Be to God on High	—	—	283
How Blest Is He (Ps.) (tune: Munich)	—	281	—
Jesus, Lead the Way	—	334	441
Thine Is the Glory	—	209	—
Thine Arm, O Lord	—	179	—
O for a Thousand Tongues	199	141	493

ANTHEMS FOR THE DAY

I Cor. 10:31 to 11:1　*Turn Back, O Man*, Gustav Holst (Galaxy). SATB (M)

Mark 1:40-45　*Come Down, O Love Divine*, William Harris (Novello). SATB (E)

To My Humble Supplication, Gustav Holst (Augener). SATB (M)　　BH

COLLECT FOR THE DAY

Lord God, we ask you to keep your family, the Church, always faithful to you, that all who lean on the hope of your promises may gain strength from the power of your love; through your Son, Jesus Christ our Lord. (LBW)

READINGS

Isa. 43:18-25 Here the lectionary may combine portions of two different songs, vs. 18-21 and vs. 22-25. Israel has wearied Yahweh by her perfunctory religious observances, not to mention outright sinfulness. Well, Yahweh, who is always trying something new, will forgive and, indeed, forget. He will wipe away the past, and in compassion offer a new future for Israel.

II Cor. 1:18-22 In obedience, Christ said "Yes" to the Father's will. We look at his life and say "Amen," so be it! But more, Christ is the great, echoing "Yes" that speaks to all, saying, "Yes, God's promises are sure!" We see him, we hear him, and we believe.

Mark 2:1-12 Two stories have been merged, the healing of a paralytic and a controversy over forgiveness. Who does Jesus think he is? Only God can forgive sins! But then, at Christ's command, the paralytic walks, demonstrating the power of God. So "you may know that the Son of man has authority on earth to forgive sins," says Jesus. DB

PSALM FOR THE DAY: Psalm 41

HYMNS FOR THE DAY	HL	HB	WB
Praise, My Soul, the King of Heaven	14	31	551
Lord Jesus, Think on Me	239	270	—
Lord, from the Depths to You I Cry	240	277	459
Seal Us, O Holy Spirit	—	238	—
Christ Is the World's Redeemer (tune: Llangloffan)	—	136	—
Come, Christians, Join to Sing	191	131	333

ANTHEMS FOR THE DAY

Isa. 43:18-25 *Springs in the Desert*, Arthur B. Jennings (H. W. Gray). SATB (M)

I Thank You, God, Lloyd Pfautsch (G. Schirmer). SATB (M)

II Cor. 1:18-22 *God Is a Spirit*, Alexander Kopylov (E. C. Schirmer). SATB (M)

Mark 2:1-12 *Glory to God*, J. S. Bach (Colombo). SATB (E)

All Things Are Thine, Leo Sowerby (H. W. Gray). SATB (D) BH

THE EIGHTH SUNDAY AFTER EPIPHANY (B)

COLLECT FOR THE DAY

Almighty and everlasting God, ruler of heaven and earth: Hear our prayer and give us your peace now and forever; through your Son, Jesus Christ our Lord. (LBW)

READINGS

Hos. 2:14-20 Poor Yahweh, like a husband with a tramp wife, he must cope with an unfaithful Israel. Instead of punishment, he decides that he himself will seek a reconciliation. He will woo Israel again. No longer will she whisper the name of her lover, "My Baal," but she will speak to Yahweh, saying, "My husband." She will be faithful in a brave, bright, new world called Mercy.

II Cor. 3:17 to 4:2 We look at Christ, we learn of Christ, we see the glory of God in Christ and we are changed. All this occurs by the Holy Spirit, who sets us free to follow Christ. Therefore, we don't want to con people into grabbing at Christ, as do self-seeking evangelists. All we do is to present Christ, the mercy of God, openly. The Lord's Spirit will do the rest.

Mark 2:18-22 When the "new man" Jesus Christ arrives, old religious ways are inappropriate. Likewise, the new life he gives—free and completely forgiven—cannot be contained in old habits of behavior. So, fresh selves for new wine! DB

PSALM FOR THE DAY: Psalm 103:1-13

HYMNS FOR THE DAY	HL	HB	WB
Rejoice, the Lord Is King	193	140	562
Make Me a Captive, Lord	247	308	—
O Light, Whose Beams Illumine All	180	145	—
The True Light That Enlightens Man	—	—	598
Fairest Lord Jesus	194	135	360
The Church's One Foundation	333	437	582

ANTHEMS FOR THE DAY

Hos. 2:14-20 *All Ye Saints Be Joyful*, K. K. Davis (Warner). SATB (ME)

Lord, for Thy Tender Mercies' Sake, Richard Farrant (E. C. Schirmer). SATB (M)

II Cor. 3:17 to 4:2 *Jesus, Sun of Life, My Splendor*, G. F. Handel (Concordia). SATB (ME)

Choristers of Light, K. K. Davis (Galaxy). SATB (M) JTF

COLLECT FOR THE DAY
Almighty and ever-living God, you hate nothing you have made and
you forgive the sins of all who are penitent. Create in us new and honest
hearts, so that, truly repenting of our sins, we may obtain from you, the
God of all mercy, full pardon and forgiveness; through your Son, Jesus
Christ our Lord, who lives and reigns with you and the Holy Spirit, one
God, now and forever.   (LBW)

READINGS
Isa. 58:3-12 True fasting involves liberation of those in bondage, the
freeing of the oppressed, the sharing of bread and housing with the hungry
and homeless.

James 1:12-18 The promise of life awaits those who endure trials, tests,
and temptations.

Mark 2:15-20 Jesus eats with tax collectors and sinners, who need him.
Fasting will be appropriate after the bridegroom is taken away.   LAB

PSALM FOR THE DAY: Psalm 51:1-17

HYMNS FOR THE DAY	HL	HB	WB
God of Compassion, in Mercy Befriend Us	290	122	392
Lord, from the Depths to You I Cry	240	277	459
O Brother Man, Fold to Your Heart	403	474	484
I'm So Glad Troubles Don't Last Always	—	—	432
The Church's One Foundation	333	437	582
Lord, Who Throughout These Forty Days	144	181	470

ANTHEMS FOR THE DAY

Isa. 58:3-12 *Blest Are They Whose Spirits Long,* G. F. Handel (Choristers
Guild). 2-Part Mixed (E)

James 1:12-18 *Show Me Thy Ways,* Walter Pelz (Augsburg). SATB (M)

Lord, in Distress We Cry to Thee, G. F. Handel (Flammer). SATB (M)

Mark 2:15-20 *Jesu, Friend of Sinners,* Edvard Grieg (H. W. Gray).
SSAATTBB (MD)

O Lamb of God Most Holy, Johann Hermann Schein (Concordia). 2-Part (M)

God So Loved the World, John Stainer (B. F. Wood). SATB (M)   HH

COLLECT FOR THE DAY

O Lord God, you led your ancient people through the wilderness and brought them to the promised land. Guide now the people of your Church, that, following our Savior, we may walk through the wilderness of this world toward the glory of the world to come; through your Son, Jesus Christ our Lord, who lives and reigns with you and the Holy Spirit, one God, now and forever.   (LBW)

READINGS

Gen. 9:8-15   God establishes his covenant with Noah and his descendants, and with all living creatures, and seals it with a rainbow.

I Peter 3:18-22   After his saving death Christ preaches to the spirits in prison, disobedient in the days of Noah. Now, baptism corresponds to this, as a pledge to God from a good conscience.

Mark 1:12-15   The Spirit drives Jesus into the wilderness, where he is tempted for forty days by Satan. Then, after John is arrested, Jesus begins to preach in Galilee that the kingdom is at hand.   LAB

PSALM FOR THE DAY: Psalm 25:3-9

HYMNS FOR THE DAY	HL	HB	WB
O God of Bethel, by Whose Hand	98	342	496
Amazing Grace! How Sweet the Sound	—	275	296
O Love, How Deep, How Broad, How High!	139	—	518
Lord, Who Throughout These Forty Days	144	181	470
When We Are Tempted to Deny Your Son	—	—	640
Angel Voices, Ever Singing	455	30	—
Rejoice, the Lord Is King	193	140	562

ANTHEMS FOR THE DAY

Gen. 9:8-15   *If Thou but Suffer God to Guide Thee*, Jody Lindh (Concordia). SATB (M)

Set Me as a Seal Upon Thine Heart, William Walton (Oxford). SATB (D)

I Peter 3:18-22   *Thy Love Brings Joy*, Schütz-Coggin (Augsburg). SATB (M)

Mark 1:12-15   *Thy Kingdom Come, O Lord*, F. Melius Christiansen (Augsburg). SATB (E)   HH

COLLECT FOR THE DAY
Almighty God, on the mountain you showed your glory in the transfiguration of your Son. Give us the vision to see beyond the turmoil of our world and to behold the king in all his glory; through your Son, Jesus Christ our Lord, who lives and reigns with you and the Holy Spirit, one God, now and forever. (LBW)

READINGS
Gen. 22:1-2, 9-13 (or 22:1-13) Abraham's faith survives an ultimate test in his willingness to sacrifice his only son, Isaac. God provides a ram instead.

Rom. 8:31-39 The God who did not spare his own Son will give us all things. Is there anything that can separate us from such love?

Mark 9:1-9 The transfiguration of Jesus. "This is my beloved Son. Hear him." LAB

PSALM FOR THE DAY: Psalm 50:1-6

HYMNS FOR THE DAY	HL	HB	WB
All Hail the Power of Jesus' Name!	192	132	285, 286
The God of Abraham Praise	8	89	587
O Christ, Whose Love Has Sought Us Out	—	—	485
O Wondrous Type, O Vision Fair	142	182	531
Where Cross the Crowded Ways of Life	410	507	642

ANTHEMS FOR THE DAY

Gen. 22:1-2, 9-13 *Fight the Good Fight*, John Gardner (Oxford). SATB (M)

Christus factus est (Jesus Christ Was Made Obedient), Juan Bautista Comes (Leeds). SATB (M)

Rom. 8:31-39 *Canticle of Affirmation*, Carlton Young (Hope). SATB (E). Text from Romans 8

Who Shall Separate Us, Heinrich Schütz (Chantry). SATB (M)

Mark 9:1-9 *Christ, Upon the Mountain Peak*, Peter Cutts (in *Ecumenical Praise*, No. 67, Hope). (E) HH

COLLECT FOR THE DAY

Eternal Lord, your kingdom has broken into our troubled world through the life, death, and resurrection of your Son. Help us to hear your Word and obey it, so that we become instruments of your redeeming love; through your Son, Jesus Christ our Lord, who lives and reigns with you and the Holy Spirit, one God, now and forever.   (LBW)

READINGS

Ex. 20:1-3, 7-8, 12-17 (or 20:1-17) The Ten Commandments, beginning with the affirmation of God as the liberator: "I am the Lord your God, who brought you out of . . . bondage."

I Cor. 1:22-25 The Christ we preach seems like foolishness, but he is really the saving power and wisdom of God.

John 2:13-25 Jesus cleanses the Temple and speaks of the destruction of the temple of his body and resurrection after three days.   LAB

PSALM FOR THE DAY: Psalm 19:7-14

HYMNS FOR THE DAY

	HL	HB	WB
Christ Is Made the Sure Foundation	336	433	325
O Word of God Incarnate (Ps.)	215	251	532
In the Cross of Christ I Glory	154	195	437
The Day of Resurrection!	166	208	584
At the Name of Jesus	—	143	303

ANTHEMS FOR THE DAY

Ex. 20:1-3, 7-8, 12-17 *We Praise Thee, O God*, Handel-Peek (H.W. Gray). SATB (M)

The Lord Is a Mighty God, Mendelssohn (Kjos). 2-Part Mixed (E)

I Cor. 1:22-25 *Christ, Be Thine the Glory! (Ehre sei dir, Christe)*, Heinrich Schütz (G. Schirmer). SATB (M)

John 2:13-25 *My Eternal King*, Jane Marshall (C. Fischer). SATB (M) HH

COLLECT FOR THE DAY

God of all mercy, by your power to heal and to forgive, graciously cleanse us from all sin and make us strong; through your Son, Jesus Christ our Lord, who lives and reigns with you and the Holy Spirit, one God, now and forever.   (LBW)

READINGS

II Chron. 36:14-21   Unfaithful priests and people stubbornly reject God's messengers of mercy, until they are carried off into exile, where a remnant is finally faithful.

Eph. 2:1-10   God is rich in mercy even when we are dead in sin. By grace we are saved through faith, not by anything we do. It is the gift of God.

John 3:14-21   "God so loved the world that he gave his only Son." "Not to condemn the world, but that the world might be saved through him." Even so, some prefer darkness to light.   LAB

PSALM FOR THE DAY: Psalm 137:1-6

HYMNS FOR THE DAY	HL	HB	WB
We Love Your Kingdom, Lord (Ps.)	337	435	626
There's a Wideness in God's Mercy	93	110	601
Come, Thou Fount of Every Blessing	235	379	341
Let All Together Praise Our God	—	—	450
Christ Is the World's True Light	—	492	326

ANTHEMS FOR THE DAY

II Chron. 36:14-21   *Bless the Lord, O My Soul*, William Mathias (Oxford). SATB (D)

There Is a Balm in Gilead, arr. William Dawson (Tuskegee Music Institute). SATB (M)

Bow Down Thine Ear, Fatyeff-Tkach (Kjos). SATB (M)

Eph. 2:1-10   *Nature with Open Volume Stands*, Erik Routley (in *Ecumenical Praise*, No. 38, Hope). (E)

John 3:14-21   *Wondrous Love*, Paul Christiansen (Augsburg). SATB (M)

Sing, My Soul, His Wondrous Love, Ned Rorem (Peters). SATB (M)   HH

THE FIFTH SUNDAY IN LENT (B)

COLLECT FOR THE DAY
Almighty God, our redeemer, in our weakness we have failed to be your messengers of forgiveness and hope in the world. Renew us by your Holy Spirit, that we may follow your commands and proclaim your reign of love; through your Son, Jesus Christ our Lord, who lives and reigns with you and the Holy Spirit, one God, now and forever.

(LBW)

READINGS
Jer. 31:31-34 "I will make a new covenant with the house of Israel." "I will put my law within them, and write it upon their hearts; and I will be their God, and they shall be my people."

Heb. 5:7-10 Even Christ, a high priest like Melchizedek, learned obedience through suffering. Those who obey him find eternal salvation.

John 12:20-33 Anyone who wants to serve Christ must follow him, and prefer Christ to this life. Before a grain of wheat can bear fruit, it must fall into the earth and die. LAB

PSALM FOR THE DAY: Psalm 51:10-16

HYMNS FOR THE DAY

	HL	HB	WB
The Head That Once Was Crowned with Thorns	195	211	589
Father, We Thank You that You Planted	—	—	366
Throned Upon the Awful Tree	—	197	605
Glorious Is Your Name, Most Holy	—	—	378
A Mighty Fortress	266	91	274
Jesus Shall Reign	377	496	443

ANTHEMS FOR THE DAY

Jer. 31:31-34 *Song of Jeremiah*, Hal Hopson (from *The People of God*, Triune Music). For children's voices (E)

Heb. 5:7-10 *Adoramus te*, Jacopo Perti (G. Schirmer). SATB (M)

A Hymn of Supplication, Don McAfee (H. W. Gray). 2-Part Mixed (E)

John 12:20-33 *Walk in the Light*, Cassler (Augsburg). SATB (E) HH

COLLECT FOR THE DAY
>Almighty God, you sent your Son, our Savior Jesus Christ, to take our flesh upon him and to suffer death on the cross. Grant that we may share in his obedience to your will and in the glorious victory of his resurrection; through your Son, Jesus Christ our Lord, who lives and reigns with you and the Holy Spirit, one God, now and forever.
>
>(LBW)

READINGS
>**Zech. 9:9-12** "Behold your king comes to you, triumphant and victorious, humble and riding on an ass."
>
>**Heb. 12:1-6** "Since we are surrounded by so great a cloud of witnesses," we ought to put sin aside and run our race with perseverance. Christ endured the cross and despised shame, and is the pioneer and perfecter of our faith.
>
>**Mark 11:1-11** Jesus enters Jerusalem on a colt, with garments and leafy branches spread on his way and the people shouting hosannas.   LAB

PSALM FOR THE DAY: Psalm 24

HYMNS FOR THE DAY	HL	HB	WB
The Son of God Goes Forth to War	271	354	—
Lift Up Your Heads (Ps.)	114	152	454
Christ, Above All Glory Seated	—	—	324
So Lowly Does the Savior Ride	—	—	571
O How Shall We Receive You	—	—	506
Hosanna, Loud Hosanna	147	185	424

ANTHEMS FOR THE DAY

>**Zech. 9:9-12** *Song of Zechariah*, Hal Hopson (Flammer). Unison (E)
>
>*Rejoice Greatly*, Johannes Petzold (in *Music for the Contemporary Choir*, Augsburg). Unison (E)
>
>**Heb. 12:1-6** *Nature with Open Volume Stands*, Erik Routley (in *Ecumenical Praise*, No. 38, Hope). (E)
>
>**Mark 11:1-11** *Hosanna to the Son of David*, Bartholomäus Gesius (Concordia). SATB (M)
>
>*On Humble Beast Now Rides the King*, Hal Hopson (Flammer). Unison (E). Also available for SAB voices
>
>*The Glory of Our King*, Dale Wood (in *Music for the Contemporary Choir*, Augsburg). Unison (E)   HH

COLLECT FOR THE DAY

Lord God, in a wonderful Sacrament you have left us a memorial of your suffering and death. May this Sacrament of your body and blood so work in us that the way we live will proclaim the redemption you have brought; for you live and reign with the Father and the Holy Spirit, one God, now and forever.   (LBW)

READINGS

Deut. 16:1-8 Instructions for the celebration of the Passover.

Rev. 1:4-8 "John to the seven churches in Asia." "To him who loves us and has freed us from our sins by his blood and made us a kingdom of priests."

Matt. 26:17-30 The institution of the Lord's Supper at the Last Supper.   LAB

PSALM FOR THE DAY: Psalm 116:12-19

HYMNS FOR THE DAY	HL	HB	WB
The Day of Resurrection!	166	208	584
Love Divine, All Loves Excelling	308	399	471
The Lord's My Shepherd	97	104	592
Deck Yourself, My Soul	—	—	351
Alone You Journey Forth, O Lord	—	—	294
The Son of God Goes Forth to War	271	354	—

ANTHEMS FOR THE DAY

Deut. 16:1-8 *By Gracious Powers,* Joseph Gelineau (in *Ecumenical Praise,* No. 57, Hope). (E). Text by Dietrich Bonhoeffer

Rev. 1:4-8 *I Am the Alpha and the Omega,* Daniel Moe (Augsburg). SATB (M)

God, Who Spoke in the Beginning, Erik Routley (in *Ecumenical Praise,* No. 80, Hope). (E). Text by Fred Kaan

Matt. 26:17-30 *Litany of Celebration,* Hal Hopson (Gentry). Unison (E)

Take, Believe, Wetzler (Art Masters). SATB or Unison (E)

Communion Hymn, Hal Hopson (Abingdon). SATB (M)   HH

COLLECT FOR THE DAY
   Almighty God, we ask you to look with mercy on your family, for whom our Lord Jesus Christ was willing to be betrayed and to be given over to the hands of sinners and to suffer death on the cross; who now lives and reigns with you and the Holy Spirit, one God, forever and ever.

(LBW)

READINGS
   Lam. 1:7-12   The sad plight of Jerusalem. "Is it nothing to you who pass by? . . . Is there any sorrow like my sorrow?"

   Heb. 10:4-18   Christ established the new covenant. "When he had offered for all time a single sacrifice for sins, he sat down at the right hand of God."

   Luke 23:33-46   The crucifixion of Jesus. In spite of the mocking and scoffing, he prays, "Father, forgive them, for they know not what they do." The promise to the repentant criminal.   LAB

PSALM FOR THE DAY: Psalm 31:1-5, 9-16

HYMNS FOR THE DAY	HL	HB	WB
O Come and Mourn with Me Awhile	159	192	—
O Sacred Head	151	194	524
Behold the Lamb of God!	153	(585)	307
When We Are Tempted to Deny Your Son	—	—	640
I'm Not Ashamed to Own My Lord	—	292	—

ANTHEMS FOR THE DAY

   Lam. 1:7-12   *O Vos Omnes (All Ye People)*, Tomás Luis de Victoria (Elkan-Vogel). SATB (M)

   O Vos Omnes (Is It Nothing . . .), Palestrina (G. Schirmer). SATB (MD)

   Heb. 10:4-18   *Lord of All Most Holy*, Hal Hopson (Flammer). 2-Part Mixed (E)   HH

COLLECT FOR THE DAY

O God, you gave your only Son to suffer death on the cross for our redemption, and by his glorious resurrection you delivered us from the power of death. Make us die every day to sin, so that we may live with him forever in the joy of the resurrection; through Jesus Christ our Lord, who lives and reigns with you and the Holy Spirit, one God, now and forever.

(LBW)

READINGS

Isa. 25:6-9 The Messianic Banquet. "He will swallow up death for ever, and the Lord God will wipe away tears from all faces." "Let us be glad and rejoice in his salvation."

I Peter 1:3-9 "By his great mercy we have been born anew to a living hope through the resurrection of Jesus Christ from the dead."

Mark 16:1-8 The resurrection of Jesus. "Go, tell his disciples and Peter that he is going before you to Galilee." The women leave, trembling in amazement and fear.

LAB

PSALM FOR THE DAY: Psalm 118:1-2, 14-24

HYMNS FOR THE DAY

	HL	HB	WB
(1) *For an early Eucharist (or Vigil)*			
"Welcome, Happy Morning!"	169	207	—
Christ Jesus Lay in Death's Strong Bands	—	—	327
Through the Night of Doubt (tune: Ebenezer)	345	475	—
Wake, Awake, for Night Is Flying	—	—	614
(2) *For a Service of the Word*			
A Hymn of Glory Let Us Sing	—	—	273
"Christ the Lord Is Risen Today"	165	—	330
The Strife Is O'er, the Battle Done	164	203	597
The Lord Is Risen (use throughout service)	—	—	265
O Sons and Daughters	167	206	527

ANTHEMS FOR THE DAY

Isa. 25:6-9 *Sing, Joyous Christians*, Antonio Lotti (Concordia). SATB (ME)

Round the Earth a Message Runs, Austin Lovelace (E. C. Kerby). 2-Part (E)

Alleluia, Jane Marshall (Sacred Music). SAB, brass, string bass, drums (M)

I Peter 1:3-9 *Come Let's Rejoice*, John Amner (Oxford). SATB (M)

Joy Dawns Again, Garry A. Cornell (Art Masters). 2 voices (E). Youth Choir

A Joyful Song, Robert Leaf (Augsburg). SA (E). For Children's Voices

Mark 16:1-8 *Christ Rising Again*, John Amner (Oxford). SATB (M)

Sing Praise to Christ, J. S. Bach (Concordia). SATB (M)

The Festal Day Is Here, Hal Hopson (Flammer). SATB (M)

HH

THE SECOND SUNDAY OF EASTER (B)

COLLECT FOR THE DAY
Almighty God, we have celebrated with joy the festival of our Lord's resurrection. Graciously help us to show the power of the resurrection in all that we say and do; through your Son, Jesus Christ our Lord, who lives and reigns with you and the Holy Spirit, one God, now and forever. (LBW)

READINGS
Acts 4:32-35 Life in the post-resurrection community of believers, holding all their possessions in common, and full of "great grace."

I John 5:1-6 "Every one who believes that Jesus is the Christ is a child of God." Our faith is "the victory that overcomes the world."

Matt. 28:11-20 Amidst attempts to discredit his resurrection, the resurrected Christ gives the Great Commission to his disciples: "Go therefore and make disciples of all nations . . ." LAB

PSALM FOR THE DAY: Psalm 148

HYMNS FOR THE DAY	HL	HB	WB
Jesus Christ Is Risen Today	163	204	440
The Easter Day with Joy Was Bright	—	—	581
Praise the Lord! (Ps.)	10	3	554
Go, Tell It on the Mountain	—	—	380
We Bear the Strain of Earthly Care	179	227	621
Heralds of Christ	379	498	416
O Master, Let Me Walk with Thee	364	304	520

ANTHEMS FOR THE DAY

Acts 4:32-35 *We Meet You, O Christ*, Erik Routley (in *Ecumenical Praise*, No. 112, Hope). (E)

I John 5:1-6 *Blessed Is the Man*, Jane Marshall (Abingdon). SATB (E)

Matt. 28:11-20 *Go Ye Into All the World*, Robert Wetzler (Augsburg). 2-Part Mixed (E) HH

COLLECT FOR THE DAY

O God, by the humiliation of your Son you lifted up this fallen world, rescuing us from the hopelessness of death. Grant your faithful people a share in the joys that are eternal; through your Son, Jesus Christ our Lord, who lives and reigns with you and the Holy Spirit, one God, now and forever.

(LBW)

READINGS

Acts 3:13-15, 17-19   Peter daringly witnesses to the resurrection of Christ and calls all to repentance, especially those who were complicitous.

I John 2:1-6   "If we win, we have a defense attorney with the Father, Jesus Christ the righteous." "If we say we abide in him, we ought to walk in the same way he walked."

Luke 24:36-49   The risen Christ invites his disciples to see and touch his wounds, eats with them, and interprets his death and resurrection from the Scriptures. He commands them to "stay in the city" until they are "clothed with power from on high."

LAB

PSALM FOR THE DAY: Psalm 139:1-12

HYMNS FOR THE DAY

	HL	HB	WB
Praise the Lord, His Glories Show	12	4	552
God Is Love: Let Heaven Adore Him	—	—	386
Be Thou My Vision	325	303	304
Christ Is the World's Redeemer	—	136	—
God Has Spoken—by His Prophets	—	—	382
They Cast Their Nets	—	421	—
Good Christian Men, Rejoice	—	—	406

ANTHEMS FOR THE DAY

Acts 3:13-15, 17-19   *A Hymn of Praise*, arr. Samuel Adler (Lawson-Gould). SATB (E)

I John 2:1-6   *If Ye Love Me, Keep My Commandments*, Thomas Tallis (G. Schirmer). (M)

Luke 24:36-49   *The Kingdom of the Lord*, Natalie Sleeth (Art Masters). 2-Part (E)

Eternal God, Whose Power Upholds, George Brandon (Concordia). 2-Part Mixed, SATB or SAB (M)

HH

THE FOURTH SUNDAY OF EASTER (B)

COLLECT FOR THE DAY
God of all power, you called from death our Lord Jesus, the great shepherd of the sheep. Send us as shepherds to rescue the lost, to heal the injured, and to feed one another with knowledge and understanding; through your Son, Jesus Christ our Lord, who lives and reigns with you and the Holy Spirit, one God, now and forever.   (LBW)

READINGS
Acts 4:8-12 Peter and John defend themselves before the religious authorities after their arrest for preaching the gospel. Christ is "the cornerstone" and the only one "under heaven given among men by whom we must be saved."

I John 3:1-3 "See what love the Father has given us, that we should be called children of God; and so we are."

John 10:11-18 "I am the good shepherd. The good shepherd lays down his life for the sheep."   LAB

PSALM FOR THE DAY: Psalm 23

HYMNS FOR THE DAY	HL	HB	WB
All Hail the Power of Jesus' Name!	192	132	285
How Sweet the Name of Jesus Sounds	310	130	—
Take Thou Our Minds, Dear Lord	245	306	579
The King of Love My Shepherd Is (Ps.)	99	106	590
Saviour, like a Shepherd Lead Us	458	380	—
My Shepherd Will Supply My Need	—	—	477

ANTHEMS FOR THE DAY

Acts 4:8-12 *Christ Is Made the Sure Foundation,* Dale Wood (Schmitt, Hall & McCreary). SATB (E)

I John 3:1-3 *The Praises of a King,* Austin Lovelace (Augsburg). 2-Part Mixed (E)

John 10:11-18 *I Am the Good Shepherd,* Dale Wood (in *Music for the Contemporary Choir,* Augsburg). Unison (M)   HH

COLLECT FOR THE DAY

O God, form the minds of your faithful people into a single will. Make us love what you command and desire what you promise, that, amid all the changes of this world, our hearts may be fixed where true joy is found; through your Son, Jesus Christ our Lord, who lives and reigns with you and the Holy Spirit, one God, now and forever.   (LBW)

READINGS

Acts 9:26-31   After his Damascus road conversion, Saul is introduced by Barnabas to the Jerusalem apostles. He preaches boldly, but is resisted by some.

I John 3:18-24   "This is his commandment, that we should believe in the name of his Son Jesus Christ and love one another." "We know that he abides in us, by the Spirit which he has given us."

John 15:1-8   "I am the true vine, and my Father is the vinedresser. . . . You are the branches."   LAB

PSALM FOR THE DAY: Psalm 22:25-31

HYMNS FOR THE DAY

	HL	HB	WB
O Sing a Song of Bethlehem	138	177	526
Put Forth, O God, Your Spirit's Might	—	477	559
O Love, How Deep, How Broad, How High!	139	—	518
Where Charity and Love Prevail	—	—	641
In Heavenly Love Abiding	284	417	—
O Holy Saviour, Friend Unseen	—	214	—

ANTHEMS FOR THE DAY

Acts 9:26-31   *How Lovely Are the Messengers,* Mendelssohn (G. Schirmer). SATB (M)

I John 3:18-24   *Day by Day,* Carlton Young (Hope). SSAATTBB (M)

If Ye Love Me, Keep My Commandments, Thomas Tallis (G. Schirmer). (M)

John 15:1-8   *Blessed Is the Man,* Jane Marshall (Abingdon). SATB (E)

                                                                          HH

THE SIXTH SUNDAY OF EASTER (B)

COLLECT FOR THE DAY

O God, from whom all good things come: Lead us by the inspiration of your Spirit to think those things which are right, and by your goodness help us to do them; through your Son, Jesus Christ our Lord, who lives and reigns with you and the Holy Spirit, one God, now and forever. (LBW)

READINGS

Acts 10:34-48 Peter's sermon in the home of Cornelius, summarizing the gospel story. The Holy Spirit is then poured out on Gentiles.

I John 4:1-7 "Do not believe every spirit, but test the spirits to see whether they are of God. . . . Let us love one another; for love is of God, and he who loves is born of God and knows God."

John 15:9-17 "As the Father has loved me, so have I loved you; abide in my love. . . . You did not choose me, but I chose you. . . . This I command you, to love one another." LAB

PSALM FOR THE DAY: Psalm 98

HYMNS FOR THE DAY	HL	HB	WB
Son of God, Eternal Savior	393	—	573
God Is Working His Purpose Out	—	500	389
In Christ There Is No East or West	341	479	435
We Are One in the Spirit	—	—	619
O Zion, Haste	382	491	—
O Be Joyful in the Lord!	—	—	482
The Friends of Christ Together	—	—	586
Through Love to Light!	499	—	—

ANTHEMS FOR THE DAY

Acts 10:34-48 *Jesus Christ, Lord and King,* Rameau-Lowe (Choristers Guild). Unison (E). Children's Choir

I John 4:1-7 *O God, Whose Will Is Life,* Thomas Tallis (in *Ecumenical Praise,* No. 50, Hope). (E)

John 15:9-17 *Whoever Would Be Great Among You,* Ronald A. Nelson (Augsburg). SAB (E)

Greater Love Hath No Man, John Ireland (Galaxy). SATB, Soprano and Baritone Solos. (M) HH

ASCENSION DAY (B)

COLLECT FOR THE DAY

Almighty God: your Son Jesus promised that if he was lifted up, he would draw all to himself. Draw us to him by faith, so that we may live to serve you, and look toward life eternal; through Jesus Christ the Lord.

(WB)

READINGS

Acts 1:1-11 Having promised the apostles that "before many days you shall be baptized with the Holy Spirit," Jesus "was lifted up, and a cloud took him out of their sight."

Eph. 1:16-23 God has made Christ to "sit at his right hand" and "has put all things under his feet and has made him the head over all things for the church."

Luke 24:44-53 (Continues the Gospel pericope of Easter 3.) Jesus led the disciples out to Bethany, where he blessed them, and "while he blessed them, he parted from them."

LAB

PSALM FOR THE DAY: Psalm 110

HYMNS FOR THE DAY

	HL	HB	WB
Come, Christians, Join to Sing (Ps.)	191	131	333
The Lord Ascendeth Up on High	172	212	—
Light of Light, Enlighten Me	21	73	—
Christ, Whose Glory Fills the Skies	26	47	332
Crown Him with Many Crowns	190	213	349

ANTHEMS FOR THE DAY

Acts 1:1-11 *Come Away to the Skies,* arr. Parker (G. Schirmer). SATB (M)

At the Name of Jesus, R. Vaughan Williams (Oxford). SATB (M)

Eph. 1:16-23 *Alleluia! Sing to Jesus,* Hal Hopson (Augsburg). 2-Part (E)

My Jesus Is My Lasting Joy, Buxtehude-Bitgood (H. W. Gray). Unison (E). Children's Choir

Luke 24:44-53 *The Praises of a King,* Austin Lovelace (Augsburg). 2-Part Mixed (E)

HH

THE SEVENTH SUNDAY OF EASTER (B)

COLLECT FOR THE DAY

God, our creator and redeemer, your Son Jesus prayed that his followers might be one. Make all Christians one with him as he is one with you, so that in peace and concord we may carry to the world the message of your love; through Jesus Christ our Lord, who lives and reigns with you and the Holy Spirit, one God, now and forever. (LBW)

READINGS

Acts 1:15-17, 21-26 At Peter's suggestion, the brethren cast lots to choose Matthias to fill the vacancy among the twelve apostles created by the defection of Judas Iscariot.

I John 4:11-16 No one "has ever seen God; if we love one another, God abides in us and his love is perfected in us. . . . God is love, and he who abides in love abides in God, and God abides in him."

John 17:11-19 "Holy Father, keep them in thy name, which thou hast given me, that they may be one, even as we are one. . . . As thou didst send me into the world, so I have sent them into the world." LAB

PSALM FOR THE DAY: Psalm 47

HYMNS FOR THE DAY	HL	HB	WB
All Hail the Power of Jesus' Name!	192	132	285, 286
God of the Prophets!	481	520	398
God Is Love: Let Heaven Adore Him	—	—	386
He Is the Way	—	—	413
Crown Him with Many Crowns	190	213	349

ANTHEMS FOR THE DAY

Acts 1:15-17, 21-26 *How Lovely Are the Messengers*, Mendelssohn (G. Schirmer). SATB (M)

I John 4:11-16 *My Lord, My Brother*, Garry A. Cornell (Hope). 2-Part Mixed (E)

John 17:11-19 *Go Ye Into All the World*, Robert Wetzler (Augsburg). 2-Part Mixed (E) HH

COLLECT FOR THE DAY

God, the Father of our Lord Jesus Christ, as you sent upon the disciples the promised gift of the Holy Spirit, look upon your Church and open our hearts to the power of the Spirit. Kindle in us the fire of your love, and strengthen our lives for service in your kingdom; through your Son, Jesus Christ our Lord, who lives and reigns with you in the unity of the Holy Spirit, one God, now and forever.   (LBW)

READINGS

Joel 2:28-32 "I will pour out my spirit on all flesh; your sons and your daughters shall prophesy, your old men shall dream dreams, and your young men shall see visions."

Acts 2:1-13 The outpouring of the Holy Spirit at Pentecost and the speaking in other tongues.

John 16:5-15 "I am going to him who sent me. . . . If I do not go away, the Counselor will not come to you; but if I go, I will send him to you." LAB

PSALM FOR THE DAY: Psalm 104:1-4, 24-33

HYMNS FOR THE DAY

	HL	HB	WB
Come to Us, Mighty King	52	244	343
Come Down, O Love Divine	—	—	334
Come, Holy Ghost, Our Souls Inspire	—	237	335
Come, O Come, Great Quickening Spirit (for Holy Communion)	—	—	338
Descend, O Spirit, Purging Flame	—	—	353
Send Down Your Truth, O God	—	—	566
O Spirit of the Living God	207	242	—
The Day of Pentecost Arrived	—	—	583
Holy Spirit, Truth Divine	208	240	422

ANTHEMS FOR THE DAY

Joel 2:28-32 *Come, Holy Spirit, Come,* S. Drummond Wolff (Concordia). SA (E). Children's Choir

Speak to One Another of Psalms, Jean Berger (Augsburg). SATB (M)

Acts 2:1-13 *Carol for Pentecost,* Judy Hunnicutt (Augsburg). Unison (E). Children's Choir

John 16:5-15 *Veni Creator,* Orlando Gibbons (A. Broude). SATB (E)

The Lone, Wild Bird, David N. Johnson (Augsburg). SATB (E)

Temples of God, Ronald A. Nelson (Augsburg). 2-Part Mixed (E)   HH

COLLECT FOR THE DAY

Almighty and ever-living God, you have given us grace, by the confession of the true faith, to acknowledge the glory of the eternal Trinity and, in the power of your divine majesty, to worship the unity. Keep us steadfast in this faith and worship, and bring us at last to see you in your eternal glory, one God, now and forever.   (LBW)

READINGS

Isa. 6:1-8 This particular passage describes three essential liturgical components: the ascription of praise, confession of sin and assurance of pardon, and the call to discipleship. Isaiah receives his call, to which he replies, "Here am I! Send me."

Rom. 8:12-17 Paul describes the life in the Spirit with emphasis upon the believer's inheritance as a child of God. As a child of God one is to live not according to the flesh but as an heir with Christ, in order that one "may also be glorified with him."

John 3:1-8 The Pharisee named Nicodemus asks Jesus how one can be born anew. Jesus replies, "Unless one is born of water and the Spirit, he cannot enter the kingdom of God." That which is of the flesh is conditioned by fleshly requirements. That which is of the Spirit is led by the Spirit. JGK

PSALM FOR THE DAY: Psalm 149

HYMNS FOR THE DAY	HL	HB	WB
O Trinity of Blessed Light	59	245	—
We Believe in One True God	—	—	622
Glory Be to God the Father	60	—	—
Holy God, We Praise Your Name	—	—	420
I Sing as I Arise Today	—	—	428
The Apostles' Creed (I Believe in God)	—	—	259
All Creatures of Our God and King	—	100	282
Earth and All Stars (Ps.)	—	—	354

ANTHEMS FOR THE DAY

Isa. 6:1-8 *In the Year That King Uzziah Died*, David McK. Williams (H. W. Gray). SATB (D)

Laudate Dominum, W. A. Mozart (Presser). SATB and Soprano Solo (MD)

Lord, Here Am I, Paulus (Art Masters). SATB (E). Youth Choir

Alleluia! Let Praises Ring! S. Drummond Wolff (Concordia). SATB (M)

Rom. 8:12-17 *Temples of God*, Ronald A. Nelson (Augsburg). 2-Part Mixed (E)

Father, We Praise Thee, Richard Peek (Brodt). SATB (E)

John 3:1-8 *We Know that Christ Is Raised*, C. V. Stanford (in *Ecumenical Praise*, No. 111, Hope). (E)   HH

COLLECT FOR THE DAY

Lord God of all nations, you have revealed your will to your people and promised your help to us all. Help us to hear and to do what you command, that the darkness may be overcome by the power of your light; through your Son, Jesus Christ our Lord. (LBW)

READINGS

Deut. 5:12-15 The Sabbath Day is proclaimed a day of rest, a day during which the people of the covenant recall the mighty acts of God. Called from labor to rest, rest then conditions and interprets further labor.

II Cor. 4:6-11 The Christian is afflicted, but not crushed; perplexed, but not driven to despair; persecuted, but not forsaken; struck down, but not destroyed. Suffering is no longer terminal, but in order that the life of Jesus may be manifested in our mortal flesh.

Mark 2:23 to 3:6 Taken from the conflict portion of Mark's Gospel, our text cites the fourth and fifth offenses. Both relate to Jesus' teaching concerning the Sabbath. Its narrow interpretation by the Jewish authorities is broadened to serve the needs of those who observe it. JGK

PSALM FOR THE DAY: Psalm 81:1-10

HYMNS FOR THE DAY	HL	HB	WB
God Himself Is with Us	51	13	384
This Is the Day of Light	20	72	—
O My Soul, Bless God, the Father	—	—	523
This Is the Day the Lord Hath Made	23	69	—
Whate'er Our God Ordains Is Right	291	366	633

ANTHEMS FOR THE DAY

Deut. 5:12-15 *Blessed Art Thou, O Lord*, Eric Reid (in *Ecumenical Praise*, No. 2, Hope). (E)

II Cor. 4:6-11 *We Thank Thee, Lord*, Bortniansky (Kjos). SATB (E) HH

COLLECT FOR THE DAY

O God, the strength of those who hope in you: Be present and hear our prayers; and, because in the weakness of our mortal nature we can do nothing good without you, give us the help of your grace, so that in keeping your commandments we may please you in will and deed; through your Son, Jesus Christ our Lord.   (LBW)

READINGS

Gen. 3:9-15   This particular creation narrative describes both promise and curse. There is promise in the fact that God continually seeks after those whom God has created. There is curse in the fact that the creatures continually seek to hide themselves from God.

II Cor. 4:13 to 5:1   Paul continues his thoughts on discipleship with emphasis upon the eternal nature of those things which are unseen. Therein lies the believer's hope. To borrow a line from the Hebrews, "Now faith is the assurance of things hoped for, the conviction of things not seen."

Mark 3:20-35   Jesus' friends claim, "He is beside himself." The scribes say, "He is possessed by Beelzebul." How can he be so possessed when his whole action is hostile to Satan? Indeed, the scribes may be guilty of blasphemy! As for his family, their lack of sympathy leads Jesus to broaden the concept of family.   JGK

PSALM FOR THE DAY: Psalm 61:1-5, 8

HYMNS FOR THE DAY	HL	HB	WB
I'm So Glad Troubles Don't Last Always	—	—	432
Jesus, Thou Joy of Loving Hearts	354	215	—
Jesus, Priceless Treasure	—	414	442
Lord of the Strong, When Earth You Trod	—	—	466
Lord God of Hosts, Whose Purpose	368	288	460
Jerusalem the Golden	435	428	—

ANTHEMS FOR THE DAY

Gen. 3:9-15   *In Adam We Have All Been One,* arr. Carl Schalk (Concordia). SATB (E)

II Cor. 4:13 to 5:1   *Immortal, Invisible, God Only Wise,* Barbara Terry (Chantry). SATB (E)

Mark 3:20-35   *Christian! Dost Thou See Them?* Lloyd Pfautsch (Abingdon). SATB (M)   HH

THE FOURTH SUNDAY AFTER PENTECOST (B)

COLLECT FOR THE DAY

God, our maker and redeemer, you have made us a new company of priests to bear witness to the Gospel. Enable us to be faithful to our calling to make known your promises to all the world; through your Son, Jesus Christ our Lord.   (LBW)

READINGS

Ezek. 17:22-24   A prophecy of messianic hope in which God will establish the house of David firmly on Mt. Zion. It will bear fruit, provide shelter, and show forth what great things the Lord can do.

II Cor. 5:6-10   Just as the believer's hope lies in the eternal nature of things unseen, so also the believer's courage comes from walking in faith. Being for the time at home in the body, the believer is so to walk in faith that God will be pleased.

Mark 4:26-34   Jesus cites two parables on the kingdom of God. The one teaches that the growth of the kingdom depends upon forces hidden within the truth itself. The other relates how even though the truth may have modest beginnings, its growth may be great.   JGK

PSALM FOR THE DAY: Psalm 92

HYMNS FOR THE DAY	HL	HB	WB
God of Grace and God of Glory	—	358	393
Lord, Speak to Me	399	298	—
Father, We Thank You that You Planted (for Holy Communion)	—	—	366
Come, You Thankful People, Come	460	525	346
Rejoice, the Lord Is King	193	140	562

ANTHEMS FOR THE DAY

II Cor. 5:6-10   *On God and Not on Human Trust,* Johann Pachelbel (Concordia). SATB (M)

Mark 4:26-34   *How Wonderful This World,* Austin Lovelace (Hope). Unison (E). Children's Choir   HH

COLLECT FOR THE DAY

O God our defender, storms rage about us and cause us to be afraid. Rescue your people from despair, deliver your sons and daughters from fear, and preserve us all from unbelief; through your Son, Jesus Christ our Lord. (LBW)

READINGS

Job 38:1-11 A portion of Yahweh's answer to Job in which Yahweh assails Job with questions he cannot answer about the wonders of nature and control of the world. Can one indeed doubt God's wisdom and justice?

II Cor. 5:16-21 As hope and courage are signs of walking in faith, so also is reconciliation a sign of the new life in Jesus Christ. The old has passed away! The believer is then commissioned as ambassador for Christ, entrusted with the ministry of reconciliation.

Mark 4:35-41 The hope and courage which Paul has been emphasizing are not evident in the disciples as the storm arises on the lake. Jesus calms the sea and rebukes the disciples for their lack of faith JGK

PSALM FOR THE DAY: Psalm 107:1-3, 23-32

HYMNS FOR THE DAY

	HL	HB	WB
We Sing the Mighty Power of God	65	84	628
Love Divine, All Loves Excelling	308	399	471
Your Love, O God, Has All Mankind Created	—	—	646
Jesus Calls Us	223	269	439
Jesus, Lover of My Soul	233	216	—
Eternal Father, Strong to Save	492	521	356

ANTHEMS FOR THE DAY

Job 38:1-11 *O Lord of Stars and Sunlight*, arr. Austin Lovelace (Hope). SATB (E)

We Praise Thee, O God (Cantata 29), J. S. Bach (Augsburg). SATB (D)

Cosmic Festival, Richard Felciano (E. C. Schirmer). Unison voices and tape (E)

II Cor. 5:16-21 *Reconciliation*, Lloyd Pfautsch (Abingdon). (M)

Mark 4:35-41 *O Lord, in Thee We Put Our Trust*, G. F. Handel (Flammer). 2-Part Mixed (E) HH

COLLECT FOR THE DAY

O God, you have prepared for those who love you joys beyond understanding. Pour into our hearts such love for you that, loving you above all things, we may obtain your promises, which exceed all that we can desire; through your Son, Jesus Christ our Lord.   (LBW)

READINGS

Gen. 4:3-10 The story of Cain and Abel casts in bold strokes the conflict between the pastoral and agricultural ways of life.

II Cor. 8:7-15 Paul counsels the Corinthian church to follow the example of the Macedonian churches in their benevolence. Paul's goal is that through mutual generosity each Christian church may have enough for its necessities.

Mark 5:21-43 Two accounts are given of Jesus' healing power: the raising of the daugher of Jairus and the healing of the woman with an issue of blood. Emphasizing either the responsibilities of stewardship or the new life to be found in Jesus the Christ will relate the Genesis reading to the New Testament readings.   JGK

PSALM FOR THE DAY: Psalm 30

HYMNS FOR THE DAY

	HL	HB	WB
Father, We Praise You	24	43	365
"Am I My Brother's Keeper?"	—	—	295
We Give Thee but Thine Own	394	312	—
Give to the Winds Your Fears	294	364	377
Thine Arm, O Lord	—	179	—
Father, Whose Will Is Life and Good	—	309	368

ANTHEMS FOR THE DAY

Gen. 4:3-10 *"Am I My Brother's Keeper?"* (WB, p. 295). (E)

II Cor. 8:7-15 *See Them Building,* Sven-Erik Bäck (in *Ecumenical Praise,* No. 99, Hope). (E)

Mark 5:21-43 *They Saw You as the Local Builder's Son,* Verner Ahlberg (in *Ecumenical Praise,* No. 105, Hope). (E)

Give Me Jesus, arr. Larry L. Fleming (Augsburg). SATB (MD)   HH

COLLECT FOR THE DAY

God of glory, Father of love, peace comes from you alone. Send us as peacemakers and witnesses to your kingdom, and fill our hearts with joy in your promises of salvation; through your Son, Jesus Christ our Lord. (LBW)

READINGS

Ezek. 2:1-5 The commission of Ezekiel which sends him into the midst of the people of Israel. He is given the warning that they might reject him. Nevertheless, he is to stand firm in the affirmation, "Thus says the Lord God."

II Cor. 12:7-10 Paul recounts for the people his own physical weakness, and the grace that has been his in spite of it. Indeed, rather than limiting, it has strengthened his ministry. For the power of Christ is "made perfect in weakness."

Mark 6:1-6 Jesus is rejected by his own people, who question the wisdom and power of one whose beginnings were indeed so humble. Except for a few isolated instances Jesus is unable to minister and returns to the villages to teach. That of which Ezekiel was warned Jesus encountered! JGK

PSALM FOR THE DAY: Psalm 123

HYMNS FOR THE DAY	HL	HB	WB
God of Compassion, in Mercy Befriend Us	290	122	392
O Son of Man, Our Hero Strong and Tender	177	217	—
Strong Son of God, Immortal Love	175	228	578
Amazing Grace! How Sweet the Sound	—	275	296
O Sing a Song of Bethlehem	138	177	526
God Moves in a Mysterious Way	103	112	391

ANTHEMS FOR THE DAY

Ezek. 2:1-5 *He Who Would Valiant Be,* arr. Gerald Near (Augsburg). SATB (E)

II Cor. 12:7-10 *Fight the Good Fight,* John Gardner (Oxford). SATB (M)

Mark 6:1-6 *They Saw You as the Local Builder's Son,* Verner Ahlberg (in *Ecumenical Praise,* No. 105, Hope). (E) HH

COLLECT FOR THE DAY

Lord God, use our lives to touch the world with your love. Stir us, by your Spirit, to be neighbor to those in need, serving them with willing hearts; through your Son, Jesus Christ our Lord.   (LBW)

READINGS

Amos 7:12-17   Priest and prophet clash in this brief exchange of words. Priest Amaziah is the appointed protector of the king's sanctuary and says what is fitting and proper. Amos makes no claim to bear the credentials of prophet. He is God's man and his words are as pointed as the sword by which Jeroboam will die.

Eph. 1:3-10   "To unite all things in him, things in heaven and things on earth," is the apostle's theme. In Jesus Christ the plan for all time becomes reality as the faithful respond to his saving grace.

Mark 6:7-13   The disciples are sent out with authority to confront unclean spirits, to cast out demons, to anoint and heal the sick, to preach repentance. Sandals on their feet and a tunic are all the earthly equipment they need to minister in Jesus' name.   RSM

PSALM FOR THE DAY: Psalm 85:7-13

HYMNS FOR THE DAY

	HL	HB	WB
Praise, My Soul, the King of Heaven	14	31	551
O God of Bethel, by Whose Hand	98	342	496
Pardoned Through Redeeming Grace	—	—	550
God Gives His People Strength	—	—	381
Lead On, O King Eternal	371	332	448
O Master, Let Me Walk with Thee	364	304	520

ANTHEMS FOR THE DAY

Amos 7:12-17   *Haste Thee, O God, to Deliver Me*, Adrian Batten (Oxford). SATB (M)

Turn Back, O Man, Gustav Holst (Stainer). SATB (ME). Hymn-anthem

Remember, O Lord, Carl Schalk (in *Four Choruses from the Lamentations*, Concordia). SATB (M). Text concludes: ". . . woe unto us, that we have sinned!"

Eph. 1:3-10   *O Christ, Our Hope*, Hugo Distler (Augsburg). SSA or SAT (MD)

Lord Jesus, Who Didst Redeem Us, Johann Heinrich Rolle (H. W. Gray). SATB, string parts available (M). Moravian Anthem

Pardoned Through Redeeming Grace, attr. to Martin Herbst (WB, p. 550)

Mark 6:7-13   *Go Ye Into All the World*, Robert Wetzler (Augsburg). 2-Part Mixed (E)   RD

COLLECT FOR THE DAY

Pour out upon us, O Lord, the spirit to think and do what is right, that we, who cannot even exist without you, may have the strength to live according to your will; through your Son, Jesus Christ our Lord.

(LBW)

READINGS

Jer. 23:1-6 Leadership that destroys, confuses, and scatters the Lord's people will come to an end. A new day is coming. No more fear, dismay, or lostness. The new leader will be wise, just, righteous. He will be called "The Lord is our righteousness." Israel and Judah will be safe.

Eph. 2:11-18 Resurrection power is a present reality for those who were dead through their alienation from God. He "made us alive together with Christ . . . and raised us up with him." Reconciliation, regardless of the past, is accomplished through the cross. Our common unity (community) is possible as we "have access in one Spirit to the Father."

Mark 6:30-34 Jesus is concerned for the well-being of the disciples as they return from their first experience of ministry. "Come away by yourselves to a lonely place, and rest a while." The crowds anticipate where Jesus and the disciples are going. They are as sheep without a shepherd.   RSM

PSALM FOR THE DAY: Psalm 23

HYMNS FOR THE DAY	HL	HB	WB
In Christ There Is No East or West	341	479	435, 436
The King of Love My Shepherd Is (Ps.)	99	106	590
The Lord's My Shepherd (Ps.)	97	104	592
My Shepherd Will Supply My Need (Ps.)	—	—	477
Saviour, like a Shepherd Lead Us	458	380	—
Forgive, O Lord, Our Severing Ways	344	476	—

ANTHEMS FOR THE DAY

Jer. 23:1-6 *Lo, My Shepherd Is Divine,* F. J. Haydn, ed. Carlton (Boosey & Hawkes). SATB (ME)

Eph. 2:11-18 *Christ Is the World's True Light,* W. K. Stanton (Oxford). Unison or 2-part (E). Text combines concepts of Christ as source of salvation, reconciliation, and peace

Lord of Our Life and God of Our Salvation, S. Drummond Wolff (Concordia). SATB (ME)

Mark 6:30-34 *The Lord My Faithful Shepherd Is,* J. S. Bach, arr. Jennings (Augsburg). SATB (M)

My Shepherd Will Supply My Need, arr. Virgil Thomson (H. W. Gray). Available for SA, SSA, SAB, TTBB, SSAA, and SATB (ME)

Psalm 23, Heinz Werner Zimmermann (Augsburg). SATB, string bass (M)   RD

COLLECT FOR THE DAY

O God, your ears are open always to the prayers of your servants. Open our hearts and minds to you, that we may live in harmony with your will and receive the gifts of your Spirit; through your Son, Jesus Christ our Lord.

(LBW)

READINGS

II Kings 4:42-44 Elisha, a man of God, demonstrates his faith in God's power. Feeding 100 men with 20 loaves of barley and grain has a familiar ring to it. The doubt expressed by the servant, "How am I to set this before a hundred men?" is echoed by the disciples when Jesus faced the 5,000. The story of this miraculous feeding ends in similar fashion: "And they ate, and had some left . . . "

Eph. 4:1-6, 11-16 Unity in ministry does not imply uniformity or equality. "Grace was given to each of us according to the measure of Christ's gift." Equipment is supplied, work is assigned, and we reach toward the goal: "unity of the faith and of the knowledge of the Son of God." In our reaching we grow. In our growth toward a mature faith, true unity is found in love.

John 6:1-15 Reminiscent of the story of Elisha is Jesus' feeding the 5,000 people, and much food is left over. Memory of the past is in sharp focus when the people recognize the sign of Jesus' power. They said, "This is indeed the prophet who is to come into the world!"

RSM

PSALM FOR THE DAY: Psalm 145

HYMNS FOR THE DAY

	HL	HB	WB
O Lord, You Are Our God and King (Ps.)	—	5	517
The Church's One Foundation	333	437	582
Built on the Rock	—	432	320
We Are One in the Spirit	—	—	619
Put Forth, O God, Your Spirit's Might	—	477	559
Guide Me, O Thou Great Jehovah	104	339	409

ANTHEMS FOR THE DAY

II Kings 4:42-44 *The Hand of God Doth Supply All Our Needs,* Antonio Vivaldi, ed. Vree (Presser). SA (M)

Eph. 4:1-6, 11-16 *Christ: Foundation, Head and Cornerstone,* Lloyd Pfautsch (Lawson-Gould). SATB, optional brass (ME)

Join Hands, Brothers, Dale Wood (Art Masters). SATB (E). Text: "In Christ There Is No East or West"

We Are One in the Spirit, Peter Scholtes (WB, p. 619)

John 6:1-15 *This Is Indeed the Prophet,* Jan Bender (Concordia). SA/TB (E)

RD

THE ELEVENTH SUNDAY AFTER PENTECOST (B)

COLLECT FOR THE DAY
> Gracious Father, your blessed Son came down from heaven to be the true bread which gives life to the world. Give us this bread, that he may live in us and we in him, Jesus Christ our Lord.   (LBW)

READINGS

Ex. 16:2-4, 12-15   Moses and Aaron are confronted by the Children of Israel in their wanderings through the wilderness. A month and a half away from things familiar in Egypt, they cannot cope with the uncertainties. The leaders are blamed. Hostility and hunger are linked together. God is testing them. Food is provided, and when they inquire as to what it is, Moses says to them, "It is the bread which the Lord has given you to eat."

Eph. 4:17-24   Newness of life is affirmed when the old life of separation from God is past history. "Be renewed in the spirit of your minds." The Ephesians are well aware of what the writer means when he uses such terms as "uncleanness" and "deceitful lusts." For them to "put on the new nature" and to live in "true righteousness and holiness" is a complete turnaround.

John 6:24-35   Jesus adds another dimension to the matter of hunger and feeding when he says, "Do not labor for the food which perishes, but for the food which endures to eternal life, which the Son of man will give to you." He is that food: "I am the bread of life." In him there is no longer hunger or thirst.   RSM

PSALM FOR THE DAY: Psalm 78:14-20, 23-29

HYMNS FOR THE DAY	HL	HB	WB
Now Israel May Say	—	357	—
Take My Life, and Let It Be	242	310	—
Take Thou Our Minds, Dear Lord	245	306	579
Sinner, Please Don't Let This Harvest Pass	—	—	570
Break Thou the Bread of Life	216	250	317
O God of Bethel, by Whose Hand	98	342	496
Hope of the World	—	291	423

ANTHEMS FOR THE DAY

Ex. 16:2-4, 12-15   *O Bread of Life from Heaven,* Louis Bourgeois and Claude Goudimel, French Psalm VI (Concordia). SATB (E)

Brethren, We Have Met to Worship (Early American hymn "Holy Manna"), arr. by Randolph Currie (Choristers Guild). SA (E)

Eph. 4:17-24   *Put Ye on the Lord Jesus,* Joseph Roff (Colombo). SATB (M)

John 6:24-35   *Thou Hast Given Us Bread from Heaven,* J. C. Geisler (H. W. Gray). SATB, string parts available (M). Moravian Anthem

Bread of Heaven, on Thee We Feed, traditional (WB, p. 313)   RD

COLLECT FOR THE DAY

Almighty and everlasting God, you are always more ready to hear than we are to pray, and to give more than we either desire or deserve. Pour upon us the abundance of your mercy, forgiving us those things of which our conscience is afraid, and giving us those good things for which we are not worthy to ask, except through the merit of your Son, Jesus Christ our Lord.   (LBW)

READINGS

I Kings 19:4-8 Elijah is running scared. Jezebel is after him and he takes to the wilderness despairing for his life. "It is enough; now, O Lord, take away my life." His despair turns to strength and renewal as ministering angels feed him and send him on his way to the mount of God.

Eph. 4:30 to 5:2 What Christ did for us should be reflected through attitudes and relationships. "Do not grieve the Holy Spirit of God" is a statement about the sensitivity and compassion of God. "Therefore be imitators of God, as beloved children."

John 6:41-51 How difficult it is for Jesus' contemporaries to be receptive to a carpenter's son who says of himself, "I came down from heaven," or "I am the bread of life," or "The bread which I shall give for the life of the world is my flesh."   RSM

PSALM FOR THE DAY: Psalm 34:1-8

HYMNS FOR THE DAY

	HL	HB	WB
Through All the Changing Scenes of Life (Ps.)	83	—	—
Give to the Winds Your Fears	294	364	377
The Lord I Will at All Times Bless (Ps.)	—	412	—
The Friends of Christ Together	—	—	586
Bread of the World	353	445	—
Bread of Heaven, on Thee We Feed	—	—	313
Jesus, Thou Joy of Loving Hearts	354	215	—

ANTHEMS FOR THE DAY

I Kings 19:4-8 *How Long, O Lord,* Orlando di Lasso (Schmitt, Hall & McCreary). SATB (MD).

It Is Enough, Mendelssohn (from *Elijah,* G. Schirmer). Tenor Solo

Eph. 4:30 to 5:2 *Be Ye Kind One to Another,* K. K. Davis (Galaxy). SATB (ME). Text: Eph. 4:32, 31

The Fruit of the Spirit Is Love, J. C. Geisler (Boosey & Hawkes). SATB, flute (M). Moravian Anthem

Brotherly Love, Alice Parker (E. C. Schirmer). Canon for 2 to 5 voices, optional guitar (ME)

John 6:41-51 *I Am the Bread of Life,* Sven-Erik Bäck (G. Schirmer). SATB. English and Latin text   RD

COLLECT FOR THE DAY
Almighty and ever-living God, you have given great and precious promises to those who believe. Grant us the perfect faith which overcomes all doubts, through your Son, Jesus Christ our Lord.

(LBW)

READINGS
Prov. 9:1-6 Contrast the banquet set by Wisdom: "Come, eat of my bread and drink of the wine I have mixed. Leave simpleness . . . and walk in the way of insight" and the invitation of the foolish woman (vs. 13-18): "And to him who is without sense she says, 'Stolen water is sweet, and bread eaten in secret is pleasant.' But he does not know that the dead are there, that her guests are in the depths of Sheol." Both Wisdom and the foolish woman say the same: "Whoever is simple, let him turn in here . . . " The outcomes are quite different.

Eph. 5:15-20 The foolish and the wise are in contrast once again. Walking in wisdom means understanding, perception, celebration, thanksgiving.

John 6:51-59 Capernaum and the synagogue are the setting for the discourse on bread and Jesus' identification of bread and wine, flesh and blood, with his own call to a life-giving, life-sustaining ministry.   RSM

PSALM FOR THE DAY: Psalm 34:9-14

HYMNS FOR THE DAY	HL	HB	WB
O Holy City, Seen of John	409	508	505
Come, We That Love the Lord (Ps.)	—	408	—
O Sing a New Song	68	37	525
Now Thank We All Our God	459	9	481
Christ Jesus Lay in Death's Strong Bands	—	—	327

ANTHEMS FOR THE DAY
Prov. 9:1-6 *Walk in the Light*, Sven Lekberg (G. Schirmer). SATB

Eph. 5:15-20 *Speak to One Another of Psalms*, Jean Berger (Augsburg). SATB (M)

Sing Ye to the Lord, Gerhard Krapf (Abingdon). SAB (MD). Exciting

Sing a Song of Joy, Jane Marshall (C. Fischer). SATB (M). Nice rhythmic vitality

John 6:51-59 *Lord, I Trust Thee, I Adore Thee*, G. F. Handel (from *The Passion of Christ*, Oxford). (E). Text continues: ". . . For the bread of life I'm sighing"

The Eyes of All, Geoffrey Schroth (J. Fischer). SATB (M). Text: Psalm 145:15-16; John 6:56-57

Verily, Verily, I Say Unto You, Thomas Tallis (Oxford). SATB (MD). Text: John 6:53-56. Short—worth the effort   RD

COLLECT FOR THE DAY

God of all creation, you reach out to call people of all nations to your kingdom. As you gather disciples from near and far, count us also among those who boldly confess your Son Jesus Christ as Lord.

(LBW)

READINGS

Josh. 24:14-18 Joshua recalls before the tribal heads of Israel the details of their history under God. Theirs is a great history. This is a moving moment when he, like a grandfather surrounded by his children, challenges them to make a choice. Will their future be with the Lord or will they choose the "gods of the Amorites in whose land you dwell"? "Choose this day whom you will serve."

Eph. 5:21-33 Ephesian Christians are instructed by the apostle to test their interpersonal relationships by the standard of Christ's relationship to the church. He focuses on the husband-wife relationship as one that calls for love, feeding, cherishing, respect, subjection.

John 6:60-69 Many of the disciples had second thoughts as Jesus emphasized the nourishing effect of his body and blood. Apparently they could not comprehend the faith response Jesus was demanding. Aware of a widening gap, Jesus says to the inner circle, "Do you also wish to go away?" Peter's response is classic: "Lord, to whom shall we go? You have the words of eternal life."

RSM

PSALM FOR THE DAY: Psalm 34:15-22

HYMNS FOR THE DAY

	HL	HB	WB
Guide Me, O Thou Great Jehovah	104	339	409
The Church's One Foundation	333	437	582
O Light, Whose Beams Illumine All	180	145	—
I'm Not Ashamed to Own My Lord	—	292	—
When We Are Tempted to Deny Your Son	—	—	640
God of Our Life	88	108	395

ANTHEMS FOR THE DAY

Josh. 24:14-18 *Serve the Lord with Gladness*, G. F. Handel (Lawson-Gould). SSA (M)

God Is My Strong Salvation (tune from *The Sacred Harp*), arr. Austin Lovelace (Canyon). SATB (E)

Once to Every Man and Nation, Thomas John Williams (WB, p. 540)

Eph. 5:21-33 *Ah, Jesus, Lord, Thy Love to Me* (Southern folk tune), arr. David N. Johnson (Augsburg). SATB (ME)

John 6:60-69 *Lord of Our Life and God of Our Salvation*, S. Drummond Wolff (Concordia). SATB (ME)

RD

COLLECT FOR THE DAY

O God, we thank you for your Son who chose the path of suffering for the sake of the world. Humble us by his example, point us to the path of obedience, and give us strength to follow his commands; through your Son, Jesus Christ our Lord.   (LBW)

READINGS

Deut. 4:1-8   Israel is called to be an obedient people. Moses taught them the statutes and ordinances. As they enter the lands of their conquest the people will be aware that the laws of their conquerors make a difference in their lives: "Surely this great nation is a wise and understanding people."

James 1:19-25   The word is not only to be heard, but is to be acted out in life situations. Don't be a hearer that forgets, but a doer that acts.

Mark 7:1-8, 14-15, 21-23   Jesus puts in balanced perspective the traditions of man and the law of God. Lip service religion is hypocrisy. Evil intentions come from within and show themselves in behavior. Food that does not meet certain ceremonial rules cannot make a person unclean.   RSM

PSALM FOR THE DAY: Psalm 15

HYMNS FOR THE DAY	HL	HB	WB
God of Our Fathers	414	515	394
Blest Are the Pure in Heart (Ps.)	—	226	—
Not Alone for Mighty Empire	416	512	479
The Light of God Is Falling	400	482	—
Rejoice, O Pure in Heart	297	407	561

ANTHEMS FOR THE DAY

Deut. 4:1-8   *Teach Me, O Lord* (Psalm 119), William Byrd (Oxford). SSATB (E)

Teach Me, O Lord, the Way of Thy Statutes, Thomas Attwood (E. C. Schirmer). SATB (ME)

James 1:19-25   *To Do God's Will,* Jean Berger (Augsburg). SATB (M)

Mark 7:1-8   *Lord, Keep Us Steadfast in Thy Word,* Buxtehude (Concordia). SATB with 2 violins and continuo (ME). Short chorale cantata

Lord, Keep Us Steadfast, Hugo Distler (Augsburg). SAB (M)   RD

COLLECT FOR THE DAY
Almighty and eternal God, you know our problems and our weaknesses
better than we ourselves. In your love and by your power help us in our
confusion and, in spite of our weakness, make us firm in faith; through
your Son, Jesus Christ our Lord.   (LBW)

READINGS
Isa. 35:4-7 God's saving power is for the fearful, the blind, the deaf, the
lame, the dumb. Their transformation to whole persons will be as dramatic
as burning sands to pools of water; from thirsty ground to springs; from
dangerous nests of jackals to grasses where all may walk without fear.

James 2:1-5 Partiality, discrimination, favoritism on the side of the rich at
the expense of the poor are not consistent with the faith in the Lord of glory.
God chose those who are poor to be rich in faith and heirs of the kingdom.

Mark 7:31-37 In the region of Decapolis, Jesus heals a man before a large
crowd. Deafness and a speech impediment, which often go together, are
cured by the great Physician. When Jesus charges the people to say nothing
about what happened, their enthusiasm for him increases all the more.

RSM

PSALM FOR THE DAY: Psalm 146

HYMNS FOR THE DAY	HL	HB	WB
Come, Thou Long-expected Jesus	113	151	342
Praise We Our Maker (Ps.)	—	—	558
The Lord Is Rich and Merciful	82	—	—
The Magnificat	56(back)	596	—
O for a Thousand Tongues	199	141	493
Open Now the Gates of Beauty	—	40	544

ANTHEMS FOR THE DAY

Isa. 35:4-7 *God Is My Strong Salvation* (tune from *The Sacred Harp*), arr.
Austin Lovelace (Canyon). SATB (E)

They Shall See the Glory of the Lord, Joseph W. Rhodes (Warner). SATB (M).
Text: Isa. 35:1-4, 10

James 2:1-5 *Defend the Poor and Desolate,* George Brandon (World
Library). 2-Part Mixed (E)

Mark 7:31-37 *He Hath Done All Things Well,* Jan Bender (Concordia).
SATB (ME)

God Hath Done All Things Well, Melchior Franck, ed. Buszin (Concordia).
SATB (M)   RD

COLLECT FOR THE DAY

O God, you declare your almighty power chiefly in showing mercy and pity. Grant us the fullness of your grace, that, pursuing what you have promised, we may share your heavenly glory; through your Son, Jesus Christ our Lord.   (LBW)

READINGS

Isa. 50:4-9   Steadfastness and acceptance of God's help are keys to faith and obedience. The teacher's endowment of tongue and sensitive ear may bring suffering and reproach, but God is faithful to those whom he calls to servanthood whether it be individual or nation.

James 2:14-18   Faith is not complete in itself. If it is not accompanied with works, it is dead. Faith is real when others can see it at work in our lives.

Mark 8:27-35   Jesus polls his disciples to get a reading on public opinion concerning him. He is identified with John the Baptist and the prophets. Peter's confession of Jesus as the Christ was right and proper. However, against the background of impending suffering and resurrection, Peter remonstrates to the point where Jesus has to say to him, "Get behind me, Satan! For you are not on the side of God, but of men."   RSM

PSALM FOR THE DAY: Psalm 116:1-9

HYMNS FOR THE DAY	HL	HB	WB
O God, You Are the Father			
(tune: Ellacombe or Lancashire)	—	93	504
Whate'er Our God Ordains (Ps.)	291	366	633
O Brother Man, Fold to Your Heart	403	474	484
In the Cross of Christ I Glory	154	195	437
When I Survey the Wondrous Cross	152	198	635

ANTHEMS FOR THE DAY

Isa. 50:4-9   *In Thee, O Lord, Have I Trusted,* G. F. Handel (E. C. Schirmer). SATB (ME)

James 2:14-18   *Give Alms of Thy Goods,* Christopher Tye (Oxford, revised). SATB (M)

Lord, We Pray Thee, S. Drummond Wolff (Concordia). SATB (ME). Text continues " . . . and make us continually to be given to all good works."

A Hymn of Brotherhood, Alec Wyton (H. W. Gray). Unison, 2-Part, or SATB (ME). Text: ". . . Follow with reverent steps the great example of him whose holy work was doing good."

Mark 8:27-35   *Take Up Thy Cross,* Austin Lovelace (C. Fischer). SATB (ME)

Thou Art Jesus, Savior and Lord, Heinrich Schütz, ed. Coggin (Augsburg). SATB (M)

He Who Would Valiant Be, C. Winfred Douglas (WB, p. 414)   RD

COLLECT FOR THE DAY
> Lord God, you call us to work in your vineyard and leave no one standing idle. Set us to our tasks in the work of your kingdom, and help us to order our lives by your wisdom; through your Son, Jesus Christ our Lord.   (LBW)

READINGS
> **Jer. 11:18-20** Jeremiah's own family has turned against him because he actively supports the reforms of King Josiah. Such reforms have economic consequences and touch the pocketbooks of the custodians of the shrine at Anathoth. Resentment leads to plotting and scheming against Jeremiah's life. He calls for God's vengeance.

> **James 3:13 to 4:3** True wisdom is pure. It "makes for peace, and is kindly and considerate; it is full of compassion and shows itself by doing good." When the human scene is controlled by earthly wisdom, the result is alienation, ambition, disharmony, distortion of truth, human degradation. The writer points to the source of disunity among Christians—uncontrolled ambition.

> **Mark 9:30-37** True greatness is humble like a servant, innocent like a child. Jesus instructs his disciples in the events of his arrest, death, and rising again. He knows they do not understand what he is saying. Their bickering about greatness opens the door for him to reorient their thinking and give them a glimpse of their future ministry.   RSM

PSALM FOR THE DAY: Psalm 54

HYMNS FOR THE DAY	HL	HB	WB
A Hymn of Glory Let Us Sing	—	—	273
Christ Is the World's True Light	—	492	326
Christ for the World We Sing	378	489	—
The Son of God Goes Forth to War	271	354	—
We Love Your Kingdom, Lord	337	435	626
Upon Your Great Church Universal	—	—	611

ANTHEMS FOR THE DAY

> **Jer. 11:18-20** *O Lord God, Unto Whom Vengeance Belongeth*, Robert Baker (H. W. Gray). SATB (MD)

> **James 3:13 to 4:3** *The Golden ABC* (from *Two Mennonite Hymns*), arr. by Alice Parker (Lawson-Gould). SATB (E). Partial text: "By righteous works and quiet faith I'll rise to heaven's glory . . . " Tune: Kedron

> *The Fruit of the Spirit Is Love*, J. C. Geisler (Boosey & Hawkes). SATB, flute (M). Moravian Anthem

> **Mark 9:30-37** *Whoever Would Be Great Among You*, Ronald A. Nelson (Augsburg). SAB (E)   RD

COLLECT FOR THE DAY

God of love, you know our frailties and failings. Give us your grace to overcome them; keep us from those things that harm us; and guide us in the way of salvation; through your Son, Jesus Christ our Lord.

(LBW)

READINGS

Num. 11:24-30 Moses feels the weight of responsibility of leadership. It is even more burdensome because of the unrest and complaints of the people. God promises that Moses can now delegate to 70 men the responsibilities of leadership. At a special meeting, the leaders gather with Moses and receive from God their measure of spiritual gifts. Two men who are absent from the meeting still receive this spiritual power. Their right to prophesy is challenged. Moses replies, "Would that all the Lord's people were prophets."

James 5:1-6 Those who have built up earthly treasure by taking advantage of the misfortunes of others stand in a precarious position before the judgment of God. Their luxury and pleasure now mock them.

Mark 9:38-48 John is concerned about a man who is casting out demons in Jesus' name. Jesus' response is reminiscent of Moses' experience with Eldad and Medad, who received prophetic powers while absent from the tent meeting (Num., ch. 11). Jesus responds, "He that is not against us is for us." The name of Jesus is power in ministry. When anyone is an obstacle to another's faith, when any part of the body is a cause for sin, it is better to enter God's kingdom physically incomplete than to be thrown into hell.   RSM

PSALM FOR THE DAY: Psalm 135:1-7, 13-14

HYMNS FOR THE DAY	HL	HB	WB
All Hail the Power of Jesus' Name!	192	132	285, 286
Spirit of God, Descend Upon My Heart	204	236	575
The Lord Will Come and Not Be Slow	185	230	—
How Sweet the Name of Jesus Sounds	310	130	—
Where Cross the Crowded Ways of Life	410	507	642
At the Name of Jesus	—	143	303

ANTHEMS FOR THE DAY

Num. 11:24-30 *God of the Prophets*, Paul Bunjes (Concordia). Chorale Concertato for SATB (optional Junior Choir), Congregation, trumpet, organ (ME). Tune: Old 124th

James 5:1-6 *Say Ye to the Righteous* (from *The Peaceable Kingdom*), Randall Thompson (E. C. Schirmer). SATB (D). Text continues: " . . . Woe unto the wicked. . . . Ye shall howl for vexation of spirit."

Mark 9:38-48 *Grant, We Beseech Thee, Merciful Lord*, John Okeover, ed. Morchen (Concordia). SATB (MD). Text continues: " . . . that they may be cleansed from all their sins and serve thee . . . "

Cause Us, O Lord (from *Three Ancient Prayers*), Ron Nelson (Boosey & Hawkes). SATB (M)   RD

COLLECT FOR THE DAY

Our Lord Jesus, you have endured the doubts and foolish questions of every generation. Forgive us for trying to be judge over you, and grant us the confident faith to acknowledge you as Lord.   (LBW)

READINGS

Gen. 2:18-24 Man's need for a helper is not satisfied with the creation of beasts and birds. Woman appears, not from the soil as did other creatures, but from the body of man himself. "She shall be called Woman, because she was taken out of Man." The editorial comment follows which often appears in the marriage service. It speaks of man leaving father and mother, cleaving to his wife, and becoming one flesh. There is no shame in nakedness when the first man and woman are created.

Heb. 2:9-13 Jesus identifies himself with all humankind. He tasted death for everyone. He was made perfect through suffering. Those for whom he suffered and died he was not ashamed "to call . . . brethren" and to celebrate that relationship in the worship and praise of God.

Mark 10:2-16 This reading deals with relationships at the most intimate levels. Jesus is being tested by the Pharisees concerning divorce. They quote from the law in Deut. 24:1. He, in reply, gets at the basic relationship established at the time of creation as found in the Genesis reading for today. For him there are no grounds for divorce. Relationships with children are a testing ground for entrance into the kingdom of God. If we do not know children, appreciate their openness and freshness, enjoy their warmth and trust, we cannot understand the things of God.   RSM

PSALM FOR THE DAY: Psalm 128

HYMNS FOR THE DAY

	HL	HB	WB
For the Beauty of the Earth	71	2	372
From All That Dwell Below the Skies	388	33	373
Crown Him with Many Crowns	190	213	349
Our Father, by Whose Name	—	—	546
Where Charity and Love Prevail	—	—	641
Children of the Heavenly King	347	340	—

ANTHEMS FOR THE DAY

Gen. 2:18-24 *God, Our Creator, Father,* Marc Antonio Ingegneri, ed. Coggin (Augsburg). SATB (ME)

O Father, All Creating, Buxtehude (in *Wedding Blessings,* Concordia). Unison or Solo (M)

Heb. 2:9-13 *Christ Atoned for Our Transgressions,* Johann Ernst Eberlin (Schmitt, Hall & McCreary). SATB (MD). Text continues: " . . . For this love the Father has raised Him over all."

Mark 10:2-16 *Suffer the Little Children,* George Lynn (Presser). SATB (ME)   RD

THE TWENTY-FIRST SUNDAY AFTER PENTECOST (B)

COLLECT FOR THE DAY

Almighty God, source of every blessing, your generous goodness comes to us anew every day. By the work of your Spirit lead us to acknowledge your goodness, give thanks for your benefits, and serve you in willing obedience; through your Son, Jesus Christ our Lord.   (LBW)

READINGS

Prov. 3:13-18 In a poetic discourse between father and son, wisdom is singled out for its value to the human condition.

Heb. 4:12-16 Loving, active, sharp, piercing, discerning—these are words descriptive of the "word of God." They take us from the printed page and our discussions of words and help us to sense the activity of the Spirit of God. We are reminded of the phrases of the prayer, "unto whom all hearts are open, all desires known, and from whom no secrets are hid." Jesus in his humanness opens the door for us, "that we may receive mercy and find grace to help in time of need."

Mark 10:17-27 Contrary to earlier teachings and traditions, which equated great possessions with God's favor, Jesus is inviting a righteous man to choose a new basis for his relationship with God. He could not give up his wealth. Jesus did not condemn him, either for his faithful observance of the law or his worldly goods. The discussion that follows reveals the disciples' inability to handle the problem. "Then who can be saved?" they ask of Jesus. His answer places the power where it belongs, in the hands of God. RSM

PSALM FOR THE DAY: Psalm 90:1-8, 12-17

HYMNS FOR THE DAY

	HL	HB	WB
Our God, Our Help in Ages Past (Ps.)	77	111	549
Lord, Thou Hast Been Our Dwelling Place (Ps.)	—	88	—
O Come, O Come, Emmanuel	108	147	489
God's Word Is like a Flaming Sword	—	—	405
Approach, My Soul, the Mercy Seat	—	386	—
God of Pity, God of Grace	252	—	—
Father Eternal, Ruler of Creation	—	486	362

ANTHEMS FOR THE DAY

Prov. 3:13-18 *Happy Is the Man Who Finds Wisdom,* Keith Clark (Lawson-Gould). SATB (MD). Text: Prov. 3:13-14, 17-18

Happy Is the Man, Jean Berger (G. Schirmer). SATB (MD)

Heb. 4:12-16 *Lord, Keep Us Steadfast in Thy Word,* arr. Donald Johns (Augsburg). SAB (M)

That God Doth Love the World We Know, F. W. Wadely (Oxford). SAB (E)

Our Faith Is in the Christ Who Walks with Men, William Knapp (WB, p. 545)

Mark 10:17-27 *Lay Up Treasures in Heaven,* James Neff (Schmitt, Hall & McCreary). 2-Part Mixed (E)   RD

COLLECT FOR THE DAY

Almighty and everlasting God, in Christ you have revealed your glory among the nations. Preserve the works of your mercy, that your Church throughout the world may persevere with steadfast faith in the confession of your name; through your Son, Jesus Christ our Lord.

(LBW)

READINGS

Isa. 53:10-12 This passage causes us to reflect once again on the dual causes of suffering. There is suffering we bring upon ourselves. There is also suffering which must be endured out of obedience to principle or as the result of responsible action. Israel, as the suffering servant, is the model for responsive obedience to the will of God.

Heb. 5:1-10 Priesthood and servanthood are closely linked in compassionate activity on behalf of the people. Jesus is the merging of the two roles: "He learned obedience through what he suffered; and being made perfect he became the source of eternal salvation to all who obey him."

Mark 10:35-45 James and John, seeking favored positions in Christ's glory, provide the occasion for Jesus to speak to all the disciples about true greatness.   RSM

PSALM FOR THE DAY: Psalm 91:9-16

HYMNS FOR THE DAY

	HL	HB	WB
Call Jehovah Your Salvation (Ps.)	292	123	322
The Man Who Once Has Found Abode (Ps.)	—	—	594
Throned Upon the Awful Tree	—	197	605
Look, Ye Saints	201	133	—
O Son of Man, Our Hero Strong and Tender	177	217	—
O Master, Let Me Walk with Thee	364	304	520
You Servants of God	198	27	645

ANTHEMS FOR THE DAY

Isa. 53:10-12 *Surely He Hath Borne Our Griefs*, Karl Heinrich Graun (Concordia). SATB (M)

Surely He Hath Borne Our Griefs, John Antes (Boosey & Hawkes). SATB, optional strings (M). Moravian Anthem

Heb. 5:1-10 *Salvation Unto Us Has Come*, Hugo Distler (Concordia). SATB (M)

Salvation Unto Us Has Come, Carl Schalk (Concordia). Unison (ME)

See also the anthems listed under the Epistle reading for Pentecost 21 (B)

Mark 10:35-45 *Whoever Would Be Great Among You*, Ronald A. Nelson (Augsburg). SAB (E)   RD

COLLECT FOR THE DAY
  Almighty and everlasting God, increase in us the gifts of faith, hope, and
  charity; and, that we may obtain what you promise, make us love what
  you command; through your Son, Jesus Christ our Lord.   (LBW)

READINGS
  Jer. 31:7-9   A promise is fulfilled. "The Lord has saved his people, the
  remnant of Israel." This remnant will come from all parts of the world and be
  representative of all conditions, "among them the blind and the lame."

  Heb. 5:1-6   The repeated passages (last Sunday, Heb. 5:1-10) give
  opportunity to develop further the concept of priesthood as an appointment
  by God on behalf of his people. The priest is gentle with those who are lost or
  ignorant, since he himself is no paragon of virtue. He offers sacrifice for his
  own sins as well as for those of the people. Jesus had no exaggerated opinion
  of his own importance and therefore represented the needs of the people he
  loved and served.

  Mark 10:46-52   Blind Bartimaeus, a beggar, could not make any claims to
  fame. Nevertheless, he addresses Jesus as "Son of David." He is perceptive at
  the point of knowing what people are saying about Jesus' ministry. By his
  peers he is treated like a bum. By Jesus he is accepted on the basis of his need
  and his faith. Healing comes and a new follower is added.   RSM

PSALM FOR THE DAY: Psalm 126

HYMNS FOR THE DAY

	HL	HB	WB
Come, You People, Rise and Sing	—	39	345
I'm So Glad Troubles Don't Last Always (Ps.)	—	—	432
If You Will Only Let God Guide You (Ps.)	105	344	431
How Sweet the Name of Jesus Sounds	310	130	—
Hail to the Lord's Anointed	111	146	—
I to the Hills Will Lift My Eyes	—	377	430

ANTHEMS FOR THE DAY

  Jer. 31:7-9   *Sing Ye to the Lord*, Gerhard Krapf (Abingdon). SAB (MD)

  Sing Unto the Lord a New Song, Harald Rohlig (Abingdon). SATB (M)

  Heb. 5:1-6   *Unto Which of the Angels* (Recitative, tenor) and *Let All the
  Angels of God Worship Him*, G. F. Handel (from *Messiah*, Part II, any
  edition). SATB, Chorus (MD)

  Mark 10:46-52   *I'll Praise My Maker*, Lloyd Pfautsch (Abingdon). SATB,
  optional brass (ME). Text combines concepts of praise, Christ's concern for
  physical needs, and our need to have faith   RD

COLLECT FOR THE DAY

Lord, when the day of wrath comes we have no hope except in your grace. Make us so to watch for the last days that the consummation of our hope may be the joy of the marriage feast of your Son, Jesus Christ our Lord.

(LBW)

READINGS

Deut. 6:1-9 Israel is confronted with the imperatives of law and obedience. The greatest commandment of all, the "Hear, O Israel," is the touchstone for the devotional and educational life of the Jewish community in later years.

Heb. 7:23-28 Only the living Christ can serve in perpetual priesthood. Therefore, only he "is able for all time to save those who draw near to God through him." The daily offerings of sacrifice for sin are no longer required because "he did this once for all when he offered up himself."

Mark 12:28-34 Jesus and the scribe discuss the first and greatest commandment. Jesus adds to the "Hear, O Israel" a second commandment as found in Lev. 19:18, "You shall love your neighbor as yourself." The two are in agreement on the oneness of God, our full response to him, to our neighbor, and the precedence of these two commandments over a sacrificial system. Jesus affirms the scribe's response with "You are not far from the kingdom of God."

RSM

PSALM FOR THE DAY: Psalm 119:1-16

HYMNS FOR THE DAY

	HL	HB	WB
We Come Unto Our Fathers' God	342	16	623
O God, Beneath Your Guiding Hand	462	523	495
How I Love Thy Law (Ps.)	—	253	—
How Shall the Young Direct Their Way? (Ps.)	—	258	—
As Men of Old Their Firstfruits Brought	—	—	301
Sing Praise to God	—	15	568

ANTHEMS FOR THE DAY

Deut. 6:1-9 *Teach Me, O Lord, the Way of Thy Statutes*, Thomas Attwood (E. C. Schirmer). SATB (ME)

Hear, O Israel (from *Three Ancient Prayers*), Ron Nelson (Boosey & Hawkes). SATB (M). Text: Deut. 6:4-6. Beautiful anthem

Heb. 7:23-28 *Jesus Christ from the Law Hath Freed Us*, Johann Hermann Schelle (Concordia). SSAB/ATBB (MD). Motet for double chorus

Mark 12:28-34 *The Only Lord*, Bob Daniels (Augsburg). Unison with flute, guitar, piano (E). Text: Mark 12:29-31; Psalm 100:2-4

You Shall Love the Lord Your God, Richard Hillert (Concordia). SATB (MD)

Thou Shalt Love the Lord Thy God, Joseph Roff (Kjos). SATB (M)   RD

COLLECT FOR THE DAY
Stir up, O Lord, the wills of your faithful people to seek more eagerly the help you offer, that, at the last, they may enjoy the fruit of salvation; through our Lord Jesus Christ. (LBW)

READINGS
I Kings 17:8-16 Elijah's first miracle is accomplished on behalf of a widow (in those days, a neglected and pitied figure) of Zarephath (*not* an Israelite, as Jesus pointed out to his angry hometown synagogue, Luke 4:26). That miracle of providing food paralleled the Lord's providing Elijah himself with food and drink (I Kings 17:6).

Heb. 9:24-28 Christ's ministry is not only prophetic, it is priestly, as Hebrews teaches. A priest is, at best, one who "sacrifices himself." Christ makes us all both prophets and priests.

Mark 12:38-44 Both sections of this reading admit of easy moralizing: vs. 38-40 were thrown at John Calvin to protest his robes, and vs. 41-44 have often been used to justify small gifts. Read together, however (the word "widow" is the link), they juxtapose the perils of religion and the freedom of those who have suffered much and possess very little. And these verses are central to Christ's teaching about his kingdom. HTA

PSALM FOR THE DAY: Psalm 107:1-3, 33-43

HYMNS FOR THE DAY	HL	HB	WB
Now Thank We All Our God	459	9	481
Praise the Lord, for He Is Good (Ps.)	—	115	—
Praise We Our Maker	—	—	558
Lo! He Comes, with Clouds Descending	184	234	—
Come, You Thankful People, Come	460	525	346
When I Survey the Wondrous Cross	152	198	635

ANTHEMS FOR THE DAY

Lo, He Comes with Clouds Descending, D. H. Williams (H. W. Gray). SATB (E)

Whoever Would Be Great Among You, Ronald A. Nelson (Augsburg). SAB (E)

We Would Offer Thee This Day, Jane Marshall (Sacred Music). SATB (M)

Help Us to Help Each Other, Lord, S. Drummond Wolff (Concordia). SATB (ME)

I'll Praise My Maker, Lloyd Pfautsch (Abingdon). SATB (ME) LLH

COLLECT FOR THE DAY

Lord God, so rule and govern our hearts and minds by your Holy Spirit that, always keeping in mind the end of all things and the day of judgment, we may be stirred up to holiness of life here and may live with you forever in the world to come, through your Son, Jesus Christ our Lord. (LBW)

READINGS

Dan. 12:1-4 As we come to the end of a liturgical year we are reminded by the lessons of these weeks of the end of all the years. Inevitably we are confronted with ultimate choices ("virtue" and "wickedness") and symbols of finality: Michael the archangel, and the Book.

Heb. 10:11-18 Christ the High Priest is at the center of time and history. "At various times in the past . . . God spoke" (Heb. 1:1), but Christ has "achieved the eternal perfection of all whom he is sanctifying" (10:14), and so is "now . . . far above the angels" (1:4), including even Michael.

Mark 13:24-32 As Christ comes to the end of his ministry of announcing the kingdom, and to the violent end of his incarnate life, he confronts his hearers with the ultimacy of that kingdom and the finality of the choice he has forced. He uses the "Son of Man" title from Daniel. He identifies his own generation as the crucial time. We too, in our generation, are witnesses of those things that have taken place (v. 30). His words still ring in our ears (v. 31). Have we ears to hear? HTA

PSALM FOR THE DAY: Psalm 16

HYMNS FOR THE DAY	HL	HB	WB
O Worship the King	2	26	533
O Thou Who Makest Souls to Shine (tune: Wareham)	480	305	—
O What Their Joy	430	424	—
The Head That Once Was Crowned with Thorns	195	211	589
Lift Up Your Heads	114	152	454
O Where Are Kings and Empires Now	334	431	530

ANTHEMS FOR THE DAY

Christian! Dost Thou See Them? Lloyd Pfautsch (Abingdon). SATB (ME)

Arise, the Kingdom Is at Hand, Gilbert Martin (Flammer). SATB (E)

Thou Who Wast God, K. K. Davis (Galaxy). SATB (E)

The King Shall Come When Morning Dawns, Ludwig Lenel (Concordia). 2-Part (E)

LLH

COLLECT FOR THE DAY
almighty and everlasting God, whose will it is to restore all things to
your beloved Son, whom you anointed priest forever and king of all
creation: Grant that all the people of the earth, now divided by the
power of sin, may be united under the glorious and gentle rule of your
Son, our Lord Jesus Christ, who lives and reigns with you and the Holy
Spirit, one God, now and forever.   (LBW)

READINGS
Dan. 7:13-14 Here is the Old Testament antecedent of the vision of the
book of Revelation which identifies Christ with Daniel's Son of Man, who is
given "sovereignty, glory and kingship."

Rev. 1:4-8 Here is a king who "loves us." He is not far away from us either:
"He is coming . . . everyone will see him." He is also a priest who "has
washed away our sins with his blood." And St. John the Divine adds his own
word of prophecy: "This is the truth."

John 18:33-37 St. John the Evangelist brilliantly uses the scene of Christ
before Pilate (i.e., Christ in confrontation with the whole mighty Roman
Empire) to define Christ as prophet ("to bear witness to the truth"), priest (v.
32), and king ("Yes, I am a king . . . "). Did Pilate finally believe? He wrote:
"Jesus the Nazarene, King of the Jews" (19:19). And he wrote that in
"Hebrew, Latin, and Greek" (19:20). All nations . . . all races, as in Daniel
and Revelation.   HTA

PSALM FOR THE DAY: Psalm 111

HYMNS FOR THE DAY	HL	HB	WB
Ancient of Days	58	246	297
Round the Lord in Glory Seated	15	—	—
All Glory Be to God on High	—	—	283
All Praise Be Yours	—	—	290
Look Ye Saints	201	133	—
Christ Is the World's Redeemer (tune: Ellacombe or Lancashire)	—	136	—
Christ, Above All Glory Seated	—	—	324

ANTHEMS FOR THE DAY

I Am the Alpha and the Omega, Daniel Moe (Augsburg). SATB (M)

Praise the Lord Who Reigns Above, Halsey Stevens (Mark Foster). 2-Part (E)

Christ Is the King, Lloyd Pfautsch (Agape). SATB and handbells (M)

Christ Is the King, Richard Peek (Brodt). SATB (M)   LLH

COLLECT FOR THE DAY
Lord Jesus Christ, you said to your apostles:
I leave you peace, my peace I give you.
Look not on our sins, but on the faith of your Church,
and grant us the peace and unity of your kingdom
where you live for ever and ever.   (RC)

READINGS
Isa. 25:6-9 Isaiah expresses the Old Testament's fondest hope: that God's
Messiah ("anointed one") would gather all the nations into a joyful banquet
("from east and west and from north and south," WB, p. 34) on Jerusalem's
highest mountain to celebrate the death of death and the unity of all.

Rev. 7:9-17 Isaiah's hope is embodied in Revelation's vision of the
triumphant throng of saints and martyrs whose robes have been washed in
Christ's blood (what a metaphor!). They do in heaven what we do every
Sunday on earth: they sing hymns of praise to the Lamb. They shout
"Amen." Why are we afraid even to whisper it? Our black friends aren't.

Luke 24:13-35 The Messianic Banquet begins . . . in an inn on the way to
Emmaus, for two perplexed people. When they get the point, they rush back
to Jerusalem, where Isaiah had said it would all happen. "Yes, it is true,"
they are told there. Death is dead. The banquet has begun. It began, and
always begins again in "the breaking of bread."   HTA

PSALM FOR THE DAY: Psalm 34

HYMNS FOR THE DAY

	HL	HB	WB
All People That on Earth Do Dwell	1	24	288
The Lord I Will at All Times Bless (Ps.)	—	412	—
For All the Saints	429	425	369
Be Known to Us in Breaking Bread	356	446	—
Become to Us the Living Bread	—	—	305

ANTHEMS FOR THE DAY

Isa. 25:6-9 *Our Soul Waits for the Lord*, George Heussenstamm (Concordia). SATB (D)

I Waited for the Lord, Mendelssohn (G. Schirmer). SATB, Soprano Solo.

Rev. 7:9-17 *Blessing, Glory, Wisdom and Thanks*, J. S. Bach (Fox). SATB (MD)

Canticle of the Lamb, Ned Rorem (Boosey & Hawkes). SATB (MD)

Blessing, Glory, Wisdom, and Thanks, Georg Gottfried Wagner (Lawson-Gould). SATB (M)

Luke 24:13-35 *Jesus, Sun of Life, My Splendor*, G. F. Handel (Concordia). SATB, optional violins (ME)

Breaking of the Bread (Emmaus), Austin Lovelace (Hope). SATB (E).   RD

COLLECT FOR THE DAY

> God of all the ages: we look for the coming of your kingdom. We await the advent of our king. Help us so to hear his word as to become children of light and servants of justice. May his Day not find us sleeping in sin. We pray in his own strong name.   HTA

READINGS

> **Jer. 33:14-16** Merging of the priestly and the kingly offices seems to be promised in the two terms "a righteous branch" and "the Lord is our righteousness."

> **I Thess. 5:1-6** The day of the Lord will come as a thief in the night. Paul is reminding the church that this need not take them by surprise. They are children of the day, and of light. He admonishes them to stay awake, alert, and sober. A false sense of security will surely lull them to sleep.

> **Luke 21:25-36** Signs of the times spell endings and beginnings, Jesus paints the picture with broad strokes and vivid realities. He is the herald of what is and what is to come. Therefore, "look up and raise your heads, because your redemption is drawing near." Watch and pray, for no one knows when or where, but read the signs, and live as though it will happen tomorrow.   RSM

PSALM FOR THE DAY: Psalm 25:1-10

HYMNS FOR THE DAY	HL	HB	WB
Hail to the Lord's Anointed	111	146	—
Savior of the Nations, Come	—	—	565
Grace and Truth Shall Mark the Way (Ps.)	—	372	—
I'm Not Ashamed to Own My Lord	—	292	—
Wake, Awake, for Night Is Flying	—	—	614
The King Shall Come	187	232	—
O Where Are Kings and Empires Now	334	431	530

ANTHEMS FOR THE DAY

> **Jer. 33:14-16** *Advent Carol (Let the Earth Bud Forth the Savior)*, Dale Wood (Art Masters). SATB (ME). Lovely

> **I Thess. 5:1-6** *The Lord, Your God, Will Come*, Evert Westra (Concordia). SATB (ME)

> **Luke 21:25-36** *And There Shall Be Signs*, Jan Bender (Concordia). Unison (ME)

> *See the Fig Tree*, Heinrich Schütz, arr. Bowman (G. Schirmer). 2-Part Mixed (M). Text: Luke 21:29-33. This piece provides an excellent opportunity for a choir of limited resources to experience the music of Schütz

> *And Take Heed to Yourselves*, Heinrich Schütz (Peters). SSATTB, optional instruments (D). Text: Luke 21:34-36   RD

COLLECT FOR THE DAY

God of all peoples: your servant John came baptizing and calling for repentance. Help us to hear his voice of judgment that we may also rejoice in his word of promise. So may we receive the Prince of Peace and be found pure and blameless in his glorious Day. We pray in his own strong name.   HTA

READINGS

Isa. 9:2, 6-7   For those walking in darkness, the dawning of a new day gives cause for rejoicing. For those longing for a righteous leader, the birth of a son who will satisfy all their hopes for Messiah ushers in a new age.

Phil. 1:3-11   Paul deeply appreciates the Christians at Philippi. Their affection and partnership in ministry is heartwarming. His hope is that they will continue to prosper in their work and in faithfulness to Christ.

Luke 3:1-6   Echoing Isaiah's prophetic announcement, "Prepare the way of the Lord," John the Baptist lays the groundwork for what is to come in his own day.   RSM

PSALM FOR THE DAY: Psalm 126

HYMNS FOR THE DAY

	HL	HB	WB
God Himself Is with Us	51	13	384
The Race That Long in Darkness Pined	—	153	—
If You Will Only Let God Guide You	105	344	431
Make Me a Captive, Lord	247	308	—
Heralds of Christ	—	498	416

ANTHEMS FOR THE DAY

Isa. 9:2, 6-7   *The People That Walked in Darkness*, Houston Bright (Shawnee). SATB (MD). A fresh setting of this text

The People That in Darkness Walked, Johannes Herbst (H. W. Gray). SATB (M). Moravian Anthem

To Us a Child of Hope Is Born, Michael Praetorius (in *The Road to Bethlehem*, Concordia). SATB (ME)

For Us a Child Is Born, Johann Kuhnau (from the cantata *How Brightly Shines the Morning Star*, H. W. Gray). SSATB (M)

Phil. 1:3-11   *He Which Has Begun a Good Work in You*, Jan Bender (Concordia). SAB (ME)

Luke 3:1-6   *Prepare the Way, O Zion*, Marie Pooler (Canyon). SAB (E)

Lo, I Am the Voice of One Crying in the Wilderness, Heinrich Schütz (G. Schirmer). SSATBB (MD)

The Way of Jehovah, Halsey Stevens (Mark Foster). SATB (MD). Effective   RD

COLLECT FOR THE DAY

God of all joyfulness: how eagerly we anticipate the Lord who is very near. Cover us with his baptism and fill our minds with everything that is true and pure and worthy of praise. Make us ministers of justice and honesty. We pray in his own strong name.   HTA

READINGS

Zeph. 3:14-18 The coming of the Lord into the midst of Israel calls for celebration. With his coming are promises of protection against enemies, evil, and disaster. They will know gladness, love, security because the Lord will be with them in their time of rejoicing.

Phil. 4:4-9 Paul is in prison when he writes about joy and forbearance and thanksgiving and peace. It all seems to be wrapped up in his word "Rejoice." It says something about him. It says something about the Christians at Philippi. Verses 8 and 9 focus attention on those plus factors in life that make it worth living. Paul invites them to imitate what virtues they have seen him emulate.

Luke 3:10-18 The affluent, the tax collectors, the soldiers, the people in general respond to John the Baptist with personal concerns. His answers are forthright. He assures them that he is not the Christ, but another is coming. "He preached good news to the people."   RSM

PSALM FOR THE DAY: Isaiah 12:2-6

HYMNS FOR THE DAY	HL	HB	WB
O Zion, Haste	382	491	—
Rejoice, O Pure in Heart	297	407	561
He Did Not Want to Be Far	—	—	412
Come, You Thankful People, Come	460	525	346
Hark! the Glad Sound, the Savior Comes	—	—	410
Hark, What a Sound	110	150	—

ANTHEMS FOR THE DAY

Zeph. 3:14-18 *Daughter of Zion, Now Rejoice,* G. F. Handel (E. C. Schirmer). SA (ME)

Daughter of Zion, Shout for Joy, G. F. Handel (Warner). SATB and Junior Choir (M)

O Sing for Joy, Luise Mueller (Abingdon). SATB (ME)

Phil. 4:4-9 *Rejoice in the Lord Alway,* Henry Purcell (Concordia). SATB, optional strings (MD). Also editions by Belwin, C. Fischer, Novello, Oxford, E. C. Schirmer, some abridged

Rejoice in the Lord Always, Daniel Moe (Abingdon). SATB (M)

Luke 3:10-18 *This Is the Record of John,* Orlando Gibbons (Lawson-Gould). SAATB, Tenor Solo, optional strings (MD). Text: John 1:19-23; also appropriate for Advent 2   RD

COLLECT FOR THE DAY

God of all praise: we join Elizabeth and Mary awaiting the moment of our Lord. Let their humility and patience be our welcome of him who will feed his flock in strength and majesty. We pray in his own strong name. HTA

READINGS

Micah 5:1-4 Out of Bethlehem, a lesser clan in weak Judah, shall come the true ruler of Israel. "He shall stand and feed his flock in the strength of the Lord." His greatness will be known throughout the world.

Heb. 10:5-10 The writer is reminding the Hebrew Christians of their heritage. In Christ a new order has been established. The body of Christ offered in sacrifice was once and for all.

Luke 1:39-47 Two pregnant women find fulfillment in their condition and in their separate destinies. Elizabeth, soon to be the mother of John the Baptist, acknowledges that Mary, her cousin, is to bear one who is to be her Lord. Mary responds with praise and joy. RSM

PSALM FOR THE DAY: Psalm 80:1-7

HYMNS FOR THE DAY	HL	HB	WB
O Come, O Come, Emmanuel	108	147	489
O Little Town of Bethlehem	121	171	511
Born in the Night, Mary's Child	—	—	312
Come, Thou Long-expected Jesus	113	151	342
Come, My Soul, You Must Be Waking	487	44	337

ANTHEMS FOR THE DAY

Micah 5:1-4 *He Shall Feed His Flock*, G. F. Handel (from *Messiah*, Part I, any edition). Alto Solo

Savior of the Nations, Come, Gerhard Krapf (Augsburg). SATB, optional congregation (M)

And You, O Bethlehem, Richard Hillert (Concordia). SA/TB (ME)

Heb. 10:5-10 *All Glory Be to God on High* and *The Only Son from Heaven*, Johann Crüger (in *Four Christmas Chorales*, Concordia). SATB with 2 descant instruments (ME). Both texts develop the concept of Christ as Redeemer

Luke 1:39-47 *My Soul Doth Magnify the Lord*, J. S. Bach (E. C. Schirmer). SATB (ME). Chorale

My Soul Doth Magnify the Lord, Henry Purcell (C. Fischer). SATB (M)

The Magnificat, Heinrich Schütz (Chantry). SATB (MD)

Magnificat, Halsey Stevens (Mark Foster). SATB, trumpet (MD)

O Magnify the Lord with Me, arr. George Lynn (Presser). SATB (M) RD

COLLECT FOR THE DAY
God of all glory: this holy night eclipses the silence of eternity with the song of angels and the praise of shepherds. Inspire in us as well, songs of glory, who come so late to your Son's manger and throne. We pray in his own strong name. HTA

READINGS
Zech. 2:10-13 Not only will the Lord cause rejoicing in Jerusalem and in Judah, but many nations will respond to him and look to Zion as the seat of his presence.

Phil. 4:4-7 This reading is nearly the same as for the third Sunday in Advent. The important emphasis is that "the Lord is at hand." It is most fitting that such emphasis be made on the eve of the nativity.

Luke 2:15-20 Mystery fills the air over Bethlehem and permeates the human scene as shepherds journey from hillside to manger side. "And all who heard it wondered at what the shepherds told them." Mary has her own secrets, "pondering them in her heart." Mystery gives way to "glorifying and praising God." RSM

PSALM FOR THE DAY: Psalm 98

HYMNS FOR THE DAY	HL	HB	WB
All My Heart This Night Rejoices	125	172	287
Joy to the World! (Ps.)	122	161	444
On a Bethlehem Hill	—	—	536
Of the Father's Love Begotten	—	7	534
Let All Mortal Flesh Keep Silence (for Holy Communion)	112	148	449
Silent Night	132	154	567

ANTHEMS FOR THE DAY

Zech. 2:10-13 *Sing and Rejoice, O Zion,* J. C. Geisler (Boosey & Hawkes). SSAB or SATB (M). Moravian Anthem

Let All Mortal Flesh Keep Silence, Gustav Holst (Stainer). SATB (ME)

Let All Mortal Flesh Keep Silence (French carol) (WB, p. 449)

See also anthems listed for the Zephaniah reading for Advent 3

Phil. 4:4-7 See anthems listed for Advent 3

Luke 2:15-20 *As It Fell Upon a Night* (English carol), arr. K. K. Davis (Galaxy). Arranged for SA, SSA, SATB, or TTBB (E). A Youth Choir favorite

All My Heart This Night Rejoices, arr. Kenneth Jennings (Augsburg). SATB, 2 flutes, optional Children's Choir (ME)

Today Is Born Emmanuel, Michael Praetorius (Mark Foster). SATB (ME)

Star Carol, John Rutter (Oxford). SATB (M). Refrain: "Follow me joyfully; Hurry to Bethlehem and see the Son of Mary!" RD

COLLECT FOR THE DAY
God of heaven and earth: by your word alone everything was created and by your Word made flesh everything has been renewed. By the birth this day of your beloved Son we all win adoption. All praise, thanks, and glory be to you today and forever; through his own great and strong name.
                                                                    HTA

READINGS
Isa. 52:6-10 The time has come for captive Israel to be set free. The messenger of God, the herald of good tidings, will be announced by the watchmen, and joy will echo and reecho across the nation and the world. "All the ends of the earth shall see the salvation of our God."

Eph. 1:3-10 Christ is the answer to our yearning for salvation. Such a plan was in the mind of God "before the foundation of the world." Christians have a destiny. By the richness of God's grace in Christ we have been blessed beyond our ability to comprehend either his purpose or his blessings. In God's appointed time all of creation will be united in Christ.

John 1:1-14 It all began with the Word God expressed to the created order, a light shining in darkness. John came to bear witness to the light, who came unrecognized by the world. To those who did receive him, he gave "power to become children of God." The Word came in human form, and "we have beheld his glory."
                                                                    RSM

PSALM FOR THE DAY: Psalm 97

HYMNS FOR THE DAY	HL	HB	WB
Watchman, Tell Us of the Night	109	149	617
The Lord Is King! (Ps.)	—	83	—
We Greet You, Sure Redeemer from All Strife	—	144	625
Lo, How a Rose E'er Blooming	—	162	455
O Come, All Ye Faithful	116	170	486

ANTHEMS FOR THE DAY

Isa. 52:6-10 *How Beautiful Upon the Mountains,* John Antes (Boosey & Hawkes). SATB (M). Moravian Anthem

How Beautiful Upon the Mountains, Daniel Moe (Presser). SATB (M)

Break Forth Into Joy, Don Whitman (Summy-Birchard). SATB (ME)

Eph. 1:3-10 *When the Time Had Fully Come,* H. Leroy Baumgartner (Concordia). SATB, or SAB, B solo (M). Text concludes with Eph. 1:3-6

John 1:1-14 *Let Our Gladness Know No End* (Bohemian carol), arr. Schroeder (Concordia). SATB, 2 flutes and cello (ME). See especially stanza 3: "Into flesh is made the Word." Lovely carol arrangement

And the Word Was Made Flesh, Heinz Werner Zimmermann (from *Five Hymns,* Concordia). SATB or Unison (ME)   RD

COLLECT FOR THE DAY
> Righteous God and Savior: you have turned to us so that we might turn to you and be saved. All the ends of the earth worship you. Help us, with Mary's Son, to offer ourselves, our souls and bodies, in the temple of your service and world; through his own sweet name.   HTA

READINGS
> **Isa. 45:18-22**   God proclaims himself as the God of Israel, a righteous God and Savior. He is the only God: "To me every knee shall bow, every tongue shall swear" (v. 23).

> **Rom. 11:33 to 12:2**   Riches, wisdom, and knowledge are attributes of God we cannot fathom. The human intellect is no match for the ways of God.

> **Luke 2:41-52**   Jesus and his parents make their annual pilgrimage to Jerusalem for the Passover celebration. The dialogue between Jesus and the teachers in the Temple amazes everyone who listened to his questions and answers. Jesus' mother is not impressed when she finds him, nor with his answer to her inquiry as to why. She does ponder over its implications.   RSM

PSALM FOR THE DAY: Psalm 111

HYMNS FOR THE DAY

	HL	HB	WB
Let All Together Praise Our God	—	—	450
All Beautiful the March of Days	471	96	281
God Moves in a Mysterious Way	103	112	391
As Men of Old Their Firstfruits Brought	—	—	301
O Master Workman of the Race	140	178	—
Crown Him with Many Crowns	190	213	349

ANTHEMS FOR THE DAY

> **Isa. 45:18-22**   *Thou Alone Art Israel's Shield,* Jean Berger (Augsburg). SATB (M). Text: "Give thy whole nation and every tribe the knowledge that thou alone art God . . . "

> *I Am the Lord,* Ernst Pepping (Concordia). SATB (MD)

> *Now Israel May Say* (Old 124th), arr. George Brandon (Waterloo). SAB (E)

> **Rom. 11:33 to 12:2**   *Greater Love Hath No Man,* John Ireland (Stainer). SATB (M). Text concludes with Rom. 12:1. Great anthem

> *Do Not Be Conformed,* Philip Landgrave (C. Fischer). SATB (ME). Text: Rom. 12:2 and Phil. 2:5-11; semi-pop idiom

> **Luke 2:41-52**   *And Jesus Increased in Wisdom,* Harvey Hahn (Concordia). SAB (ME)

> *My Son, Wherefore Hast Thou Done This to Us?* Heinrich Schütz (Concordia). SATB, SAB solo, strings (D)   RD

COLLECT FOR THE DAY

God of all wisdom: seers have sought you through all the ages. Your servant Anna announced your Son as the one for whom they waited. Let us never be so foolish as to fail him on his wise way to a cross. We pray in Jesus' name, God with us.   HTA

READINGS

Job 28:20-28 Job asks where wisdom and understanding have their source. Man and beast and bird cannot see it. Even rumors are inconclusive. God knows because he is the only one who is all and knows all. To man, "the fear of the Lord, that is wisdom; and to depart from evil is understanding."

I Cor. 1:18-25 The cross is both folly and the power of God. Christ crucified is a stumbling block and the power and wisdom of God. Those who have answered the call of God in Christ are on the side of power and wisdom.

Luke 2:36-40 Anna, a prophetess of God, is an old, dedicated servant. She influenced Mary and Joseph and also participated in Jesus' development as a young boy. "And the child grew and became strong, filled with wisdom; and the favor of God was upon him."   RSM

PSALM FOR THE DAY: Psalm 147:12-20

HYMNS FOR THE DAY

	HL	HB	WB
Great God, We Sing That Mighty Hand	470	527	408
God of Our Life (tune: Sandon)	88	108	395
Praise Ye the Lord, for It Is Good (Ps.)	—	36	—
God of Grace and God of Glory	—	358	393
O Thou Whose Feet Have Climbed Life's Hill	490	468	—

ANTHEMS FOR THE DAY

Job 28:20-28 *Wisdom and Understanding,* Kent A. Newbury (Somerset). SATB or SSA (M). Text: Job 28:20-21, 23-28

Fear God and Give Glory to Him, Milton Dieterich (Southern). SATB (M)

I Cor. 1:18-25 *Christus factus est,* Niccolo Zingarelli, ed. Kaplan (Lawson-Gould). SATB (M). Text: "Jesus for us became obedient unto death. . . . Wherefore God exalted Him."

Christ Was Made Obedient, Anton Bruckner (G. Schirmer). SATB (M)

Luke 2:36-40 *And the Child Grew,* Randall Thompson (from *Nativity According to St. Luke,* E. C. Schirmer). SATB (M). Text: Luke 2:40, with Alleluias. Fine festival type of piece   RD

COLLECT FOR THE DAY
Gracious God: you have given us your Son, our Lord Jesus Christ. We
have brought to him gifts of treasure and of treachery. Reveal to us, we
pray, the mystery of his wide love for saints and sinners, kings and
common folk. Lead us from his cradle to his cross, there to offer
ourselves in his service. We offer our prayer through that same Jesus
Christ our Lord.   HTA

READINGS
Isa. 60:1-6 Keys to the attractive force of God are light and glory. All the
nations respond to him and produce their own radiance and wealth. Gold
and frankincense are symbols of response to God in praise and rejoicing.

Eph. 3:1-6 The apostle is in a favored position as a steward of God's grace.
Apostles and prophets by the Spirit know what was not revealed in other
generations. Gentiles are fellow heirs, members of the same body, and
partakers of the promises in Christ.

Matt. 2:1-12 Familiar is the story of the nativity as it recalls the prophecy
concerning the Messiah. The Wise Men fulfill prophecy (Isaiah) in the
giving of gifts of gold, frankincense, and myrrh. What is in the dream that
warns them to return home another way?   RSM

PSALM FOR THE DAY: Psalm 72:1-19

HYMNS FOR THE DAY

	HL	HB	WB
Brightest and Best	136	175	318
The Morning Light Is Breaking	389	499	—
Jesus Shall Reign (Ps.)	377	496	443
O Morning Star, How Fair and Bright	321	415	521
We Three Kings	—	176	—

ANTHEMS FOR THE DAY

Isa. 60:1-6 *Arise, Shine, for Thy Light Has Come*, Kenneth Jennings
(Augsburg). SATB (M)

For Your Light Has Come, Ronald A. Nelson (Augsburg). SATB, trumpets (E)

All from Saba Shall Come, Gerhard Schroth (G.I.A.). SA or TB, optional
guitar (E). Text: Isa. 60:6 and 1

Eph. 3:1-6 *Arise, O God, and Shine*, arr. S. Drummond Wolff (Concordia).
SATB, trumpet (ME). Hymn-anthem. Text includes reference to the
spreading of light to the Gentiles

Matt. 2:1-12 *To Jesus from the Ends of Earth* (Huron Indian carol), arr.
Kenneth Jewell (Concordia). SATB or SSA (E). Text continues: "Three Wise
Men came this day"

Saw You Never in the Twilight, Wilbur Held (Augsburg). Unison (E)

Epiphany Alleluias, John Weaver (Boosey & Hawkes). SATB (ME)   RD

COLLECT FOR THE DAY
God of light: at the dawn of creation your Spirit hovered over the water.
Again at the Jordan River your Spirit descended as a dove upon your
Son Jesus, to anoint him for his ministry of reconciliation. Grant us his
peace always we pray; in his name.   HTA

READINGS
Gen. 1:1-5 Creation begins with the separation of light and darkness, day
and night. The epiphany is the spreading of that light.

Eph. 2:11-18 Separation between Jew and Gentile comes to an end through
the reconciling power of Christ. The separated, the unreconciled now
become one through the cross.

Luke 3:15-17, 21-22 At the hand of John, Jesus receives baptism. At the
hand of God, he is set apart for ministry. "Thou art my beloved Son; with
thee I am well pleased."   RSM

PSALM FOR THE DAY: Psalm 29:1-4, 9-10

HYMNS FOR THE DAY	HL	HB	WB
Guide Me, O Thou Great Jehovah	104	339	409
Morning Has Broken	—	464	—
O Day of Rest and Gladness	18	70	—
Here, O Lord, Your Servants Gather	—	—	417
The Lone, Wild Bird	496	540	591
Descend, O Spirit, Purging Flame	—	—	353

ANTHEMS FOR THE DAY

Gen. 1:1-5 *In the Beginning of Creation,* Daniel Pinkham (E. C. Schirmer).
SATB, electronic tape (E). Text: Gen. 1:1-3. A good piece to explore the use
of electronic tape

Eph. 2:11-18 See the anthems listed for Pentecost 9 (B)

Here, O Lord, Your Servants Gather, Isau Koizumi (WB, p. 417)

Luke 3:15-17, 21-22 *At the Name of Jesus,* R. Vaughan Williams (Oxford).
SATB (ME)

O Jesus, King Most Wonderful, Robert Wetzler (Augsburg). SATB (E) RD

THE SECOND SUNDAY AFTER EPIPHANY (C)

COLLECT FOR THE DAY

God of love: you have entered into the heart of human life through Jesus Christ our Lord. At a marriage in Cana of Galilee he made glad the hearts of all and so declared us to be your delight. Give us that same Spirit of love that we who are many may become one body; through Jesus Christ our Lord. .... HTA

READINGS

Isa. 62:2-5 Israel's role and identity will change and become the occasion for celebration. Dazzling beauty in the hand of God will be her lot instead of the names "Desolate" and "Forsaken." God has chosen Israel to be great and glorious.

I Cor. 12:4-11 The unifying power of the Spirit is demonstrated in the arenas of many gifts and ministries. The same inspires them all for the common good.

John 2:1-12 Water and wine are the center of attention at the wedding at Cana. The tense interchange of words between Jesus and his mother reveals that she knows what he can do. This first miracle affirms his lordship and the discipleship of the twelve. .... RSM

PSALM FOR THE DAY: Psalm 36:5-10

HYMNS FOR THE DAY

	HL	HB	WB
Christ, Whose Glory Fills the Skies	26	47	332
The Church's One Foundation	333	437	582
Thy Mercy and Thy Truth, O Lord	—	82	—
Put Forth, O God, Your Spirit's Might	—	477	559
Jesus, Priceless Treasure	—	414	442
Thanks to God, Whose Word Was Spoken	—	—	580

ANTHEMS FOR THE DAY

Isa. 62:2-5 *They Shall See the Glory of the Lord*, Joseph W. Rhodes (Warner). SATB (MD)

I Cor. 12:4-11 *Draw Us in the Spirit's Tether*, Harold Friedell (H. W. Gray). SATB (ME)

O Lord, Give Thy Holy Spirit, Thomas Tallis (Chappell). SATB (M)

John 2:1-12 *Lord, Who at Cana's Wedding Feast*, Buxtehude (in *Wedding Blessings*, Concordia). Solo or Unison (ME). Suitable if emphasis is on Christ's presence in marriage rather than on miracle .... RD

COLLECT FOR THE DAY

Giver of the Word: you are never without a witness among us. Prophets and reformers have spoken your truth. Apostles and teachers have edified your people. And your living Word Jesus has come among us to fulfill all their words in our world. Give us attentive hearts; through that same Jesus Christ our Lord.

HTA

READINGS

Neh. 8:1-3, 5-6, 8-10 Ezra reads and explains the law. The occasion becomes a time of worship and celebration in the city square. The people respond in sadness upon hearing the law, but their weeping turns to joy and gladness.

I Cor. 12:12-30 The apostle uses the body as a model for describing the functions of the community of faith. If one member suffers, all suffer; if one member is honored, all are glad. In the body of Christ, the church, various gifts and functions are needed.

Luke 4:14-21 In his home synagogue at Nazareth, Jesus reads from Isa., ch. 61, which describes the mission and ministry of Messiah. His commentary sets the seal on his own future.

RSM

PSALM FOR THE DAY: Psalm 113

HYMNS FOR THE DAY

	HL	HB	WB
Praise God, Ye Servants of the Lord (Ps.)	—	19	—
A Mighty Fortress	266	91	274, 276
Onward, Christian Soldiers	365	350	542
We Are One in the Spirit	—	—	619
O Sing a Song of Bethlehem	138	177	526
Spread, O Spread the Mighty Word	—	—	577

ANTHEMS FOR THE DAY

Neh. 8:1-3 *Behold, God Is My Salvation,* Eugene Butler (Leonard Pub.). SATB (M). Text continues: "For the Lord is my strength and my song"

I Will Rejoice in the Lord, Gottfried Homilius, ed. Kaplan (Lawson-Gould).SATB (ME)

I Cor. 12:12-30 *Dismiss Me Not Thy Service, Lord,* Austin Lovelace (H. W. Gray). SATB (ME). Text includes: ". . . All works are good, and each is best As most it pleases thee"

All Praise to Our Redeeming Lord, Van Wyatt (Pro Art). SATB (E). Folk-like in character. Text continues: ". . . He bids us build each other up; and gathered into one. . . We hand in hand go on"

Luke 4:14-21 *Good News,* Jane Marshall (C. Fischer). SATB, Narrator, B solo (E). Text: Luke 4:16-19

Hark the Glad Sound, Robert J. Powell (Flammer). Unison or 2-Part (E). Text based on Luke 4:18-19

RD

THE FOURTH SUNDAY AFTER EPIPHANY (C)

COLLECT FOR THE DAY

Patient God: your plans for us precede our birth and overrule our unreadiness. Your own Son was rejected by his neighbors and betrayed by his friends. Equip us, we pray, with the gifts of faith, hope, and love that we may fulfill your plans for us; through Jesus our Lord.   HTA

READINGS

Jer. 1:4-10 Jeremiah's call to the prophetic office is by divine initiative and under divine authority. Even though he feels ill equipped and inexperienced, God assures him of his credentials for this responsibility.

I Cor. 13:1-13 Prophetic powers, wisdom, oratory, understanding, faith, self-giving dedication are all valid gifts. However, these of themselves are not complete. They are significant gifts when the power of love is at the heart of each. Love opens avenues of understanding and insight not otherwise perceived. This is best seen against the background of 12:31, "But earnestly desire the higher gifts. And I will show you a still more excellent way."

Luke 4:22-30 Jesus is not surprised at the negative reaction of his townspeople in Nazareth. He cites instances in the ancient Scriptures where other than the "in crowd" were shown favor by God. They try to destroy him, but their attempts on his life do not prevail.   RSM

PSALM FOR THE DAY: Psalm 71:1-6, 15-17

HYMNS FOR THE DAY

	HL	HB	WB
O Word of God Incarnate	215	251	532
Who Trusts in God (Ps.)	—	375	—
Where Charity and Love Prevail	—	—	641
Love Came Down	133	—	—
God of the Prophets!	481	520	398
God of Grace and God of Glory	—	358	393

ANTHEMS FOR THE DAY

I Cor. 13:1-13 *The Gift of Love,* Hal Hopson (Hope). Unison or 2-Part (E).

Though I Speak with the Tongues of Men, Edward Bairstow (Oxford). SATB/SAB (M)

The Corinthians, Ned Rorem (Peters). SATB (D). Text includes entire thirteenth chapter; important organ score

Though with the Tongues of Men and Holy Angels, Johannes Brahms (in *Four Scriptural Songs,* G. Schirmer). Available for high or low solo voice (MD). Text: I Cor. 13:1-3, 12-13

The Greatest of These Is Love, Daniel Moe (Augsburg). Solo (M). Text: I Cor. 13:1-2, 4-5a, 6-8a

Luke 4:22-30 *He Was Despised,* Karl Heinrich Graun (Presser). SATB (M)

Hail, Thou Once Despised Jesus, Leland Sateren (Schmitt, Hall & McCreary). SATB (ME)   RD

COLLECT FOR THE DAY

Eternal Lover of humanity: constantly you call. We confess with prophets and apostles that we are not worthy, not even able. Draw us back from all the dead ends of our lives by the grace given us through the resurrection of Jesus Christ our Lord.   HTA

READINGS

Isa. 6:1-8 Isaiah's call to ministry is colorful, dramatic, and filled with symbolism. Each action, each step in the sequence has deep personal significance for Isaiah and are keys to the ordering of worship.

I Cor. 15:1-11 Paul defends himself and his ministry as he recites his priorities for preaching. Christ's death, resurrection, and appearances have highest claim on him. Faced by suspicion, he is unconcerned about his own credentials. It is by God's grace that he ministers.

Luke 5:1-11 Jesus' teaching from the boat as the people sit along the shore is the setting for the call of the disciples. At the close of his discourse, Jesus turns to Peter, who is cleaning his nets, and invites him to cast his nets once more. The result is a great catch. Peter is personally threatened by it. Jesus assures him and his companions that there is nothing to fear. "Henceforth you will be catching men." They follow him.   RSM

PSALM FOR THE DAY: Psalm 138

HYMNS FOR THE DAY

	HL	HB	WB
Round the Lord in Glory Seated	15	—	—
Holy, Holy, Holy!	57	11	421
Holy God, We Praise Your Name	—	—	420
Lord, Speak to Me	399	298	—
This Is the Good News	—	—	263
Jesus Calls Us	223	269	439
They Cast Their Nets	—	421	—

ANTHEMS FOR THE DAY

Isa. 6:1-8 *Isaiah, Mighty Seer*, Martin Luther, setting by Melchior Vulpius (Concordia). SSATTBB (ME). Text: Isa. 6:1-4

Holy Is God the Lord (Isaiah, Mighty Seer), arr. Paul Bunjes (Concordia). Unison (E)

Holy, Holy, Holy (Sanctus and Hosanna), F. J. Haydn (Mercury). SATB (ME)

Holy Is the Lord, Andreas Hammerschmidt (Concordia). SSATB with 2 obbligato instruments (M). Text: Isa. 6:3 with concluding doxology.

I Cor. 15:1-11 *Christ Atoned for Our Transgressions*, Johann Ernst Eberlin (Schmitt, Hall & McCreary). SATB (MD)

O Christ, Our Hope, Hugo Distler (Augsburg). SSA or SAT (MD)

Luke 5:1-11 *Master, We Have Toiled All Night*, Gerhard Krapf (Concordia). Unison or Solo (M)   RD

THE SIXTH SUNDAY AFTER EPIPHANY (C)

COLLECT FOR THE DAY

Lord of life: your word illumines even the darkness. You set before us blessing or curse, life or death, wilderness or waterside. As you raised Christ from the grave, lift us up to fruitfulness and happiness; through Jesus Christ the Lord. HTA

READINGS

Jer. 17:5-8 There is a close parallel in this passage with Psalm 1. In both, the contrast is made between the one who trusts in himself and turns away from the Lord, and the one who trusts in the Lord and finds his life sustained like a tree near a stream of water.

I Cor. 15:12-20 Faith is meaningless apart from the power of the resurrection. Hope is empty without the knowledge that God raised Jesus from the dead.

Luke 6:17-26 Jesus' teaching and healing give powerful evidence of his lordship. The Sermon on the Plain is a combination of beatitude and judgment. RSM

PSALM FOR THE DAY: Psalm 1

HYMNS FOR THE DAY	HL	HB	WB
Sing to the Lord of Harvest (Ps.)	—	—	569
Cast Your Burden on the Lord	288	—	323
Come, You Faithful, Raise the Strain	168	205	344
Blest Are the Pure in Heart	—	226	—
"Thy Kingdom Come"	363	484	—
Rejoice, the Lord Is King	193	140	562

ANTHEMS FOR THE DAY

Jer. 17:5-8 *Happy the Man Who Fears the Lord*, Richard Proulx (Augsburg). SS with flute and oboe (M)

Blessed Is He Who Walks Not in the Path of the Wicked, Heinrich Schütz (Concordia). SA (MD)

Blessed Is the Man, Peter Waring (E. C. Schirmer). SATB (M)

I Cor. 15:12-20 *Christ Being Raised from the Dead*, John Blow (Concordia). SATB (D). Text includes I Cor. 15:20-22

Medway, William Billings (in *Two Fuguing Tunes*, Hope). SATB (E). Text: "Sing to the Lord. . . . When His salvation is our theme Exalted be our voice."

Luke 6:17-26 *The Beatitudes*, Lloyd Pfautsch (Flammer). SATB (M)

The Beatitudes, Jan Bender (Concordia). SA (ME)

The Beatitudes, Edmund Rubbra (Lengnick). SSA (D). Recommended for ensemble of mature musicians

The Beatitudes (from *Triptych*), Alan Hovhaness (AMP). SATB (D)　RD

COLLECT FOR THE DAY

God of compassion: lead us to love our enemies. We are such children of flesh that we love only those who love us. Show us the better way of your kingdom and Spirit; through Jesus our Lord, who gave his life for many.

HTA

READINGS

I Sam. 26:6-12   David and his companions are tempted to kill Saul while he is sleeping. However, David's wisdom and patience do not allow it to happen. He knows that Saul is king by the anointing of God to the sacred office. He also knows that in God's good time an end will come to Saul's reign.

I Cor. 15:42-50   Flesh and spirit, Adam and Christ, man of dust and man from heaven, physical then spiritual—these are in proper sequence according to Paul. He applies this argument to the resurrection as well as to the kingdom of God and those who inherit it.

Luke 6:27-36   The teachings of Jesus are hard sayings. Love does not expect love in return. Doing good is in itself its own reward. Lending, kindness, unselfishness are acts of mercy. Why expect anything in return?   RSM

PSALM FOR THE DAY: Psalm 37:3-10

HYMNS FOR THE DAY

	HL	HB	WB
Let There Be Light, Lord God of Hosts	402	480	451
The Steps of Those Whom He Approves (Ps.)	—	422	—
O God of Love, O King of Peace	421	483	—
O God, Whose Will Is Life and Peace	—	—	503
O God of Every Nation	—	—	498
God of Compassion, in Mercy Befriend Us	290	122	392

ANTHEMS FOR THE DAY

I Sam. 26:6-12   *Give Thy Servant an Understanding Heart*, Virgil T. Ford (C. Fischer). SATB (ME). Text continues: ". . . that I may discern between good and evil"

I Cor. 15:42-50   *Since by Man Came Death*, G. F. Handel (from *Messiah*, Part III, any edition). (M)

I Am the Resurrection and the Life, Heinrich Schütz (Peters). SATB/SATB (D). Double chorus. Text: John 11:25-26

Luke 6:27-36   *Be Merciful, Even as Your Father Is Merciful*, Gerhard Krapf (Concordia). Unison or Solo (M). Text: Luke 6:36-42

Let Us Love One Another, Alan Hovhaness (Peters). SATB,T/B Soli (MD)

Brotherly Love, Alice Parker (E. C. Schirmer). Canon for 2 to 5 voices, optional guitar (ME)   RD

THE EIGHTH SUNDAY AFTER EPIPHANY (C)

COLLECT FOR THE DAY

Redeemer of us all: convert our hearts that we may be converted in our lives. Help us to know our own innermost thoughts without becoming insensitive to our neighbors' need. Keep us always vigilant to do your work knowing that with you we never labor in vain; through our risen Redeemer, Jesus Christ.   HTA

READINGS

Job 23:1-7 Job was an honest man: honest enough to confess he couldn't find God to plead his defense, honest enough to admit his "rebellious lament." That sort of honesty is never in vain before God, and may well be its own finest reward.

I Cor. 15:54-58 We complete our several weeks' reading of I Corinthians this week. We, with Job, are reminded that even death has been deprived of its "sting" by Christ's resurrection, so that neither our defeats nor our discipleship will ever be "in vain."

Luke 6:36-45 Here in Luke's version of the Sermon on the Mount Jesus authoritatively defines inner integrity as having two components: (1) admission of one's own faults and failings (as well as questions), and (2) congruity between inner disposition and outer deportment. As in the Matthean version: "All you need say is 'Yes' if you mean yes, 'No' if you mean no." (Matt. 5:37)   HTA

PSALM FOR THE DAY: Psalm 92

HYMNS FOR THE DAY

	HL	HB	WB
O God of Light, Your Word, a Lamp Unfailing	—	247	499
It Is Good to Sing Thy Praises (tune: Hyfrydol)	—	20	—
The Strife Is O'er	164	203	597
Come, Labor On	366	287	—
'Tis the Gift to Be Simple	—	—	606
O Master, Let Me Walk with Thee	364	304	520

ANTHEMS FOR THE DAY

O Death, Where Is Thy Sting? G. F. Handel (from *Messiah*). Alto and Tenor Duet

Thy Truth Is Great, Ron Nelson (Boosey & Hawkes). SATB (MD)

I Thank You, God, Lloyd Pfautsch (Lawson-Gould). SATB (ME)

A Prayer for Courage, Michael Moody (Augsburg). 2-Part (E)   LLH

COLLECT FOR THE DAY

Lord God of hosts: make of us pilgrims throughout these forty days. Lead us through discipline to discipleship, through fasting to feasting, through privation to freedom. Free us from our own struggles, so that we may more fully serve one another; through Jesus Christ our Lord.

HTA

READINGS

Zech. 7:4-10 Lent: fasting, discipline, and sacrifice. The prophet probes the motive of those who ask if the traditional disciplines are to be followed. How much of the spiritual life is for one's own benefit? The word from the Lord points his people toward others, so that in observing *their* needs the true spirituality of the season might be practiced. The benefits are those that make for the real life.

I Cor. 9:19-27 Paul exults in the freedom he experiences in the new life in Christ. He reports that he gladly imposes two kinds of limitations on himself: he accepts the perspectives of others in order to win them to the life in Christ; he disciplines his body—like an athlete—in order to fulfill the task he has been given.

Luke 5:29-35 Jesus has dinner with Levi, the tax collector, identifying his ministry as work with sinners, not righteous persons. When comparison is made to disciples of John and of Pharisees, Jesus replies that his disciples "feast" because the bridegroom is with them. Time enough for fasting when the bridegroom has been taken from them.   TPS

PSALM FOR THE DAY: Psalm 51:1-17

HYMNS FOR THE DAY

	HL	HB	WB
Lord, Who Throughout These Forty Days	144	181	470
O God of Bethel, by Whose Hand	98	342	496
God, Be Merciful to Me (Ps.)	—	282	—
God of Compassion, in Mercy Befriend Us (Ps.)	290	122	392
Sinners Jesus Will Receive	227	—	—

ANTHEMS FOR THE DAY

Zech. 7:4-10 *Mercy, Pity, Peace and Love,* Austin Lovelace (Canyon). SATB (E)

Luke 5:29-35 *A Lenten Motet,* Richard Purvis (Sacred Songs). SATB (M)

Blessed Jesu, God Incarnate, Gabriel Fauré, arr. Lloyd Pfautsch (Lawson-Gould). SATB (E)   DCR

THE FIRST SUNDAY IN LENT (C)

COLLECT FOR THE DAY

Ever-present Lord: in all our wilderness wanderings you have been before and behind us, beneath and around us. Conform us to Christ's confidence in you and ever give us your word with which to ward off all evil assaults. Be for us the water and bread of life; through the presence of Jesus Christ our Lord.   HTA

READINGS

Deut. 26:5-11   An affirmation of faith—perhaps the "classic" model, in that it tells the story of what God has done. This eloquent, simple narrative becomes the affirmation of faith for successive generations ("our" story) as they recognize that the account of earlier people is a part of their own autobiography. Intensely personal, yet wonderfully designed for liturgical use as the firstfruits are brought as offerings.

Rom. 10:8-13   Later models for affirmations of faith. This time it is Paul who centers his attention, and ours, on Jesus, Risen Lord. Paul indicates that the way to salvation is opened as believers name him "Lord" with lips and heart. Done as a liturgical act, this simple affirmation sustains the hope of the community of believers.

Luke 4:1-13   Led by the Spirit into the wilderness, Jesus is tempted by the devil. The temptations recapitulate the temptations of the people of Israel. Where they have succumbed, he does not. Acknowledging Jesus' victory, the devil withdraws for the time being.   TPS

PSALM FOR THE DAY: Psalm 91

HYMNS FOR THE DAY	HL	HB	WB
Lord, Who Throughout These Forty Days	144	181	470
O Love, How Deep, How Broad, How High!	139	—	518
Call Jehovah Your Salvation (Ps.)	292	123	322
When We Are Tempted to Deny Your Son	—	—	640
Who Trusts in God	—	375	—
A Mighty Fortress	266	91	274

ANTHEMS FOR THE DAY

Deut. 26:5-11   *Clap Your Hands,* John Diercks (Abingdon). SATB (ME)

O Be Joyful in the Lord, Charles Wood (Summy-Birchard). SATB (E)

Psalmkonzert I (Nun danket), Heinz Werner Zimmermann (Concordia). SATB, Children's Choir, 3 trumpets, vibraphone, and string bass (D)

Rom. 10:8-13   *At the Name of Jesus,* R. Vaughan Williams (WB, p. 303)

Salvation Is Created, Paul Tschesnokoff, arr. Norden (J. Fischer). SATTBB (M)

Luke 4:1-13   *Lord, Who Throughout These Forty Days* (HB, No. 181; WB, p. 470)

Be Strong in the Lord, Thomas Matthews (Fitzsimons). SATB (M)   DCR

COLLECT FOR THE DAY

God of glory: we thank you that you have marked out our journey to glory on mountain heights. Take us to Moriah with Abraham and to Sinai with Moses and Elijah. Dazzle us with the transfiguration of your Son and transfigure even our poor bodies for all that lies beyond, in the midst of suffering and glorious humanity; through Jesus Christ our Lord. HTA

READINGS

Gen. 15:5-12, 17-18 God has promised Abram and Sarai a son, but they are still childless and in need of reassurance. God points Abram's attention to the stars and says, "So shall your descendants be." Abram trusts the promise and God renews the covenant, this time in terms of the land.

Phil. 3:17 to 4:1 Words of encouragement, reminding the readers that their commonwealth is in heaven. A contrast is drawn with those "enemies of the cross of Christ" whose minds are set on earthly things, whose god is the belly and whose end is destruction.

Luke 9:28-36 The transfiguration. Flesh and blood exalted beyond the mind's ability to imagine. A vision that is truly startling. Compare with the crucifixion, Jesus, the Christ, suffering and dying on a garbage heap. God himself identifying with human misery in ways beyond the mind's ability to comprehend. A truly awesome sight. TPS

PSALM FOR THE DAY: Psalm 27:7-18

HYMNS FOR THE DAY	HL	HB	WB
The God of Abraham Praise	8	89	587
Father, We Greet You	—	285	364
God Is My Strong Salvation (Ps.)	92	347	388
O Wondrous Type, O Vision Fair	142	182	531
Where Cross the Crowded Ways of Life	410	507	642

ANTHEMS FOR THE DAY

Gen. 15:5-12, 17-18 *Benedictus,* William Barnard (H. W. Gray). SATB with much Unison (E)

Luke 9:28-36 *Transfiguration,* Alan Hovhaness (Peters). Cantata for SATB, Tenor Solo, 16 sections, 16 minutes (D)

Transfiguration, Alex Tchereprin (in *Six Liturgical Chants,* Peters). SATB (MD) DCR

COLLECT FOR THE DAY

God of Abraham, Isaac, and Jacob: you met Moses at the mountain and made holy the ground beneath his feet. Through him you baptized your people into freedom and gave them food and drink. Remind us of our baptism through this holy season and renew our repentance, that we too might stand in your holy presence on the day of resurrection; through Jesus Christ our Lord.   HTA

READINGS

Ex. 3:1-8, 13-15   The call of Moses: while tending sheep, the common is suddenly made holy. When charged by God to represent him to the slaves and to Pharaoh, Moses prudently asks for the Name. God said to Moses, "Say this to the people of Israel, 'I AM has sent me to you.' "

I Cor. 10:1-12   Paul describes how God dealt with the people of the exodus. Indicating the ways in which they were unfaithful, Paul urges the members of the Corinthian congregations to avoid those pitfalls, trusting rather than testing the Lord.

Luke 13:1-9   Jesus continues his teaching on watchfulness, faithfulness, judgment, and repentance. A parable about an unfruitful fig tree gives a perspective different from the story of Jesus cursing the fig tree.   TPS

PSALM FOR THE DAY: Psalm 103:1-11

HYMNS FOR THE DAY	HL	HB	WB
Praise, My Soul, the King of Heaven (Ps.)	14	31	551
Bless, O My Soul! (Ps.)	—	8	—
Guide Me, O Thou Great Jehovah	104	339	409
Lord, from the Depths to You I Cry	240	277	459
There's a Wideness in God's Mercy	93	110	601

ANTHEMS FOR THE DAY

Ex. 3:1-8, 13-15   *Hark, I Hear the Harps Eternal,* arr. Alice Parker (Lawson-Gould). Tune: Invitation. SAATBB (MD)

He, Watching Over Israel, Mendelssohn (from *Elijah,* G. Schirmer, or other editions). SATB (M)

I Cor. 10:1-12   *My God Is a Rock* (spiritual), arr. Alice Parker and Robert Shaw (Lawson-Gould). SATB and Baritone Solo (M)

Luke 13:1-9   *Thou Knowest, Lord, the Secrets of Our Hearts,* Henry Purcell (B. F. Wood). SATB (E)

Cause Us, O Lord, Ron Nelson (Boosey & Hawkes). SATB (ME)

                                                                     DCR

COLLECT FOR THE DAY

Almighty God: your Son Jesus has followed us into the far country of our disobedience. We praise you that even now he is guiding us back to your loved abode where forgiveness awaits and the Passover of gladness resounds. Receive us who once were dead but now are your new creation; through Jesus Christ our Lord.   HTA

READINGS

Josh. 5:9-12 With the crossing of the Jordan and the conquest of the Canaanites, the exodus comes to its conclusion at Gilgal. The Passover is celebrated once again; the manna ceases the next day; and the people eat the fruit of the Promised Land for the first time.

II Cor. 5:16-21 No one, including Christ, is to be perceived from a human point of view only. With the passing of the old and the coming of the new, God commissions his people as ambassadors of the new creation.

Luke 15:11-32 The parable of the prodigal son. Or is it the parable of the loving father? Or is it the parable of the bitter elder brother? Dealing with each in turn and all together, we are confronted again by the incredible power of Jesus' Word in his words.   TPS

PSALM FOR THE DAY: Psalm 34:1-8

HYMNS FOR THE DAY

	HL	HB	WB
How Firm a Foundation	283	369	425
The Lord I Will at All Times Bless (Ps.)	—	412	—
Your Love, O God, Has All Mankind Created	—	—	646
Pardoned Through Redeeming Grace	—	—	550
The Day of Resurrection!	166	208	584
Our Father, by Whose Name	—	—	546

ANTHEMS FOR THE DAY

II Cor. 5:16-21 *Reconciliation*, Lloyd Pfautsch (Abingdon). SATB and trumpet, including a very effective section for a speaking choir (M)

Now We Are Ambassadors, Mendelssohn (from *St. Paul*, G. Schirmer). Section 25 for Tenor and Bass Duet (E)

Luke 15:11-32 *Dear Lord and Father of Mankind*, Austin Lovelace (Abingdon). SATB (E)

Lord, for Thy Tender Mercies' Sake, Richard Farrant (G. Schirmer). SATB (E)   DCR

COLLECT FOR THE DAY

Your kingdom, Lord, upsets all our claims. The new deeds you do in the world overturn all our old ones. To rise with Christ, we must share his sufferings. And the greatest among us must be the servant of all. Give us grace, O God, to share our Lord's trials and to sit with him at table in the kingdom of heaven; through the same Jesus Christ our Lord.   HTA

READINGS

Isa. 43:16-21   The prophet of the exile describes how Cyrus will conquer Babylon and will then permit the people of God to return to the Promised Land. The poetry is powerful; the vision is grand. "Behold, I am doing a new thing . . ."

Phil. 3:8-14   The writer exults in the venture of the upward way. Looking to the future rather than presuming to have achieved perfection, he sees the prize as knowing Christ and experiencing the power of his resurrection.

Luke 22:14-30   The hour has arrived; Jesus and his apostles join for the Passover meal. Using the familiar words, Jesus distributes cup and bread. He then speaks of the one who will betray him. After a flurry of anxiety about this, the disciples proceed to argue about status. Jesus helps them move their dispute onto higher ground by identifying his own role as that of "one who serves."   TPS

PSALM FOR THE DAY: Psalm 28:1-3, 6-9

HYMNS FOR THE DAY	HL	HB	WB
Lead On, O King Eternal	371	332	448
Children of the Heavenly King	347	340	—
Christ of the Upward Way	277	295	—
O for a Closer Walk with God	259	319	—
O God, Our Faithful God	—	—	500
Open Now the Gates of Beauty	—	40	544

ANTHEMS FOR THE DAY

Isa. 43:16-21   *Springs in the Desert*, Arthur B. Jennings (H. W. Gray). SATB (M)

Phil. 3:8-14   *Be Thou My Vision* (HB, No. 303; WB, p. 304)

Jesus, Priceless Treasure (HB, No. 414; WB, p. 442)

Jesus So Lowly, Harold Friedell (H. W. Gray). SATB (M)

Luke 22:14-30   *Here, O My Lord, I See Thee Face to Face* (HB, No. 442; WB, p. 418, tune: Erfyniad)

For the Bread, V. Earle Copes (Abingdon). SATB (E)

My God, and Is Thy Table Spread, Eric Thiman (from *The Last Supper*, Novello). SATB (M)   DCR

PASSION (PALM) SUNDAY (C)

COLLECT FOR THE DAY

Lord, save us! We gladly greet our Lord at the gates of our cities and hearts. But justice has fled and integrity has vanished. Here too he can only be crucified. Forgive us in your endless patience, loving God, and place on our lips and in our lives songs of praise, lest the stones themselves take up the sound: Blessed is he who comes in the name of the Lord. Hosanna!

HTA

READINGS

Isa. 59:14-20 The totality of national corruption is acknowledged. The prophet tells how God saw it and wondered that no one was able to bring justice and righteousness. Recognizing this, God acted, doing himself what man would not—could not?—do.

I Tim. 1:12-17 Paul's summation of who he has been, of what Christ has done for him and through him for others.

Luke 19:28-40 Jesus arranges for a colt to be brought to him for his entrance into Jerusalem. The disciples hail him as the procession leaves the Mount of Olives and moves on to the city. Some Pharisees standing by urge him to silence his disciples, but he responds simply that if they were quiet, the stones would cry out.

TPS

PSALM FOR THE DAY: Psalm 31:1-5, 9-16

HYMNS FOR THE DAY

	HL	HB	WB
Ride On! Ride On in Majesty!	150	188	563
When, His Salvation Bringing	149	186	—
Lift Up Your Heads	114	152	454
When Jesus Wept	—	—	636
Hosanna, Loud Hosanna	147	185	424

ANTHEMS FOR THE DAY

Isa. 59:14-20 *O Lord, How Can We Know Thee,* Ron Nelson (Boosey & Hawkes). SATB (M)

I Tim. 1:12-17 *Immortal, Invisible, God Only Wise* (HB, No. 85; WB, p. 433)

Draw Nigh to Jerusalem, David H. Williams (H. W. Gray). SATB (M)

Richard de Castre's Prayer to Jesus, setting by Barbara Terry (G. Schirmer). SATB (M)

Luke 19:28-40 *O Thou Eternal Christ, Ride On,* arr. Austin Lovelace (Abingdon). Tune: Llangloffan. SATB (E)

DCR

COLLECT FOR THE DAY

Deliverer of Israel: join us to your holy people of old who in the Passover praised you as their Liberator. Christ our Passover has been sacrificed; therefore, O Lord, let us keep the feast in sincerity and truth, welcoming your kingdom with joy; through Jesus Christ our Lord. HTA

READINGS

Num. 9:1-3, 11-12 The Passover is established as a liturgical event to be observed regularly by the community of God's people.

I Cor. 5:6-8 In dealing with the bad behavior of the Corinthian Christians, Paul alludes to Christ as "the Passover Lamb." Using the festival's imagery of cleansing the household of all leaven, he exhorts them to use the "unleavened" bread of sincerity and truth.

Mark 14:12-26 Jesus and the Twelve gather in the upper room for the Passover meal. Jesus institutes the sacrament of the Lord's Supper. TPS

PSALM FOR THE DAY: Psalm 116:12-19

HYMNS FOR THE DAY	HL	HB	WB
Let Us with a Gladsome Mind	64	28	453
Praise God, Ye Servants of the Lord	—	19	—
What Shall I Render to the Lord? (Ps.)	—	32	—
Come, Risen Lord, and Deign to Be Our Guest	—	—	340
Christ Jesus Lay in Death's Strong Bands	—	—	327
According to Thy Gracious Word	358	444	—

ANTHEMS FOR THE DAY

Num. 9:1-3, 11-12 *Guide Me, O Thou Great Jehovah* (HB, No. 339; WB, p. 409)

I Cor. 5:6-8 *Christ lag in Todesbanden* (Cantata No. 4), J. S. Bach (H. W. Gray), "Christ Lay in Death's Dark Prison," sections 5 and 7 especially. (MD)

Mark 14:12-26 *Passion According to St. Mark*, J. S. Bach (Peters). Several chorales are inspired by this text. The alto aria "My Savior, Thee Will I Ne'er Forget" follows the Evangelist's reading of this text. Peters edition is in German. (D) DCR

COLLECT FOR THE DAY

We watch and wait, Lord, close by the cross. Can this be our King? Have you forsaken him? His silence shames our questions; his questions save our lives. Amen! Worthy is the Lamb that was slain. He has made us kings and priests to serve you now and forever. Sing, my tongue, the glorious battle; sing the ending of the fray!   HTA

READINGS

Hos. 6:1-6   The prophet calls the faithless people to accept God's judgment of them as accurate and appropriate. He indicates that their proper response is to repent and to offer love and the knowledge of God as their worship, rather than sacrifice and burnt offering.

Rev. 5:6-14   The vision of worship in heaven. The Lamb, slain and now victorious, receives the homage of all.

Matt. 27:31-50   Jesus is led away for crucifixion. He is mocked and tempted. He utters the cry of dereliction. He dies.   TPS

PSALM FOR THE DAY: Psalm 22:1-8, 19-31

HYMNS FOR THE DAY	HL	HB	WB
When I Survey the Wondrous Cross	152	198	635
Alone You Journey Forth, O Lord	—	—	294
All Ye That Fear God's Holy Name (Ps.)	—	35	—
Come, Let Us to the Lord Our God	—	125	—
A Hymn of Glory Let Us Sing	—	—	273
Crown Him with Many Crowns	190	213	349
Once to Every Man and Nation	373	361	540

ANTHEMS FOR THE DAY

Hos. 6:1-6   *Thanks Be to God*, Thomas Matthews (Fitzsimons). SATB (M)

Hope of the World, V. Earle Copes (Abingdon). SAB (E)

Rev. 5:6-14   *Blessing and Honor and Glory and Power* (HB, No. 137; WB, p. 311)

Worthy Is the Lamb That Was Slain, G. F. Handel (Chorus No. 53 from *Messiah*, G. Schirmer). SATB

Matt. 27:31-50   *Four Chorales* from *The Crucifixion*, John Stainer (Schmitt, Hall & McCreary): No. 1, *Cross of Jesus;* No. 2, *Jesus, the Crucified, Pleads for Me;* No. 3, *I Adore Thee;* No. 4, *All for Jesus.* (E)

Tenebrae in E-flat, J. Michael Haydn, ed. George Strickling (Schmitt, Hall & McCreary). SATB (E)

Seven Words of Love, Lloyd Pfautsch (Abingdon). Lenten cantata for Mixed Choir, Narrator, and Congregation (E)

St. Matthew Passion, J. S. Bach (G. Schirmer). English translation by Robert Shaw. Sections 64-72 are based on this text. (MD)   DCR

COLLECT FOR THE DAY

Powerful God: even death was no match for your might. We praise you this glad day that Christ our King reigned from his cross and is now the firstborn of many who believe. Moses and all the prophets live in him. May he live in us and always be known to us in the breaking of bread; through the power and presence of his resurrection.   HTA

READINGS

Ex. 15:1-11   "The Song of Moses" describes in grand terms the triumph of God over the forces of Pharaoh at the Red Sea. The song calls upon all nations to pay attention to what God has done.

I Cor. 15:20-26   Just as Adam brought the power of death into history, so Christ's resurrection has brought the power for resurrection to all people.

Luke 24:13-35   Two disciples set off for Emmaus. Joined by the risen Jesus, they do not recognize him even when he recapitulates the story of salvation. Only at supper when he breaks the bread are their eyes opened.   TPS

PSALM FOR THE DAY: Psalm 118:1-2, 14-24

HYMNS FOR THE DAY	HL	HB	WB
Fairest Lord Jesus	194	135	360
That Easter Day with Joy Was Bright	—	—	581
This Is the Day the Lord Hath Made (Ps.)	23	69	—
Come, You Faithful, Raise the Strain	168	205	344
He Did Not Want to Be Far	—	—	412
The Day of Resurrection!	166	208	584

ANTHEMS FOR THE DAY

Ex. 15:1-11   *The Day of Resurrection*, Thomas Matthews (Fitzsimons). SATB (M)

Fanfare for Easter, Jane Marshall (C. Fischer). SATB, Youth Choir, optional brass and tympani (M)

A Cantata for Easter, Cecil Effinger (G. Schirmer). SATB (MD). Prologue, Passion, Resurrection, Ascension, and Epilogue.

I Cor. 15:20-26   *Since by Man Came Death*, G. F. Handel (Chorus No. 46 from *Messiah*, G. Schirmer). SATB (M)

Luke 24:13-35   *Come, Risen Lord, and Deign to Be Our Guest* (WB, p. 340)

I Know that My Redeemer Lives, Paul Bunjes (Concordia). A choral cantata based on tune "Duke Street," for choir, congregation (or junior choir), trumpet, and organ. Organ introduction and eight verses. (M)

Sic Transit, Richard Felciano (E. C. Schirmer). SAB, chorus, organ, electronic tape, and light sources (M)

Easter Narrative, Kenneth Jennings (Augsburg). SATB, flute, and organ (M)   DCR

COLLECT FOR THE DAY

Eternal God: you have brought your Son Jesus back from death. May we hear his voice when he calls us back from all our failures, to send us into the world as disciples. Fill our hands with healing help and our lives with the bread of life, even Jesus Christ our Lord.   HTA

READINGS

Acts 5:12-16   The apostles carry on a vigorous ministry of preaching and healing. Signs and wonders attract large numbers of persons; many of them come to believe.

Rev. 1:9-13, 17-19   John is living on the island of Patmos, apparently in exile because of his faith. He is called by God to write his vision down and to send it to "the seven churches."

John 21:1-14   Seven of the disciples are fishing in the Sea of Galilee. They have no luck until the risen Jesus, unrecognized, suggests from the shore that they try the other side. Success follows; Jesus is recognized; they breakfast together on the shore.   TPS

PSALM FOR THE DAY: Psalm 149

HYMNS FOR THE DAY

	HL	HB	WB
Jesus Christ Is Risen Today	163	204	440
O Day of Rest and Gladness	18	70	—
O for a Thousand Tongues	199	141	493
Hark, My Soul, It Is the Lord!	224	263	—
Rejoice, the Lord Is King	193	140	562

ANTHEMS FOR THE DAY

Acts 5:12-16   *Prayer,* Lloyd Pfautsch (Lawson-Gould). 2-Part with accompaniment (E). Text by Dag Hammarskjöld

Tu solus, qui facis mirabilia, Josquin Desprez (AMP). (M)

Rev. 1:9-13, 17-19   *Jesus Christ Is Risen Today* (HB, No. 204; WB, p. 440)

Now Glad of Heart Be Every One, Richard Peek (Canyon). SATB (E)

There Through Endless Ranks of Angels, Carl Schalk (Augsburg). SATB (M)

John 21:1-14   *Jesus, the Bread of Life,* George Lynn (Mercury). SATB (M)

Easter Chorale, Samuel Barber (G. Schirmer). SATB divisi, brass, tympani (organ) (M)   DCR

THE THIRD SUNDAY OF EASTER (C)

COLLECT FOR THE DAY

High King of heaven: accept our praise for Jesus, the Lamb who was slain. Yes, we love him and long to serve him. Grant us courage to follow in his steps even where we would rather not go. Let our obedience to him be first in our lives; for the sake of his holy name.   HTA

READINGS

Acts 5:27-32 The apostles are brought to trial before the council. Condemned for their preaching, Peter responds for the apostles by giving a brief affirmation of their faith.

Rev. 5:11-14   (See Good Friday)

John 21:15-19 Jesus and Peter talk following breakfast. Jesus asks, "Do you love me?" The encounter renews their relationship and results in Peter's assuming the major leadership role among the apostles.   TPS

PSALM FOR THE DAY: Psalm 30

HYMNS FOR THE DAY

	HL	HB	WB
Blessing and Honor and Glory and Power	196	137	311
O Lord, by Thee Delivered (Ps.)	—	127	—
I'm Not Ashamed to Own My Lord	—	292	—
Ten Thousand Times Ten Thousand	427	427	—
They Cast Their Nets	—	421	—
Far Off I See the Goal	183	337	—
Christ, Above All Glory Seated	—	—	324

ANTHEMS FOR THE DAY

Acts 5:27-32   *Rejoice, the Lord Is King* (HB, No. 104; WB, p. 562)

Rev. 5:11-14   *Blessing and Honor and Glory and Power* (HB, No. 137; WB, p. 311)

Worthy Is the Lamb That Was Slain, G. F. Handel (Chorus No. 53 from *Messiah,* G. Schirmer). SATB (MD)

John 21:15-19   *The Lord Is My Shepherd,* Thomas Matthews (Fitzsimons). SATB (M)   DCR

THE FOURTH SUNDAY OF EASTER (C)

COLLECT FOR THE DAY

Guardian of Israel: you have raised up Jesus to be the shepherd of all humanity. He who lives again gives us new life. He who is one with you makes of us one body in the Spirit. Make us bold witnesses to the resurrection and gather us into your blessed fold forevermore; through Jesus Christ our Lord.

HTA

READINGS

Acts 13:44-52 At Antioch of Pisidia the Gentiles flock to hear Paul and Barnabas proclaim the gospel. The Jews of the city are jealous. Paul makes it plain that the gospel is for Gentiles as well as for Jews.

Rev. 7:9-17 John's vision focuses here upon the vast throng from all tribes and nations who are gathered before the throne of God.

John 10:22-30 Jesus, walking in the Temple at the time of the Feast of Dedication, is confronted by people who want an unequivocal statement from him about himself and his authority. Jesus responds by saying that those who are able to trust need no such sign.

TPS

PSALM FOR THE DAY: Psalm 100

HYMNS FOR THE DAY

	HL	HB	WB
Before the Lord Jehovah's Throne (Ps.)	63	81	306
Jesus, Stand Among Us	—	222	—
God's Word Is like a Flaming Sword	—	—	405
Behold the Lamb of God!	153	—	307
How Sweet the Name of Jesus Sounds	310	130	—
Of the Father's Love Begotten	—	7	534

ANTHEMS FOR THE DAY

Acts 13:44-52 *But Paul and Barnabas Spoke Freely,* tenor recitative, and *For So Hath the Lord,* duet for tenor(s) and bass(es), Mendelssohn (from *St. Paul,* G. Schirmer)

Rev. 7:9-17 *You Servants of God, Your Master Proclaim* (HB, No. 27; WB, p. 645)

Psalm 111, T. Charles Lee (H. W. Gray). SATB (M)

John 10:22-30 *Psalm 23,* Heinz Werner Zimmermann (Augsburg). SATB, string bass, organ (ME)

DCR

COLLECT FOR THE DAY
God with us: we rejoice in the resurrection of Jesus our Lord. Let his love for us, and our love for one another, be our strength through all hardship and trial. Bring us at the last to his new heaven and earth where tears will be wiped away and death destroyed; through Jesus Christ our Lord. HTA

READINGS
Acts 14:19-28 Paul is persecuted by his fellow Jews at Antioch and Iconium. Despite this, he continues his missionary activity among the Gentiles. New communities of believers are established by him throughout the region.

Rev. 21:1-5 John's vision culminates in the sight of a new Jerusalem. This holy city comes down to earth from heaven. Thus, "the dwelling of God is with men."

John 13:31-35 Shortly before his betrayal and arrest Jesus gives his friends a "new commandment": they are to love one another just as he has loved them. TPS

PSALM FOR THE DAY: Psalm 145:1-13

HYMNS FOR THE DAY	HL	HB	WB
Glory Be to God the Father	60	—	—
All Glory Be to God on High	—	—	283
O Lord, You Are Our God and King (Ps.)	—	5	517
Fight the Good Fight	270	359	—
Jerusalem the Golden	435	428	—
O Holy City, Seen of John	409	508	505
Jesus, Thy Boundless Love to Me	314	404	—
Where Charity and Love Prevail	—	—	641

ANTHEMS FOR THE DAY

Rev. 21:1-5 *O Holy City, Seen of John* (HB, No. 508; WB, p. 505)

Jerusalem, My Happy Home (American melody), arr. Leland Sateren (Augsburg). SATB (E)

O Holy City, Seen of God, J. S. Bach (E. C. Schirmer). SAB, or (Boosey & Hawkes) SATB (ME)

John 13:31-35 *Draw Us in the Spirit's Tether*, Harold Friedell (H. W. Gray). SATB (E)

Choristers of Light, K. K. Davis (Galaxy). SATB (E)

Prayer, Arthur Frackenpohl (Charter). Unison and organ (E) DCR

COLLECT FOR THE DAY

Lord God Almighty: send upon us the Spirit of Christ whose death has purchased peace for all. His light outshines any temple and his love fulfills all the commandments. Be our light and our life until all shadows scatter and glory is seen upon us; through Jesus Christ our Lord.

HTA

READINGS

Acts 15:1-2, 22-29   The success of Paul's work among the Gentiles of Asia Minor creates problems for the Jewish Christians of Jerusalem. Is it necessary for a Gentile to become a Jew in order to become a Christian? The council of Jerusalem decides that the answer is no. Circumcision is not a prerequisite for becoming a Christian.

Rev. 21:10-14, 22-23   The new Jerusalem has no need of a temple. The relationship of God with his people is immediate and open. All religion is unnecessary and inappropriate.

John 14:23-29   The farewell discourses of Jesus ring with the tones of the resurrection. In this portion Jesus tells of the gift of the Holy Spirit.   TPS

PSALM FOR THE DAY: Psalm 67

HYMNS FOR THE DAY

	HL	HB	WB
Sing Praise to God	—	15	568
Praise the Lord! You Heavens, Adore Him	10	3	554
Lord, Bless and Pity Us (Ps.)	—	493	456
Where High the Heavenly Temple Stands	—	389	—
Holy Spirit, Truth Divine	208	240	422
How Gentle God's Commands	279	105	—
Come Down, O Love Divine	—	—	334

ANTHEMS FOR THE DAY

Acts 15:1-2, 22-29   *Walk Tall, Christian* (WB, p. 616)

Rev. 21:10-14, 22-23   *Open Now the Gates of Beauty* (WB, p. 544)

Golden Jerusalem, Horatio Parker (No. VII from *Hora Novissima*, Novello). Tenor Solo (M). Section XI for quartet and chorus is also appropriate (D)

John 14:23-29   *Holy Spirit, Truth Divine* (WB, p. 422)

If Ye Love Me, Keep My Commandments, Thomas Tallis (E. C. Schirmer). SATB (E)

Peace I Leave with You, Knut Nystedt (Augsburg). SSATB (MD)

Serenity, Charles Ives (AMP). Unison (M)

Lord, Thou Hast Put Gladness in My Heart, Daniel Pinkham (No. III from *Songs of Peaceful Departure*, E. C. Schirmer). SATB with guitar and piano (MD)

DCR

ASCENSION DAY (C)

COLLECT FOR THE DAY

Almighty God: your Son Jesus promised that if he was lifted up, he would draw all to himself. Draw us to him by faith, so that we may live to serve you, and look toward life eternal; through Jesus Christ the Lord. (WB)

READINGS

Acts 1:1-11 Having promised the apostles that "before many days you shall be baptized with the Holy Spirit," Jesus "was lifted up, and a cloud took him out of their sight."

Eph. 1:16-23 God has made Christ to "sit at his right hand" and "has put all things under his feet and has made him the head over all things for the church."

Luke 24:44-53 (Continues the Gospel pericope of Easter 3.) Jesus led the disciples out to Bethany, where he blessed them, and "while he blessed them, he parted from them." LAB

PSALM FOR THE DAY: Psalm 110

HYMNS FOR THE DAY	HL	HB	WB
Come, Christians, Join to Sing (Ps.)	191	131	333
The Lord Ascendeth Up on High	172	212	—
Light of Light, Enlighten Me	21	73	—
Christ, Whose Glory Fills the Skies	26	47	332
Crown Him with Many Crowns	190	213	349

ANTHEMS FOR THE DAY

Acts 1:1-11 *Come Away to the Skies,* arr. Parker (G. Schirmer). SATB (M)

At the Name of Jesus, R. Vaughan Williams (Oxford). SATB (M)

Eph. 1:16-23 *Alleluia! Sing to Jesus,* Hal Hopson (Augsburg). 2-Part (E)

My Jesus Is My Lasting Joy, Buxtehude-Bitgood (H. W. Gray). Unison (E). Children's Choir

Luke 24:44-53 *The Praises of a King,* Austin Lovelace (Augsburg). 2-Part Mixed (E) HH

COLLECT FOR THE DAY

Holy God: you have revealed yourself to us in Jesus, who is the first and the last, the Beginning and the End. Enable each of us to offer him our entire spirit, soul, and body whatever the cost. And keep us in unity with one another that all the world may believe; through Jesus Christ our Lord.   HTA

READINGS

Acts 7:55-60 Stephen, one of seven deacons, is martyred. The story reminds the reader that faithful discipleship does not always yield peace and happiness.

Rev. 22:12-14, 16-17, 20 The end of John's visions. The final, "Amen. Come, Lord Jesus!"

John 17:20-26 Jesus' prayer centers on the theme of the unity of all believers. The church is to be one and universal—genuinely ecumenical. A word of judgment for us today. A word of hope, as well.   TPS

PSALM FOR THE DAY: Psalm 47

HYMNS FOR THE DAY

	HL	HB	WB
Christ, Whose Glory Fills the Skies	26	47	332
Majestic Sweetness Sits Enthroned	197	142	—
When Stephen, Full of Power and Grace	—	—	638
The Son of God Goes Forth to War	271	354	—
Put Forth, O God, Your Spirit's Might	—	477	559
Christ Is Made the Sure Foundation	336	433	325

ANTHEMS FOR THE DAY

Acts 7:55-60 *When Stephen, Full of Power and Grace* (WB, p. 638)

Stephen, Alec Wyton (Flammer). SATB and Tenor Solo (M)

Rev. 22:12-14, 16-17, 20 *Of the Father's Love Begotten* (HB, No. 7; WB, p. 534)

Come, O Thou God of Grace (WB, p. 339)

I Am the Alpha and the Omega, Daniel Moe (Augsburg). SATB (D)   DCR

PENTECOST (C)

COLLECT FOR THE DAY

Source of Spirit: send us speech to tell of all your marvels. Send us breath that we might live long and in peace. Send us fire for our cold hearts. Send us forth to tell the world of your love for all through Jesus Christ our Lord, who lives and reigns with you in the unity of the Holy Spirit, one God, now and forever.   HTA

READINGS

Isa. 65:17-25   A poetic depiction of the peaceable kingdom in which all life has meaning and joy.

Acts 2:1-13   Jews have gathered in Jerusalem from all over the world for the Feast of Pentecost. They are startled to hear (in their own languages) the apostles tell of God's mighty works in Jesus.

John 14:25-31   (See Sunday of Easter 6)   TPS

PSALM FOR THE DAY: Psalm 104:1-4, 24-33

HYMNS FOR THE DAY	HL	HB	WB
O Spirit of the Living God	207	242	528
Spirit Divine, Attend Our Prayers	212	243	574
The Race That Long in Darkness Pined	—	153	—
The Day of Pentecost Arrived	—	—	583
Our Blest Redeemer	205	—	—
Holy Ghost, Dispel Our Sadness	—	—	419
Come, Holy Ghost, Our Souls Inspire	—	237	335

ANTHEMS FOR THE DAY

Isa. 65:17-25   *Peaceable Kingdom*, Randall Thompson (E. C. Schirmer). Appropriate choruses might include *Say Ye to the Righteous* (M), *For Ye Shall Go Out with Joy* (M), and *Ye Shall Have a Song*, Double Chorus (D)

Acts 2:1-13   *The Day of Pentecost Arrived* (WB, p. 583)

O Spirit of the Living God (HB, No. 242; WB, p. 528)

Come Down, O Love Divine, R. Vaughan Williams, arr. Dietterich (Abingdon). Tune: Down Ampney. SATB (E)

Love Divine, All Love Excelling, Ned Rorem (Boosey & Hawkes). SATB (MD)

Day of Pentecost, Leland Sateren (Augsburg). SATB (M)

John 14:25-31   *How Lovely Are the Messengers*, Mendelssohn (No. 26 from St. Paul, G. Schirmer). SATB (ME)   DCR

COLLECT FOR THE DAY

Father, Son, and Spirit: your unity in love shines through the life together of the community of Christ. Share your life with us as we share forgiveness with one another; through Jesus Christ, who sends us as you sent him.   HTA

READINGS

Prov. 8:22-31   Wisdom claims to have been with God since the very beginning of creation.

I Peter 1:1-9   Jewish Christians are scattered far from Jerusalem. Peter writes this letter of encouragement to sustain them in their exile.

John 20:19-23   A post-resurrection appearance of Jesus includes his gift to the apostles of the Holy Spirit and of authority.   TPS

PSALM FOR THE DAY: Psalm 8

HYMNS FOR THE DAY	HL	HB	WB
O Worship the King	2	26	533
Earth and All Stars	—	—	354
O Trinity of Blessed Light	59	245	—
O Lord, Our Lord, in All the Earth (Ps.)	—	95	515
Holy God, We Praise Your Name	—	—	420
We Believe in One True God	—	—	622
Come to Us, Mighty King	52	244	343

ANTHEMS FOR THE DAY

Prov. 8:22-31   *O Come Let Us Sing Unto the Lord*, Emma Lou Diemer (C. Fischer). SATB (M). Accompaniment is difficult

Only Begotten Word of God Eternal, arr. Allanson Brown (H. W. Gray). (ME)

I Peter 1:1-9   *Come, You People, Rise and Sing* (HB, No. 39; WB, p. 345)

The Day of Resurrection! (HB, No. 208; WB, p. 584)

O Love, How Deep, How Broad, How High, setting by Carl Schalk (Concordia). Tune: Deo Gracias. SATB (E)

John 20:19-23   *Go Ye Therefore*, Alec Wyton (H. W. Gray). SATB (M)

Peace Be Unto You, Knut Nystedt (Augsburg). SSATBB (MD)   DCR

THE SECOND SUNDAY AFTER PENTECOST (C)

COLLECT FOR THE DAY

Lord God of all: we praise you that you are not our God only. You reveal yourself as God by your constant care for those whom we call stranger and foreigner. Open our small spirits to the healing and help you promise to all who seek you; through our loving Lord, Jesus Christ.

HTA

READINGS

I Kings 8:41-43 Solomon's prayer of dedication of the Temple includes this note of universalism: the foreigner who comes to prayer shall be heard. The passage offered support and encouragement to the exiled Jews returning from Babylonia to rebuild the Temple.

Gal. 1:1-10 Paul's letter on Christian freedom opens with his claim to God-given authority. He sets the stage by identifying those who preach another gospel.

Luke 7:1-10 Jesus follows up some teaching with the healing of the centurion's servant. The encounter with the Roman soldier provides the occasion for affirming Jesus' authority over all powers and peoples. TPS

PSALM FOR THE DAY: Psalm 117

HYMNS FOR THE DAY	HL	HB	WB
From All That Dwell Below the Skies (Ps.)	388	33	373
Praise God, Ye Servants of the Lord	—	19	—
Christ for the World We Sing	378	489	—
O God of Every Nation	—	—	498
Your Love, O God, Has All Mankind Created	—	—	646
Jesus Shall Reign	377	496	443

ANTHEMS FOR THE DAY

I Kings 8:41-43 *Behold, the Tabernacle of God,* Healy Willan (C. Fischer). SATB (ME)

Gal. 1:1-10 *Rejoice, Ye People,* tune by M. Zimmerman, setting by Daniel Moe (Augsburg). SATB (M)

Lord of Life, David Mitchell (Augsburg). SATB (ME)

Luke 7:1-10 *Where Cross the Crowded Ways of Life* (HB, No. 507; WB, p. 642)

Father, in Thy Mysterious Presence Kneeling, Van Denman Thompson (H. W. Gray). SATB (E)

DCR

COLLECT FOR THE DAY

Lord God of the lonely: we thank you for the compassion your Son Jesus had for all those who were sad and bereft. Your prophets have always cared for such as the special objects of your justice. Let your church always be careful to proclaim the gospel good news among those who most need to hear it; through Jesus Christ our Savior. HTA

READINGS

I Kings 17:17-24 Hiding from Ahab, Elijah takes up residence with a widow. It is a time of drought, and Elijah assists her with the jar of meal and the cruse of oil that are never depleted. Her son falls ill and stops breathing; Elijah revives him.

Gal. 1:11-19 An autobiographical statement by Paul covering the period of his zealous devotion to Judaism, his conversion, and his period of isolation in Arabia. The passage concludes with the description of his visit with Cephas as he takes up his new ministry.

Luke 7:11-17 Jesus encounters a funeral procession as he approaches the city of Nain. Seeing the grief of the dead man's mother, a widow, Jesus revives the young man. TPS

PSALM FOR THE DAY: Psalm 30

HYMNS FOR THE DAY	HL	HB	WB
When Morning Gilds the Skies	3	41	637
O Lord, by Thee Delivered (Ps.)	—	127	—
Give to the Winds Your Fears	294	364	377
Holy Ghost, Dispel Our Sadness	—	—	419
Now Thank We All Our God	459	9	481

ANTHEMS FOR THE DAY

I Kings 17:17-24 *Amazing Grace! How Sweet the Sound!* (HB, No. 275; WB, p. 296)

Amazing Grace, arr. John Coates (Shawnee). SSA or SATB (E). Accompaniment is in a slow blues style

On God and Not on Human Trust, Johann Pachelbel (Concordia). SATB (MD)

Gal. 1:11-19 *O Thou, the True and Only Light*, Mendelssohn (in *Four Chorales from St. Paul*, G. Schirmer). SATB (E)

Luke 7:11-17 *By the Springs of Water*, Cecil Effinger (Augsburg). SATB (M) DCR

COLLECT FOR THE DAY

Lord God of sinners: we rejoice that you always reach out to those who by sin have hurt themselves and others. You forgive kings and those of poor repute whose names are not even known. God forbid that we should glory save in the life we have through the death of Jesus Christ our Lord.   HTA

READINGS

II Sam. 12:1-7a   The prophet Nathan delivers a subtle and stinging rebuke to King David for having sacrificed Uriah in battle in order to take his wife, Bathsheba, for his own. Nathan promises the Lord's forgiveness along with a sign of punishment. God's forgiveness is as large as the sin which calls it forth.   HTA

Gal. 2:15-21   Paul is well into his argument against seeking justification by works of the law.

Luke 7:36-50   A woman known as a sinner anoints Jesus with ointment and tears. Jesus tells his host, Simon, something of the meaning of forgiveness.   TPS

PSALM FOR THE DAY: Psalm 32

HYMNS FOR THE DAY	HL	HB	WB
O Worship the King	2	26	533
How Blest Is He (Ps.)	—	281	—
There's a Wideness in God's Mercy	93	110	601
Pardoned Through Redeeming Grace	—	—	550
Master, No Offering Costly and Sweet	407	299	—
My Faith Looks Up to Thee	285	378	—

ANTHEMS FOR THE DAY

II Sam. 12:1-7a   *Create in Me, O God, a Clean Heart*, Johannes Brahms (G. Schirmer). Motet, Op. 29, No. 2. SATBB (ME)

Gal. 2:15-21   *Lord, to Thee We Turn*, Orlando di Lasso (E. C. Schirmer). SATB (M)

St. Theresa's Bookmark, Louis White (H. W. Gray). SATB (E)

Lord of Life, David Mitchell (Augsburg). SATB (E)

Luke 7:36-50   *Prayer of St. Francis*, Jan Nieland (World Library). SA or SATB (ME)   DCR

COLLECT FOR THE DAY

Protector of your people: how patiently you bear with all our arrogance and rebelliousness. Even the presence of your Son in our midst had to be a secret, and to follow him today is to take up a cross. Give us who are baptized into him the joy and the strength of that cross; through Jesus Christ our Lord.

HTA

READINGS

Zech. 12:7-10   A promise of victory to the house of David. The concluding verse tells the price of the victory, which will stir the people to compassion as much as to celebration.

Gal. 3:23-29   Before faith all were under the law. Those baptized into Christ are all one in him: there is neither male nor female, slave nor free. All are offspring of Abraham, heirs according to the promise.

Luke 9:18-24   Peter declares Jesus to be "the Christ of God." Jesus immediately tells the disciples what the future holds for him. The passage concludes with Jesus identifying the form and content of discipleship.

TPS

PSALM FOR THE DAY: Psalm 63:1-8

HYMNS FOR THE DAY

	HL	HB	WB
Come, Christians, Join to Sing	191	131	333
O Lord, Our God, Most Earnestly (Ps.)	—	327	514
We Are One in the Spirit	—	—	619
"Take Up Thy Cross "	—	293	—
Stand Up, Stand Up for Jesus	265	349	—
Am I a Soldier of the Cross	—	353	—

ANTHEMS FOR THE DAY

Zech. 12:7-10   *Jerusalem, My Happy Home,* arr. Leland Sateren (Augsburg). SATB (E)

Gal. 3:23-29   *In Christ There Is No East or West* (HB, No. 479; WB, p. 435)

Luke 9:18-24   *He Comes to Us,* Jane Marshall (C. Fischer). SATB (M). Text by Albert Schweitzer

DCR

COLLECT FOR THE DAY

Leader of your people: free us from selfish preoccupations, that we might follow where you lead and serve one another with the same zeal that took our Lord to his cross. We pray in his name.   HTA

READINGS

I Kings 19:15-21   Elijah flees from Ahab to Mt. Horeb and is encountered there by God. He is instructed to bring down the king of Israel by first arranging for a military coup in Syria. Following the anointing of a new king of Israel, he is to anoint his own successor, Elisha.

Gal. 5:1, 13-18   Paul reaffirms the freedom of the believer and the use to which freedom is to be put. The believer walks by the Spirit and does not gratify the desires of the flesh. Freedom is both the gift and the goal of the Christian life.

Luke 9:51-62   Jesus sets "his face to go to Jerusalem." Three encounters are briefly described, each focusing on Jesus' goal and his single-mindedness in pursuing it.   TPS

PSALM FOR THE DAY: Psalm 16

HYMNS FOR THE DAY

	HL	HB	WB
God Our Father, You Our Maker	—	—	399
Through All the Changing Scenes of Life	83	—	—
God of the Prophets!	481	520	398
Make Me a Captive, Lord	247	308	—
Christ of the Upward Way	277	295	—
Lead On, O King Eternal	371	332	448
Alone You Journey Forth, O Lord	—	—	294

ANTHEMS FOR THE DAY

I Kings 19:15-21   *God of the Prophets,* arr. Paul Bunjes (Concordia). SATB, congregation, trumpet, and organ (M)

Gal. 5:1, 13-18   *Hope of the World* (HB, No. 291; WB, p. 423)

The Fruit of the Spirit Is Love, J. C. Geisler, arr. Karl Kroeger (Boosey & Hawkes). SATB, flute, and organ (M). Moravian Anthem

Prayer, Arthur Frackenpohl (Charter). Unison and organ (ME)

Luke 9:51-62   *Benedictus,* William Barnard (H. W. Gray). SATB with much Unison (E)

Turn Ye, Turn Ye, Charles Ives (Mercury). SATB (MD)   DCR

COLLECT FOR THE DAY

Eternal Love: how tenderly you nourish the people of your love. You have been a mother to Israel of old and in Christ you make us children of peace. As we follow his cross may we become sharers of peace with all; through Jesus Christ our Redeemer.   HTA

READINGS

Isa. 66:10-14   A song of joyful hope, centering on the city of Jerusalem. The imagery used by the poet in describing God's action in saving and blessing the people is female in gender: a mother who nurses, cares for, and comforts her children.

Gal. 6:11-18   The conclusion of Paul's letter restates the irrelevance of the law (circumcision) for believers.

Luke 10:1-9   Jesus appoints the Seventy and sends them out in pairs. He gives them some directions for their ministry.   TPS

PSALM FOR THE DAY: Psalm 66:1-12, 16-20

HYMNS FOR THE DAY

	HL	HB	WB
Come, You People, Rise and Sing	—	39	345
Come, Ye That Fear the Lord (Ps.)	—	296	—
In the Cross of Christ I Glory	154	195	437
God Is Working His Purpose Out	—	500	389
Spread, O Spread the Mighty Word	—	—	577
Sinner, Please Don't Let This Harvest Pass	—	—	570
Come, Labor On	366	287	—

ANTHEMS FOR THE DAY

Isa. 66:10-14   *Jerusalem the Golden* (HB, No. 428)

Jerusalem the Golden, arr. Henry Pfohl (Flammer). SATB (M)

Gal. 6:11-18   *O Save Us Then,* Daniel Pinkham (No. III from *Three Lenten Poems of Richard Crashaw,* E. C. Schirmer). SATB, string quartet and handbells (or celesta, harp, or piano) (MD)

Luke 10:1-9   *All Who Love and Serve Your City* (WB, p. 293)

O Jesus Christ, to You May Hymns Be Rising (WB, p. 509)

O Jesus Christ, to Thee May Hymns Be Rising, Daniel Moe (Augsburg). Extended anthem based on the hymn by Daniel Moe (tune: City of God). SATB (M)
                                                                    DCR

THE EIGHTH SUNDAY AFTER PENTECOST (C)

COLLECT FOR THE DAY

Unseen God: we have now seen you in the face of Jesus. Your glory has shone through Golgotha's gloom. Your word has come near in acts of neighbor love. Give us neighborly hearts, and eyes to see the needy around us; through our Lord and Savior, Jesus Christ.   HTA

READINGS

Deut. 30:9-14 The blessing of God culminates in the assurance that the word is "very near you."

Col. 1:15-20 Paul testifies to the nature of Jesus Christ, identifying him as a part of the Godhead.

Luke 10:25-37 In response to a lawyer's question about the good life, Jesus tells the parable of the good Samaritan.   TPS

PSALM FOR THE DAY: Psalm 69:30, 32-36

HYMNS FOR THE DAY	HL	HB	WB
Praise the Lord, His Glories Show	12	4	552
Thy Loving-kindness, Lord, Is Good and Free (Ps.)	—	393	—
O Jesus Christ, to You May Hymns Be Rising	—	—	509
Father, Whose Will Is Life and Good	—	309	368
"Am I My Brother's Keeper?"	—	—	295
The Light of God Is Falling	400	482	—
At the Name of Jesus	—	143	303

ANTHEMS FOR THE DAY

Deut. 30:9-14 *Be Strong in the Lord*, Thomas Matthews (Fitzsimons). SATB (M)

If Ye Love Me, Keep My Commandments, Thomas Tallis (E. C. Schirmer). (E)

God Bless the Master of This House, arr. R. Vaughan Williams (in *Folksongs of the Four Seasons*, Winter, No. 4, Oxford). Unison with descant (E)

Col. 1:15-20 *Praise*, Alex Rowley (Oxford). SATB (ME)

Lord Jesus Christ, Thou Prince of Peace, J. S. Bach (Concordia). SATB, violin and cello (organ) (E)

O Heavenly Father, Thomas Matthews (Fitzsimons). SATB (E)

Luke 10:25-37 *O Jesus Christ, to You May Hymns Be Rising* (WB, p. 509)

Where Charity and Love Prevail (WB, p. 641)   DCR

COLLECT FOR THE DAY

Heavenly Visitor: we await your appearance. As Abraham and Sarah received you beside their tent, Mary and Martha received you in their home. Do come among us. Help us to believe your promises and to treasure the mystery of your presence; through Jesus Christ our Lord.
                                                                    HTA

READINGS

Gen. 18:1-11   God appears to Abraham and Sarah and makes the promise of an heir. The nature and the subject of the appearance are surprising to Abraham; he responds well.

Col. 1:24-28   Paul identifies his own pursuit of the Christian way, making the contrast with his opponents plain, if not explicit. He signals something of the cost of the Christian ministry.

Luke 10:38-42   Jesus is a guest at the home of Martha and her sister Mary. In response to Martha's fretful complaint about Mary's behavior, Jesus tries to help Martha understand that there is need to sense the value of the time given.
                                                                    TPS

PSALM FOR THE DAY: Psalm 15

HYMNS FOR THE DAY

	HL	HB	WB
God Himself Is with Us	51	13	384
Blest Are the Pure in Heart (Ps.)	—	226	—
Fight the Good Fight	270	359	—
We Greet You, Sure Redeemer from All Strife	—	144	625
O How Shall We Receive You	—	—	506
Jesus, Thou Joy of Loving Hearts	354	215	—
Jesus, Priceless Treasure	—	414	442

ANTHEMS FOR THE DAY

Gen. 18:1-11   *Seek First the Kingdom of God*, W. A. Mozart, ed. J. G. Smith (Mark Foster). SATB (M)

Col. 1:24-28   *We Greet You, Sure Redeemer from All Strife* (HB, No. 144; WB, p. 625)

Thanks Be to God, Thomas Matthews (Fitzsimons). SATB (M)

Luke 10:38-42   *Quaerite primum regnum Dei* (Seek First the Kingdom of God), Samuel Scheidt (Hanssler). SSAT and ATBB (D)
                                                                    DCR

THE TENTH SUNDAY AFTER PENTECOST (C)

COLLECT FOR THE DAY

Patient God: we children of Abraham continually cry to you, and your own Son Jesus has given us words for our prayers. May your name be hallowed and your kingdom come, now and forever.   HTA

READINGS

Gen. 18:20-33   Abraham intercedes with Yahweh on behalf of Sodom. God will withhold judgment for the sake of a very small number of innocent people. Through Abraham's prayer of intercession, through a righteous remnant, the salvation of Sodom could be at hand. God wants to save, not punish: "By his knowledge shall the righteous one, my servant, make many to be accounted righteous" (Isa. 53:11).

Col. 2:8-15   Our life is to be found and lived fully in Christ, the Righteous One, the Remnant. We are buried with him in baptism and raised with him through faith. Having been dead in sin, we have been forgiven and made alive with him. Therefore, we must allow no other way of thinking to confuse us.

Luke 11:1-13   Jesus teaches his disciples to pray the Lord's Prayer. Have no doubt that God will hear your prayer and answer your need, even more than your friend would rise in the middle of the night to share his bread with you.
                                                                                            HFA

PSALM FOR THE DAY: Psalm 138

HYMNS FOR THE DAY	HL	HB	WB
How Firm a Foundation	283	369	425
Father Eternal, Ruler of Creation	—	486	362
All Who Love and Serve Your City	—	—	293
Our Father, Which Art in Heaven	—	—	547
To God My Earnest Voice I Raise	—	387	—
Lead Us, Heavenly Father, Lead Us	304	343	—

ANTHEMS FOR THE DAY

Gen. 18:20-33   *Sing, My Soul, His Wondrous Love,* Ned Rorem (Peters). SATB (D)

Col. 2:8-15   *They That Put Their Trust in the Lord,* Robin Orr (Oxford). SATTBB (D)

Luke 11:1-13   *Rejoice in the Lord Alway,* Henry Purcell (Novello). SATB with Alto, Tenor, Bass Solos (MD)   DL

COLLECT FOR THE DAY

Giver of all good gifts: teach us to treasure Christ and his grace above all earthly possessions. So may we cast our lot with life and not with death; for we pray in his own strong name.   HTA

READINGS

Eccl. 2:18-23 In a life that has lost touch with God and experiences only the emptiness of his absence, even a person's work becomes a tragedy—incapable of providing a source of meaning to life.

Col. 3:1-11 Christ is our life. We have died with him; therefore, we must put to death the practices of our old way of life and put on our new nature which is being renewed after the image of its creator.

Luke 12:13-21 Jesus tells the parable of the rich fool. The person who concentrates on building up possessions does not know a fulfilled life, for the person is not rich toward God.   HFA

PSALM FOR THE DAY: Psalm 49:1-12

HYMNS FOR THE DAY

	HL	HB	WB
O Day of Rest and Gladness	18	70	—
Work, for the Night Is Coming	—	297	—
(use "our" in last line to avoid sexism)			
Come, You Thankful People, Come	460	525	346
Father, in Your Mysterious Presence	256	384	363
(alternate tune: Welwyn)			
In Christ There Is No East or West	341	479	436

ANTHEMS FOR THE DAY

Col. 3:1-11 *St. Teresa's Bookmark*, Louis White (Belwin). SATB (D)

Christ, Who Alone Art Light of Day, Hugo Distler (Concordia). SAB, 2 violins, keyboard (MD). Duration: 9 minutes

Luke 12:13-21 *The Righteous Live*, Leo Sowerby (Oxford). SA(T)B (M)
                                                                     DL

COLLECT FOR THE DAY
Father of our faith: keep us constant in trusting you. May we ever be awake and alive for the new city and society you are creating among us; through Jesus Christ our Lord.   HTA

READINGS
II Kings 17:33-40   God's own people stubbornly refuse to fear him alone, but continue to fear and worship other gods.

Heb. 11:1-3, 8-12   By faith we know how things are with the world: created good by God. Through faith we have hope because of God's good promises. By faith we exercise our obedience, as disciples, to God's Word—even as did Abraham, looking forward to the promises of God. Therefore, be patient in all things.

Luke 12:35-40   Be ready for the coming of the Son of Man at an hour you do not expect. Stay awake. Church leaders, especially, are expected to be servants after the will of God and not act like ruthless bosses.   HFA

PSALM FOR THE DAY: Psalm 33

HYMNS FOR THE DAY	HL	HB	WB
Guide Me, O Thou Great Jehovah	104	339	409
The God of Abraham Praise	8	89	587
City of God	338	436	—
Glorious Things of You Are Spoken	339	434	379
Wake, Awake, for Night Is Flying	—	—	614
O Day of God, Draw Nigh	—	—	492
Come, Thou Long-expected Jesus	113	151	342

ANTHEMS FOR THE DAY

II Kings 17:33-40   *Cause Us, O Lord*, Ron Nelson (Boosey & Hawkes). SATB (M)

Heb. 11:1-3, 8-12   *Bright Canaan*, arr. Robert Shaw and Alice Parker (Lawson-Gould). SATB (M)

Bless the Lord, O My Soul, William Mathias (Oxford). SATB (D)

Luke 12:35-40   *Blessed Is the Man*, Arcangelo Corelli, ed. B. J. Stone (Boston Music). SATB and SAB (ME)   DL

COLLECT FOR THE DAY

Loving Lord: your peace comes among us sometimes as strife and suffering. So it was for our Lord Jesus. Keep us close to him and in communion with all his saints. In his name we pray.   HTA

READINGS

Jer. 38:1b-13 Jeremiah is imprisoned in a cistern because he counseled surrender and life to Jerusalem's defenders during the Babylonian siege. His counsel is given at a time when the Babylonian army had to retreat from their siege positions because of the approach of an Egyptian military force. During the resultant period of false optimism by the Jerusalem inhabitants, Jeremiah's counsel appears false, unreasonable, and even sounds like treason. The prophetic word does not always find easy acceptance and frequently is followed by persecution.

Heb. 12:1-6 Since our faith is supported by the faith of so many great martyrs who have gone before us, let us then run the race set before us with perseverance. Keep the faith by keeping your life focused upon Jesus.

Luke 12:49-53 Jesus did not come to bring peace on earth, but division. The cost of discipleship may even divide families.   HFA

PSALM FOR THE DAY: Psalm 82

HYMNS FOR THE DAY	HL	HB	WB
God Has Spoken—by His Prophets	—	—	382
Lord, from the Depths to You I Cry	240	277	459
Awake, My Soul, Stretch Every Nerve	278	346	—
For All the Saints	429	425	369
O God of Every Nation	—	—	498
Judge Eternal, Throned in Splendor	417	517	447

ANTHEMS FOR THE DAY

Jer. 38:1b-13 *Jesus Christ, Our Blessed Savior*, Johann Walter and Paul Bunjes (see LH, p. 18). (M) (In spelling, do not confuse Johann Walter with Johann Gottfried Walther.) May be performed with unison, two-part or four-part choir. Good for Holy Communion. (ME)

Heb. 12:1-6 *Christ, to Thee Be Glory*, Heinrich Schütz (Mercury). SATB (M)

Luke 12:49-53 *Blest Spirit, One with God*, arr. Adolf Strube (see SAB, p. 54). (ME)

Descend, O Spirit, Purging Flame (WB, p. 353). (E)   DL

COLLECT FOR THE DAY

Lord of all: your glory is a gift to all peoples, and the door to your kingdom is open to the last and the least of all. Lead us in the narrow way and save us at the last; through Jesus Christ our Lord.   HTA

READINGS

Isa. 66:18-23   God is working to bring about the new heavens and the new earth—when everyone shall worship him. Even the heathen are called into close fellowship with God—into his service. God is to send his servants in mission to the world to the end that all may know him as the one, true, God.

Heb. 12:7-13   Even though God disciplines us, we need to know that he does it as a loving father. Therefore, strengthen your weaknesses and when you are tired, be energetic so that you might walk according to the will of God.

Luke 13:22-30   The door is narrow; not all will be able to enter and sit at table in the kingdom of God. Some of the last will be first and some of the first, last.   HFA

PSALM FOR THE DAY: Psalm 117

HYMNS FOR THE DAY	HL	HB	WB
Father, We Praise You	24	43	365
From All That Dwell Below the Skies	388	33	373
As Men of Old Their Firstfruits Brought	—	—	301
Whate'er Our God Ordains Is Right	291	366	633
One Table Spread	—	—	541
All People That on Earth Do Dwell	1	24	288

ANTHEMS FOR THE DAY

Isa. 66:18-23   *O for a Thousand Tongues* (WB, p. 493). (E)

Laudate Dominum, W. A. Mozart, ed. George Lynn (Presser). SATB and Soprano Solo. (MD) Sing it in Latin and print the English text in the bulletin

Heb. 12:7-13   *Sing a Song of Joy*, Robert J. Powell (Augsburg). Two-part choir (ME)

Luke 13:22-30   *At the Name of Jesus* (WB, p. 303). Unison (E). Or R. Vaughan Williams' own anthem setting (Oxford). SATB (MD)

Feed My Lambs, Natalie Sleeth (C. Fischer). Unison, two treble instruments, keyboard. (E)   DL

COLLECT FOR THE DAY

Lord of the lowly: you invite to your feast those who have always been left out. Give to us who hear Christ's call and join his covenant hospitable hearts to welcome the humble; through the same Jesus Christ our Lord.   HTA

READINGS

Prov. 22:1-9 Living a rich life in the service of the Lord is far better than amassing rich possessions. Share your bread with the poor.

Heb. 12:18-24 Jesus is the mediator of the new covenant. He is the one to whom you have come, in whom you live as a part of the new order of things.

Luke 14:1, 7-14 Be sure you don't get caught up playing the game of who is best or more important. Be humble, taking the seat of least honor. Do things for those who cannot repay your kindness.   HFA

PSALM FOR THE DAY: Psalm 112

HYMNS FOR THE DAY	HL	HB	WB
Father, We Praise You	24	43	365
At the Name of Jesus	—	143	303
O Holy City, Seen of John	409	508	505
"Am I My Brother's Keeper?"	—	—	295
Where Cross the Crowded Ways	410	507	642

ANTHEMS FOR THE DAY

Prov. 22:1-9 *In Christ There Is No East or West* (WB, p. 436). (E)

Heb. 12:18-24 *All Ye Servants of the Lord*, Robert Elmore (Galaxy). SATB (MD)

Luke 14:1, 7-14 *Come, Risen Lord*, Leo Sowerby (Belwin). Best for Holy Communion. SATB or Unison with descant (ME)

Jubilate Deo in C, Benjamin Britten (Oxford). SATB (MD)

Jubilate Deo, Richard Dirksen (Lawson-Gould). 2-Part (ME)   DL

THE SIXTEENTH SUNDAY AFTER PENTECOST (C)

COLLECT FOR THE DAY

Lord of wisdom: teach us to fear you and to trust you. May the cross of Christ turn our fear into faith and our service into celebration; through Jesus Christ our Lord. HTA

READINGS

Prov. 9:8-12   The fear of the Lord is the beginning of wisdom. Obedience to his will is the source of life.

Philemon 8-17   Paul appeals to the church to accept Onesimus back into their midst, not as a slave, but as a brother in Jesus Christ.

Luke 14:25-33   Whoever does not renounce all that he has cannot be Christ's disciple. Be sure first to count the cost of discipleship.   HFA

PSALM FOR THE DAY: Psalm 10:12-14, 16-18

HYMNS FOR THE DAY	HL	HB	WB
Our God, Our Help in Ages Past	77	111	549
Come, Ye That Fear the Lord (tune: Ellacombe)	—	296	—
Make Me a Captive, Lord	247	308	—
"Take Up Thy Cross"	—	293	—
Alone You Journey Forth, O Lord	—	—	294
The Son of God Goes Forth to War	271	354	—

ANTHEMS FOR THE DAY

Prov. 9:8-12   *O Lord, Give Thy Holy Spirit*, Thomas Tallis (Belwin). SATB (MD)

Philemon 8-17   *I Have Preached Righteousness*, Daniel Pinkham (Peters). SATB (D)

Luke 14: 25-33   *Jesus So Lowly*, Harold Friedell (Belwin). SATB (M)

If Thou but Suffer God to Guide Thee, arr. Friedrich Zipp (see SAB, p. 62). (ME)   DL

COLLECT FOR THE DAY

Seeker of the lost: even you can repent of your anger at your people.
Help us to repent of our sin against you and fill us with faith and love in
Christ Jesus our Lord.   HTA

READINGS

Ex. 32:7-14 After the people of Israel turn from the Lord and make the
molten calf, God prepares to destroy them. Moses intercedes for them,
appealing to God on the basis of his promises, and God repents.

I Tim. 1:12-17 Jesus Christ came into the world to save sinners—even Paul
the foremost of sinners. We need to know that his mercy is available to us.
Receiving this mercy gives us the assurance of the truth, certainty, and
validity of the gospel.

Luke 15:1-32 Jesus tells the parable of the prodigal son. God's love to a
returning sinner knows no bounds. Let us not be jealous of this sharing of
love, but join the celebration at each restoration of a person to the
fellowship.   HFA

PSALM FOR THE DAY: Psalm 51:1-17

HYMNS FOR THE DAY	HL	HB	WB
O Worship the King	2	26	533
There's a Wideness in God's Mercy	93	110	601
Amazing Grace! How Sweet the Sound	—	275	296
God of Compassion, in Mercy Befriend Us	290	122	392
Deck Yourself, My Soul	—	—	351
When I Survey the Wondrous Cross	152	198	635

ANTHEMS FOR THE DAY

Ex. 32:7-14 *O God, Wherefore Art Thou Absent from Us*, William Child (A.
Broude). SATB (MD)

I Tim. 1:12-17 *Immortal, Invisible*, Eric Thiman (Novello). SATB (MD)

Luke 15:1-32 *Amazing Grace*, arr. Robert Shaw and Alice Parker
(Lawson-Gould). SATB and Tenor Solo (M)   DL

THE EIGHTEENTH SUNDAY AFTER PENTECOST (C)

COLLECT FOR THE DAY

God of rulers, pastors, and all ordinary folk: rule over us as we pray for one another and also share such material possessions as you have entrusted to us; through Jesus Christ our only Lord.   HTA

READINGS

Amos 8:4-8 The prophet unleashes a searing indictment of the greed and avarice of the rich, merchant class of his day.

I Tim. 2:1-8 Paul counsels his young friend and assistant, Timothy, concerning matters of church order. He advises that prayers be offered in the Christian assembly for all, especially "kings and others in authority," as a sign of God's ultimate authority over all.

Luke 16:1-13 Jesus tells a curious parable about a crafty servant who uses the prerogatives of his position to gain for himself friends, as insurance against poverty after his imminent forced retirement. The parable is then interpreted as a warning against the love of money.   HTA

PSALM FOR THE DAY: Psalm 113

HYMNS FOR THE DAY	HL	HB	WB
God, the Lord, a King Remaineth	61	90	403
Praise God, Ye Servants of the Lord (Ps.)	—	19	—
God of Pity, God of Grace	252	—	—
O God of Earth and Altar	419	511	497
A Mighty Fortress	266	91	274

ANTHEMS FOR THE DAY

I Tim. 2:1-8 *O Pray for the Peace of Jerusalem*, Herbert Howells (Oxford). SATB (D)

Luke 16:1-13 *O Come, Ye Servants of the Lord*, Christopher Tye (Banks Music). SATB (MD)   DL

COLLECT FOR THE DAY

King of kings and Lord of lords: you have not only given us Moses and the prophets, but you have brought back Jesus from the dead, who calls us to faith and love, patience and gentleness. Help us so to live this life in generosity that we shall not be ashamed in the end; through Jesus Christ our Lord.   HTA

READINGS

Amos 6:1, 4-7   Those who live in ease and luxury in Zion are condemned to be the first to taste the hardship and poverty of exile.

I Tim. 6:11-16   We are urged to shun richness and the love of money so that we can work toward righteousness, godliness, faith, love, steadfastness, and gentleness.

Luke 16:19-31   The parable of the rich man and Lazarus indicates God's favor and compassion for the poor and points to the deafness of the rich to hear and obey the prophetic word. Impiety and lovelessness will not be rewarded by God.   HFA

PSALM FOR THE DAY: Psalm 146

HYMNS FOR THE DAY	HL	HB	WB
O Spirit of the Living God	207	242	528
A Charge to Keep I Have	—	301	—
Fight the Good Fight	—	359	—
That Easter Day with Joy Was Bright	—	—	581
Open Now the Gates of Beauty	—	40	544

ANTHEMS FOR THE DAY

I Tim. 6:11-16   *Fight the Good Fight,* John Gardner (No. 5 of *Five Hymns in Popular Style,* Oxford). Also in SSA, using accompaniment from SATB score. (D)

Luke 16:19-31   *Jesus So Lowly,* Harold Friedell (Belwin). SATB (MD)

When My Last Hour Has Come, Adam Gumpeltzhaimer (see I Mot, p. 74). SATB (MD)   DL

THE TWENTIETH SUNDAY AFTER PENTECOST (C)

COLLECT FOR THE DAY

Faithful God: help us to live fruitfully by what little faith is in us, always being grateful for your promises of help in time of hardship; through our Savior, Christ Jesus, who has abolished death. HTA

READINGS

Hab. 1:1-3; 2:1-4 In the midst of violence, destruction, and trouble the righteous person shall live by faith. Securities of the world which can be destroyed easily by strife and contention are not the source of life.

II Tim. 1:3-12 Paul, remembering Timothy's sincere faith, reminds him of God's gift of a spirit of power and love and self-control. Paul calls upon him to take his share of suffering for this gospel: that God saved and called us, not because of our works, but because of his purpose in Jesus Christ, in whom he has conquered death and brought life and immortality to light.

Luke 17:5-10 Christ reminds us that even the tiniest amount of faith is able to accomplish great things. Therefore we need not be presumptuous in asking the Lord to increase our faith nor in expecting thanks for doing that which we have been commanded to do. HFA

PSALM FOR THE DAY: Psalm 95:1-7

HYMNS FOR THE DAY	HL	HB	WB
God Is Working His Purpose Out	—	500	389
Faith of Our (Mothers), see II Tim. 1:5	267	348	361
I'm Not Ashamed to Own My Lord	—	292	—
If You Will Only Let God Guide You	105	344	431
Give to the Winds Your Fears	294	364	377

ANTHEMS FOR THE DAY

Hab. 1:1-3; 2:1-4 *O Vos Omnes*, Juan Esquivel, ed. M. Martens (Walton). SATB (D)

De Profundis, W. A. Mozart (see I Mot, p. 38). SATB (MD)

II Tim. 1:3-12 *He That Is Down Need Fear No Fall*, R. Vaughan Williams (Oxford). Unison, Soprano or Tenor (M)

Luke 17:5-10 *O Lord, Increase Our Faith*, Orlando Gibbons (see I Mot, p. 70). SATB (MD) DL

COLLECT FOR THE DAY

Healing and helping God: have pity on us who are so reluctant to believe in your faithfulness toward us. Remind us of Jesus' mighty resurrection as we remember our own washing in baptism, and evermore lift our hearts to you in praise and thanksgiving; through the same Jesus Christ our Lord.   HTA

READINGS

II Kings 5:9-17 Naaman's leprosy is healed through Elisha the prophet, emphasizing the healing as a free and gracious act of God's creative word. Naaman's faith is, indeed, tested as to whether or not he will trust in the word of the Lord alone, without asking for other signs or insisting on some preconceived approach to himself by God or the prophet.

II Tim. 2:8-13 Whatever our actions, Jesus Christ remains faithful.

Luke 17:11-19 Jesus cleanses ten lepers. Only one, a foreigner, makes a response of praise and thanksgiving. That one's faith has made him whole. The very ones we would expect to make such a response do not. When Jesus comes, will he find faith where one would expect?   HFA

PSALM FOR THE DAY: Psalm 98:1-4

HYMNS FOR THE DAY	HL	HB	WB
Praise, My Soul, the King of Heaven	14	31	551
When We Are Tempted to Deny Your Son	—	—	640
At Even, When the Sun Was Set	43	55	—
Father, Whose Will Is Life and Good	—	309	368
Thine Arm, O Lord	—	179	—
Sing Praise to God	—	15	568

ANTHEMS FOR THE DAY

II Kings 5:9-17 *Wash Me Thoroughly*, Samuel Sebastian Wesley (Novello). SATB (MD)

II Tim. 2:8-13 *O Taste and See*, R. Vaughan Williams (see I Mot, p. 11). SATB and Soprano Solo, or divide soprano section (MD)

Jesu, Dulcis Memoria, Paul Drayton (Oxford). SSATTB. This is very difficult, but worth the effort (D)

Luke 17:11-19 *O King Enthroned on High*, Joseph Goodman (Beekman). SATB (MD)   DL

COLLECT FOR THE DAY

God of justice: you have mercifully given your waiting people prophets and apostles to assure them of your faithfulness to your word. Now let your justice be done through us and among us by the power of Jesus Christ, judge of the living and the dead.   HTA

READINGS

Ex. 17:8-13 In a tense moment in the wilderness, Israel is given a sign of God's eternal faithfulness as Moses presides over a battle, Aaron and Hur supporting him.

II Tim. 3:14 to 4:2 Paul provides Timothy with the assurance of his "apostolic succession" by reminding him of his teachers' fidelity to Holy Scripture, and in turn exhorts Timothy to be a faithful and patient teacher.

Luke 18:1-8 Jesus assures us of God's final faithfulness in seeing justice done, but then turns the tables on us by asking if we will finally be as faithful.   HTA

PSALM FOR THE DAY: Psalm 121

HYMNS FOR THE DAY	HL	HB	WB
O God, Our Faithful God	—	—	500
Our God, Our Help in Ages Past	77	111	549
I to the Hills Will Lift My Eyes (Ps.)	—	377	430
Unto the Hills (Ps.)	96	—	—
Lord, Thy Word Abideth	—	252	—
O Word of God Incarnate	215	251	532
God Is Working His Purpose Out	—	500	389

ANTHEMS FOR THE DAY

Ex. 17:8-13 *Holy Father, Pure and Gracious*, M. Thomas Cousins (Brodt). SATB (ME)

II Tim. 3:14 to 4:2 *I Have Preached Righteousness*, Daniel Pinkham (Peters). SATB (D)   DL

COLLECT FOR THE DAY
Merciful God: forgive us when we are proud in our piety and praying; and when we are overwhelmed by misery and need, remind us of the great compassion shown for us in Jesus Christ, your Son, who was a friend of tax collectors and sinners.   HTA

READINGS
Deut. 10:16-22   Bring your heart in line with the love of the Lord your God. Fear him. Serve him.

II Tim. 4:6-8, 16-18   Paul acknowledges God's faithfulness to him, giving him strength.

Luke 18:9-14   God is the one who justifies us.   HFA

PSALM FOR THE DAY: Psalm 34:1-2, 15-22

HYMNS FOR THE DAY	HL	HB	WB
Praise We Our Maker	—	—	558
God of Our Fathers	414	515	394
God of Our Life	88	108	395
The Lord I Will at All Times Bless (Ps.)	—	412	—
The Lord Will Come and Not Be Slow	185	230	—
There's a Wideness in God's Mercy	93	110	601

ANTHEMS FOR THE DAY

Deut. 10:16-22   *Praise to the Lord,* Hugo Distler (see I Mot, p. 5). SATB (MD)

II Tim. 4:6-8, 16-18   *Who Shall Abide,* Walter Pelz (Augsburg). SAB with flute and guitar (M)

Luke 18:9-14   *Let Thy Merciful Ears, O Lord,* Thomas Weelkes (Oxford). SATB (M)

O God, Be Merciful, Christopher Tye (Oxford). SATB (M)   DL

THE TWENTY-FOURTH SUNDAY AFTER PENTECOST (C)

COLLECT FOR THE DAY

God: we call to you sure that your coming will bring joy and forgiveness. Visit us, sinners as we are, with your salvation, that we might be reconciled one with another; through Jesus Christ our Lord.   HTA

READINGS

Ex. 34:5-9   The Lord, in preparation for renewing his covenant with his people, announces his love, faithfulness, and forgiveness to Moses.

II Thess. 1:11 to 2:2   Paul's prayer for the Thessalonians is that God may make them worthy of his call. He is the one who authenticates and makes effective our good intentions and works of faith.

Luke 19:1-10   Jesus enters Jericho and invites himself to the home of the rich chief tax collector, Zacchaeus. Zacchaeus responds joyfully, offering half of his possessions to the poor. Salvation is operable in the midst of life and is recognized in sincere faith, demonstrated commitment and obedience, and concern for the poor.   HFA

PSALM FOR THE DAY: Psalm 145

HYMNS FOR THE DAY	HL	HB	WB
God of Compassion, in Mercy Befriend Us	290	122	392
Jesus Calls Us (tune: Stuttgart)	223	269	439
Come, Let Us to the Lord Our God	—	125	—
Sinner, Please Don't Let This Harvest Pass	—	—	570
Sinners Jesus Will Receive (tune: Dix)	227	—	—
O Lord, You Are Our God and King	—	5	517

ANTHEMS FOR THE DAY

Ex. 34:5-9   *My Heart Is Full Today*, Richard Proulx (Augsburg). 2-Part or Unison, triangle, tambourine, handbells or glockenspiel and harpsichord or organ (M)

Luke 19:1-10   *He Hath Done All Things Well*, Jan Bender (see I Mot, p. 20). SATB (M)

Sing, My Soul, His Wondrous Love, Ned Rorem (Peters). SATB (MD)   DL

COLLECT FOR THE DAY

God of the living: the spirits of all stand before you. With kings and priests, mothers in Israel and sisters in faith, we give you glory and blessing; through Jesus Christ the Lord, who is the Resurrection and the Life.

HTA

READINGS

I Chron. 29:10-13   King David offers a prayer of praise and adoration to the Lord, acknowledging that all things belong to the Lord.

II Thess. 2:16 to 3:5   God loves us. Through his grace our hearts are comforted and we are given hope. He is the one who guides our hearts into every good work and word and directs them to his love and Christ's steadfastness.

Luke 20:27-38   Jesus affirms the resurrection of the dead on the basis of God not being God of the dead, but God of the living.

HFA

PSALM FOR THE DAY: Psalm 148

HYMNS FOR THE DAY

	HL	HB	WB
Praise to the Lord, the Almighty	6	1	557
Hail to the Lord's Anointed	111	146	—
Blessing and Honor and Glory and Power	196	137	311
Praise the Lord! You Heavens, Adore Him (Ps.)	10	3	554
If You Will Only Let God Guide You	105	344	431
God of the Living, in Whose Eyes	—	—	397
O Lord of Life, Where'er They Be	—	—	513

ANTHEMS FOR THE DAY

I Chron. 29:10-13   *The Trumpeters and the Singers Were as One,* Thomas Matthews (Fitzsimons). SATB (M)

II Thess. 2:16 to 3:5   *If Ye Love Me,* Thomas Tallis (Oxford). SATB (MD)

Luke 20:27-38   *Sing Praise to Our Glorious Lord,* Heinrich Schütz (see I Mot, p. 15). SATB (MD)

DL

THE TWENTY-SIXTH SUNDAY AFTER PENTECOST (C)

COLLECT FOR THE DAY

Active and eternal God: you await us at the end of the day, at the end of our lives, and at the end of the world. May we ever persevere and never weary in well doing; through Jesus our Lord, the First and the Last, the Beginning and the End.   HTA

READINGS

Mal. 3:16 to 4:2   The prophet anticipates the great day of the Lord's coming to his temple (3:1), the rising of the "sun of righteousness" when perseverance in the fear of the Lord will be its own reward.

II Thess. 3:6-13   Some advice: Persevere . . . persist "night and day," avoiding idlers, never wearying in well-doing.

Luke 21:5-19   Whoever perseveres ("endures") to the end will be saved. That outlasts and outranks even the temple, to which the Lord came that day (cf. Mal.3:1) and whose destruction he anticipated, in more ways than one.   HTA

PSALM FOR THE DAY: Psalm 98:1-3

HYMNS FOR THE DAY

	HL	HB	WB
Come to Us, Mighty King	52	244	343
Hark! the Herald Angels Sing (stanza 3)	117	163	411
Christ, Whose Glory Fills the Skies	26	47	332
Work, for the Night Is Coming	—	297	—
Go, Labor On	376	283	—
Come, Labor On	366	287	—
He Is the Way	—	—	413

ANTHEMS FOR THE DAY

He That Shall Endure to the End, Mendelssohn (from *Elijah*, any edition)

Awake, Our Souls, George Brandon (Concordia). 2-Part Mixed (E)

Forth in Thy Name, O Lord, My Daily Labor to Pursue, David H. Williams (Shawnee). SATB (ME)

E'en So, Lord Jesus, Quickly Come, Paul Manz (Concordia). SATB (MD)

Come, My Way, My Truth, My Life, Philip Dietterich (H. W. Gray). SATB (ME)

O Mighty God, Our Lord, Heinrich Schütz (Mercury). 2-Part Mixed (M)
                                                                              LLH

COLLECT FOR THE DAY

Lord of all majesty and might, Monarch of all the nations: you have made yourself visible in Jesus of Nazareth, who was pushed out of the world onto a cross. Unite us to him, our head, and make of us repentant ministers of peace.   HTA

READINGS

II Sam. 5:1-4 David is anointed King of the Jews, a title later to adorn Christ's cross. From the first, therefore, that kingship was described as shepherding. Thus does Jesus describe himself as "the good shepherd" (John 10:14).

Col. 1:11-20 No title is too splendid for Christ in this early Christian hymn (vs.15-20). But the highest moment of his ministry is "making peace by the blood of the cross."

Luke 23:35-43 The religious and political establishments make fun of Jesus on his cross: Is he king? . . . Is he Christ? How he threatened them! It takes a condemned criminal, on another cross, to confess Jesus' kingly power. How he comforted him: "Today . . . Paradise!"   HTA

PSALM FOR THE DAY: Psalm 98:4-9

HYMNS FOR THE DAY	HL	HB	WB
O Worship the King	2	26	533
The King of Love My Shepherd Is	99	106	590
Immortal, Invisible, God Only Wise	66	85	433
From Shepherding of Stars	—	—	374
O Splendor of God's Glory Bright	32	46	529
Throned Upon the Awful Tree	—	197	605
Crown Him with Many Crowns	190	213	349

ANTHEMS FOR THE DAY

In Quiet Joy, Michael McCabe (Sacred Music). 2-Part (ME). Text from Psalm 98

My Eternal King, Jane Marshall (C. Fischer). SATB (M)

Cantique de Jean Racine, Gabriel Fauré (Broude Br.). SATB (M)

The Glory of Our King (folk tune: Morning Song), arr. Carlton Young (in *Ecumenical Praise*, No. 117, Hope). SATB or Unison (E)   LLH

COLLECT FOR THE DAY
God of east and west, God of bread and wine: all the earth sings to you
and rejoices to gather around the table you spread. Your kingdom come,
Lord, and your will be done, on earth as it is in heaven.　　HTA

READINGS
I Chron. 16:23-34　God's salvation is to be declared among all people.

Acts 2:42-47　The fellowship of the early church expressed community by
holding all possessions in common and redistributing them according to a
person's need, a sure indication of the presence of the messianic kingdom.

Matt. 8:5-13　In response to the centurion's faith, Jesus heals his servant.
Even Gentiles and people who feel unworthy may demonstrate faith and
will sit at table in the kingdom of God.　　HFA

PSALM FOR THE DAY: Psalm 34

HYMNS FOR THE DAY	HL	HB	WB
A Mighty Fortress	266	91	274, 276
How Dear to Me, O Lord of Hosts	—	440	—
Father, We Thank You that You Planted	—	—	366
One Table Spread	—	—	541
Jesus, Priceless Treasure	—	414	442
The Church's One Foundation (tune: St. Theodulph)	333	437	582

ANTHEMS FOR THE DAY

I Come with Joy, arr. Austin Lovelace (in *Ecumenical Praise*, No. 84, Hope)

For the Bread, V. Earle Copes (Abingdon). SATB (E)

Draw Us in the Spirit's Tether, Harold Friedell (H. W. Gray). SATB (E)

Here, O Lord, Thy Servants Gather, Richard Peek (Choristers Guild). Organ,
piano, and tam-tam accompaniment. SATB (E)

The Living Bread, Leland Sateren (Augsburg). SATB (M)

O Magnify the Lord with Me, arr. George Lynn (Presser). SATB (MD)

O Taste and See, R. Vaughan Williams (Oxford). SSA with Tenor or Soprano
Solo; SATB version available (ME)　　LLH

INDEX OF SCRIPTURE LESSONS

These readings are in the Lectionary for the Christian Year, pp. 165-175 of *The Worshipbook—Services and Hymns* (The Westminster Press, 1972; 2d printing, 1973).

I Samuel
3:1-10   Epiphany II, B
26:6-12   Epiphany VII, C

II Samuel
5:1-4   Epiphany IX, C
            Pentecost XXVII, C
5:1-5   Lent IV, A
7:8-16   Advent IV, B
7:18-22   Pentecost IX, A
12:1-7a   Pentecost IV, C

I Kings
3:5-12   Pentecost X, A
8:41-43   Pentecost II, C
17:8-16   Pentecost XXV, B
17:17-24   Pentecost III, C
19:4-8   Pentecost XII, B
19:9-16   Pentecost XII, A
19:15-21   Pentecost VI, C

II Kings
4:8-16   Pentecost VI, A
4:42-44   Pentecost X, B
5:9-17   Pentecost XXI, C
17:33-40   Pentecost XII, C

I Chronicles
16:23-34   World Communion,
            C
29:10-13   Pentecost XXV, C

II Chronicles
36:14-21   Lent IV, B

Ezra
(none)

Nehemiah
8:1-3, 5-6,   Epiphany III, C
  8-10

Esther
(none)

Job
7:1-7   Epiphany V, B
23:1-7   Epiphany VIII, C
            Pentecost XXVIII, C
28:20-28   Christmas II, C
38:1-11   Pentecost V, B

Psalms
(See *Psalter Index,* below)

Proverbs
3:13-18   Pentecost XXI, B
8:22-31   Christmas II, A
            Pentecost I (Trinity
              Sunday), C
9:1-6   Pentecost XIII, B
9:8-12   Pentecost XVI, C
22:1-9   Pentecost XV, C
31:10-13,   Pentecost XXVI, A
  19-20, 30-31

Ecclesiastes
2:18-23   Pentecost XI, C
3:1-9, 14-17 Christmas I, A
3:1-13   New Year's Eve or
              Day, B

Song of Solomon
3:1-5   Pentecost XXV, A

Isaiah
2:1-5   Advent I, A
5:1-7   Pentecost XX, A
6:1-8   Epiphany V, C
            Pentecost I (Trinity
              Sunday), B
7:10-15   Advent IV, A
9:1-4   Epiphany III, A
9:2, 6-7   Advent II, C
            Christmas Day, A
11:1-9   Christian Unity, A
11:1-10   Advent II, A
22:19-23   Pentecost XIV, A
25:6-9   Easter Day, B
            Pentecost XXI, A
            World Communion,
              B
26:1-8   Day of Civic or Na-
              tional Signifi-
              cance, B
35:1-6, 10 Advent III, A
35:3-10   Christian Unity, B
35:4-7   Pentecost XVI, B
40:1-5, 9-11 Advent II, B
42:1-7   Epiphany I, A
42:1-9   Holy Week—Tues-
              day, A,B,C

43:16-21	Lent V, C	20:7-9	Pentecost XV, A
43:18-25	Epiphany VII, B	20:10-13	Pentecost V, A
45:1-6	Pentecost XXII, A	23:1-6	Pentecost IX, B
45:18-22	Christmas I, C	31:7-9	Pentecost XXIII, B
49:1-10	New Year's Eve or Day, C	31:10-13	Christmas I, B
		31:31-34	Lent V, B
49:3-6	Epiphany II, A	33:14-16	Advent I, C
49:14-18	Epiphany VIII, A Pentecost XXVIII, A	38:1b-13	Pentecost XIII, C
49:18-23	World Communion, A	*Lamentations*	
		1:7-12	Good Friday, B
50:4-7	Passion (Palm) Sunday, A	*Ezekiel*	
50:4-9	Pentecost XVII, B	2:1-5	Pentecost VII, B
50:4-10	Holy Week—Monday, A,B,C	17:22-24	Pentecost IV, B
		18:25-29	Pentecost XIX, A
52:6-10	Christmas Day, C	33:7-9	Pentecost XVI, A
52:7-10	Christmas Eve, B	34:11-17	Epiphany IX, A Pentecost XXVII, A
52:13 to 53:12	Holy Week—Wednesday, A,B,C	37:1-4	Pentecost I (Trinity Sunday), A
	Good Friday, A	37:11-14	Lent V, A
53:10-12	Pentecost XXII, B	*Daniel*	
55:1-3	Pentecost XI, A	7:13-14	Epiphany IX, B
55:1-5	Christian Unity, C		Pentecost XXVII, B
55:6-11	Pentecost XVIII, A	9:3-10	Day of Civic or National Significance, C
55:10-13	Pentecost VIII, A		
56:1-7	Pentecost XIII, A		
58:3-12	Ash Wednesday, B	12:1-4	Pentecost XXVI, B
58:7-10	Epiphany V, A		
59:14-20	Passion (Palm) Sunday, C	*Hosea*	
		2:14-20	Epiphany VIII, B Pentecost XXVIII, B
60:1-5	Christmas II, B	6:1-6	Good Friday, C
60:1-6	Epiphany, A,B,C		Pentecost III, A
61:1-4	Epiphany I, B		
61:1-4, 8-11	Advent III, B	*Joel*	
61:10-11	Thanksgiving Day, A	2:12-18	Ash Wednesday, A
62:1-4	Christmas Eve, A	2:28-32	Pentecost (Whitsunday), B
62:2-5	Epiphany II, C		
62:6-12	Christmas Day, B		
63:16 to 64:4	Advent I, B	*Amos*	
65:17-25	Pentecost (Whitsunday), C	6:1, 4-7	Pentecost XIX, C
		7:12-17	Pentecost VIII, B
66:10-14	Pentecost VII, C	8:4-8	Pentecost XVIII, C
66:18-23	Pentecost XIV, C		
		Obadiah	
Jeremiah		(none)	
1:4-10	Epiphany IV, C		
11:18-20	Pentecost XVIII, B	*Jonah*	
17:5-8	Epiphany VI, C	3:1-5, 10	Epiphany III, B

3:21-28	Pentecost II, A
	Reformation Sunday, A
4:13-25	Pentecost III, A
5:1-5	Lent III, A
5:6-11	Holy Week — Wednesday, A,B,C
	Pentecost IV, A
5:12-15	Pentecost V, A
5:12-19	Lent I, A
6:1-11	Pentecost VI, A
8:6-11	Lent V, A
	Pentecost VII, A
8:12-17	Pentecost I (Trinity Sunday), B
	Pentecost VIII, A
8:18-25	Pentecost IX, A
8:26-30	Pentecost X, A
8:31-39	Lent II, B
	Pentecost XI, A
9:1-5	Pentecost XII, A
10:8-13	Lent I, C
11:13-16, 29-32	Pentecost XIII, A
11:33-36	Pentecost XIV, A
11:33 to 12:2	Christmas I, C
12:1-7	Pentecost XV, A
13:1-8	Day of Civic or National Significance, A
13:8-10	Pentecost XVI, A
13:11-14	Advent I, A
14:5-9	Pentecost XVII, A
15:4-9	Advent II, A
16:25-27	Advent IV, B

I Corinthians

1:1-9	Epiphany II, A
1:3-9	Advent I, B
1:10-17	Epiphany III, A
1:18-25	Christmas II, C
1:22-25	Lent III, B
1:26-31	Epiphany IV, A
2:1-5	Epiphany V, A
2:6-10	Epiphany VI, A
3:1-11	Christian Unity, B
3:16-23	Epiphany VII, A
4:1-5	Epiphany VIII, A
	Pentecost XXVIII, A
5:6-8	Maundy Thursday, C
6:12-20	Epiphany II, B

7:29-31	Epiphany III, B
7:32-35	Epiphany IV, B
9:16-19, 22-23	Epiphany V, B
9:19-27	Ash Wednesday, C
10:1-12	Lent III, C
10:31 to 11:1	Epiphany VI, B
11:23-32	Maundy Thursday, A
12:4-11	Epiphany II, C
12:4-13	Pentecost (Whitsunday), A
12:12-30	Epiphany III, C
13:1-13	Epiphany IV, C
15:1-11	Epiphany V, C
15:12-20	Epiphany VI, C
15:20-26	Easter Day, C
15:20-28	Epiphany IX, A
	Pentecost XXVII, A
15:42-50	Epiphany VII, C
15:54-58	Epiphany VIII, C
	Pentecost XXVIII, C

II Corinthians

1:18-22	Epiphany VII, B
3:17 to 4:2	Epiphany VIII, B
	Pentecost XXVIII, B
4:6-11	Pentecost II, B
4:13 to 5:1	Pentecost III, B
5:6-10	Pentecost IV, B
5:16-21	Lent IV, C
	Pentecost V, B
	Reformation Sunday, B
5:20 to 6:2	Ash Wednesday, A
8:7-15	Pentecost VI, B
9:6-15	Thanksgiving Day, C
12:7-10	Pentecost VII, B
13:5-13	Pentecost I (Trinity Sunday), A

Galatians

1:1-10	Pentecost II, C
1:11-19	Pentecost III, C
2:15-21	Pentecost IV, C
3:23-29	Pentecost V, C
5:1, 13-18	Pentecost VI, C
6:6-10	Thanksgiving Day, B
6:11-18	Pentecost VII, C

Ephesians

1:3-10	Christmas Day, C
	Pentecost VIII, B

11:1-10	Reformation Sunday, C	3:1-3	Easter IV, B
		3:18-24	Easter V, B
12:1-6	Passion (Palm) Sunday, B	4:1-7	Easter VI, B
		4:11-16	Easter VII, B
	Pentecost XIII, C	5:1-6	Easter II, B
12:7-13	Pentecost XIV, C		
12:18-24	Pentecost XV, C	*II John*	
		(none)	
James			
1:12-18	Ash Wednesday, B	*III John*	
1:19-25	Pentecost XV, B	(none)	
2:1-5	Pentecost XVI, B		
2:14-18	Pentecost XVII, B	*Jude*	
3:13 to 4:3	Pentecost XVIII, B	(none)	
5:1-6	Pentecost XIX, B		
5:7-10	Advent III, A	*Revelation*	
		1:4-8	Epiphany IX, B
I Peter			Maundy Thursday, B
1:1-9	Pentecost I (Trinity Sunday), C		Pentecost XXVII, B
1:3-9	Easter Day, B	1:9-13, 17-19	Easter II, C
	Easter II, A	3:17-22	World Communion, A
1:17-21	Easter III, A		
2:4-10	Easter V, A	5:6-14	Good Friday, C
2:11-17	Day of Civic or National Significance, C	5:11-14	Easter III, C
			Christian Unity, C
		7:9-17	Easter IV, C
2:19-25	Easter IV, A		World Communion, B
3:13-18	Easter VI, A		
3:18-22	Lent I, B	21:1-5	Easter V, C
4:12-19	Easter VII, A	21:1-7	New Year's Eve or Day, A
II Peter		21:10-14, 22-23	Easter VI, C
3:8-14	Advent II, B	21:22 to 22:2	Christmas II, B
		22:12-14,	
I John		16-17, 20	Easter VII, C
2:1-6	Easter III, B		

PSALTER INDEX

246

66:1-7, 16-20	Easter VI, A	105:1-7	Easter II, A
66:1-12, 16-20	Pentecost VII, C		Pentecost XXVII, A
67	Pentecost XIII, A	107:1-3, 23-32	Pentecost V, B
	Epiphany II, B	107:1-3, 33-43	Pentecost XXV, B
	Easter VI, C	110	Ascension Day, A,B,C
69:1-18, 34-36	Pentecost V, A		
69:30, 32-36	Pentecost VIII, C	111	Christmas I, A,B,C
70:1-2, 4-5	Wednesday in Holy Week, A,B,C		Pentecost XXVII, B
		112	Pentecost XV, C
71:1-6, 15-17	Epiphany IV, C	112:4-9	Epiphany V, A
71:1-12, 15, 17	Tuesday in Holy Week, A,B,C	113	Epiphany III, C
			Pentecost XVIII, C
72:1-19	Advent II, A	116:1-9	Lent V, A
	Epiphany, A,B,C		Pentecost XVII, B
78:14-20, 23-29	Pentecost XI, A,B	116:12-19	Maundy Thursday, A,B,C
80:1-7	Advent I, B		
	Advent IV, C	117	Pentecost II, C
80:7-15, 18-19	Pentecost XX, A		Pentecost XIV, C
81:1-10	Pentecost II, B	118:1-2, 14-24	Easter Day, A,B,C
82	Pentecost XIII, C	119:1-16	Epiphany VI, A
84	Christmas II, B		Pentecost XXIV, B
85	Advent II, B	119:33-40	Pentecost XVI, A
85:7-13	Pentecost VIII, B	119:129-136	Pentecost X, A
85:8-13	Pentecost XII, A	121	Pentecost XXII, C
86:11-17	Pentecost IX, A	122	Advent I, A
89:1-4, 14-18	Advent IV, B	123	Pentecost VII, B
89:1-4, 15-18	Pentecost VI, A	126	Pentecost XXIII, B
90:1-8, 12-17	Pentecost XXI, B		Advent II, C
91	Lent I, C	128	Pentecost XXVI, A
91:9-16	Pentecost XXII, B		Pentecost XX, B
92	Epiphany VIII, C	130	Lent I, A
	Pentecost IV, B	131	Pentecost XXIV, A
95:1-7	Pentecost XX, C	135:1-7, 13-14	Pentecost XIX, B
95:1-2, 6-11	Lent III, A	137:1-6	Lent IV, B
96	Christmas Eve, A,B	138	Pentecost XIV, A
	Christmas Day, A		Epiphany V, C
	Pentecost XXII, A		Pentecost X, C
97	Christmas Day, C	139:1-12	Easter III, B
98	Christmas Day, B	145	Pentecost VII, A
	Easter VI, B		Pentecost X, B
	Christmas Eve, C		Pentecost XXIV, C
98:1-3	Pentecost XXVI, C	145:1-13	Easter V, C
98:1-4	Pentecost XXI, C	146	Advent III, A
98:4-9	Pentecost XXVII, C		Pentecost XVI, B
100	Pentecost IV, A		Pentecost XIX, C
	Easter IV, C	147:1-12	Epiphany V, B
103:1-11	Lent III, C	147:12-20	Christmas II, A,C
103:1-13	Epiphany VII, A	148	Easter II, B
	Epiphany VIII, B		Pentecost XXV, C
	Pentecost XVII, A	149	Pentecost I (Trinity Sunday), B
104:1-4, 24-33	Pentecost (Whitsunday), A,B,C		Easter II, C

RESOURCES

COLLECTS

The Book of Common Prayer. According to the use of The Episcopal Church (Church Hymnal Corp. and Seabury Press: Charles Mortimer Guilbert, Custodian of the Standard Book of Common Prayer, 1979). P. 213.

Lutheran Book of Worship (Ministers Edition). Prepared by the churches participating in the Inter-Lutheran Commission on Worship (Minneapolis: Augsburg Publishing House; and Philadelphia: Board of Publication, Lutheran Church in America, 1978). Pp. 121-170.

The Roman Missal. Revised by Decree of the Second Vatican Ecumenical Council and published by Authority of Pope Paul VI. *The Sacramentary* (Collegeville, Minn.: Liturgical Press, 1974). P. 524.

The Worshipbook—Services and Hymns. Prepared by The Joint Committee on Worship for Cumberland Presbyterian Church, Presbyterian Church in the United States, The United Presbyterian Church in the United States of America (Philadelphia: Westminster Press, 1970, 1972). Pp. 135-157.

COMMENTARIES AND HOMILETICAL AIDS

Barth, Karl. *Church Dogmatics: An Index Volume with Aids for the Preacher,* ed. G. W. Bromiley and T. F. Torrance. Edinburgh: T. & T. Clark, 1977.

An index to all Scripture references, major and minor, in the entirety of Barth's *Church Dogmatics.* It also provides full quotations from the *Dogmatics* for lections for an entire year according to a 1958 Lutheran Lectionary. By cross-referencing into the three-year ecumenical lectionary the preacher has brilliant and suggestive theological "starters" for preaching.

Celebration—A Creative Worship Service

Leaflets for each Sunday on a subscription basis which include Bible commentary and sermon ideas, music and hymn suggestions. Special supplements with creative services for all occasions and reviews of new music. Roman Catholic but easily adaptable. Available from P.O. Box 281, Kansas City, Mo. 64141.

Fuller, Reginald H. *Preaching the New Lectionary: The Word of God for the Church Today.* Liturgical Press, 1974.

The indispensable exegetical, liturgical, and homiletical commentary for all three years. Originally published serially in *Worship* magazine; now in a paperback volume.

Good News

A monthly subscription service, also largely Roman Catholic although an ecumenical supplement is available. It includes exegetical notes, brief homilies, prayers, visual features, and articles on various liturgical topics. Available from Franciscan Communications Center, 1229 S. Santee Street, Los Angeles, Calif. 90015.

Homily Service

A monthly subscription service of The Liturgical Conference, an ecumenical liturgical renewal society. This service includes exegetical materials and sermon samples and ideas for each Sunday. It discourages use of "canned" sermons however. Its "Studying the Lectionary" leaflet is a useful instrument for small groups. The Conference also has a valuable set of seasonal packets entitled *Major Feasts and Seasons*. Available from The Liturgical Conference, 810 Rhode Island Avenue, N.E., Washington, D.C. 20018.

Interpretation—A Journal of Bible and Theology. Richmond: Union Theological Seminary in Virginia.

An excellent scholarly quarterly which will keep readers in touch with current Biblical study for background in homiletical work. Its April 1977 issue (XXXI, No. 2) was devoted entirely to a consideration of the ecumenical lectionary. It includes articles by Elizabeth Achtemeier, Lloyd R. Bailey, John Reumann, and Gerard S. Sloyan. Available from Union Theological Seminary, 3401 Brook Road, Richmond, Va. 23227.

A Lectionary. Prepared by the Commission on Worship of the Consultation on Church Union. Princeton, N.J.: Consultation on Church Union, 1974.

A 42-page pamphlet. It includes a helpful introduction to the ecumenical lectionary by Prof. James F. White, a listing of a consensus table for all three years drawn from Roman Catholic, Episcopal, Presbyterian, and Lutheran editions, and a very useful index arranged by books of the Bible. Available from the Consultation on Church Union, 228 Alexander Street, Princeton, N.J. 08540.

New Covenant Community: A Daily Lectionary for Growing Christians. Prepared by the Youth Program Office of the Program Agency, The United Presbyterian Church in the U.S.A.

A September-to-September daily lectionary (one lesson per day) for junior and senior high youth (but useful for adults as well), which anticipates one of the three Sunday lections and provides a paragraph of commentary for each week. Available from Curriculum Services UPCUSA, P.O. Box 868, William Penn Annex, Philadelphia, Pa. 19105.

Proclamation. Fortress Press.

An entire series of small paperback commentaries for specified Seasons of the Christian Year (for all three cycles of the lectionary) and of individual books of the Bible. They are written by distinguished authors of many denominations. A descriptive brochure is available from Fortress Press, 2900 Queen Lane, Philadelphia, Pa. 19129.

Seasons of the Gospel: Resources for the Christian Year. Abingdon Press, 1979.

A comprehensive study of calendar and lectionary by the excellent Methodist liturgiologist. It includes weekly resources, visual in particular.

Sloyan, Gerard S. *A Commentary on the New Lectionary.* Paulist Press, 1975.

A careful exegetical analysis of all the lections for the entire three years. Excellent as a first-stage study guide for preaching.

Word Bread Cup. Forward Movement Publications, 1978.

A pamphlet produced by the Commission on Worship of the Consultation on Church Union. It provides a flexible word-sacrament service together with illustrative texts for the eucharistic prayer and the agreed ecumenical international texts produced by the International Consultation on English Texts. A Table of Psalms is also provided for the three-year lectionary. Available from the Consultation on Church Union, 228 Alexander Street, Princeton, N.J. 08540.

Word and Table. Prepared by the Section on Worship of the Board of Discipleship of The United Methodist Church. Abingdon Press, 1976.

A basic text introducing the Word-Sacrament pattern for Sunday worship for Methodists. Commentary on the various elements of worship is provided, together with a detailed discussion of the eucharistic order and prayer. The calendar presupposed by the ecumenical lectionary is discussed, and the complete table of lessons, with psalms, is given. A good study guide for laity.

Word and Witness

An excellent subscription service edited and written by Protestant preachers. Each two-month packet includes extensive worship and homiletical helps. Edited by Professor Charles Rice. Available from 3003 South Congress Avenue, 2-E (Palm Springs), Lake Worth, Fla. 33461.

MUSICAL RESOURCES

Carols for Choirs, Book I, ed. and arr. Reginald Jacques and David Willcocks. Oxford University Press, 1961.

Carols for Choirs, Book II, ed. and arr. David Willcocks and John Rutter. Oxford University Press, 1970.

Fifty Christmas and Advent carols are contained in each volume. The range of difficulty runs from easy to very difficult. Both collections solve Advent and Christmas problems for years to come.

Ecumenical Praise, ed. Carlton R. Young. Hope Publishing Co., Agape, 1977.

An able collection of contemporary texts, tunes, or both (117 numbers), which would complement use of the lectionary and Christian Year. Almost the best of current composing and arranging. Available in melody, pew, and accompaniment editions. A good choir resource.

A First Motet Book. Concordia Publishing House.

Seventeen motets from Christopher Tye and Claude Goudimel to Hugo Distler and Ralph Vaughan Williams.

The Gelineau Gradual

The most accessible system for recovery of chanting the psalms. Easily learned antiphons provided for use with psalms for every Sunday of the three-year cycle. Psalms can be sung by cantor, choir, or minister. A variety of editions and arrangements is available from G.I.A. Publications, 7404 S. Mason Avenue, Chicago, Ill. 60638.

Lift Up Your Hearts, ed. by Paul Bunjes. Concordia Publishing House.

Twelve anthems suitable for Holy Communion with something for every season. Not all pieces require SATB.

Lutheran Book of Worship (Pew Edition). Prepared by the churches participating in the Inter-Lutheran Commission on Worship. Minneapolis: Augsburg Publishing House; and Philadelphia: Board of Publication, Lutheran Church in America, 1978.

This new hymnal is a delight visually and musically. Of all the new hymnals it is the most careful of discriminatory or exclusive language. Its hymns and service music will function well with the ecumenical lectionary. Its table of "Hymns for the Church Year" (pp. 929-931) will be especially useful.

The Psalmody for the Day, ed. Charles Frischmann. Fortress Press, 1974, 1975, 1976.

Three 8½" by 11" paperbacks (Years A, B, C) containing complete texts and music for the responsorial system of psalmody now being widely used, especially by Lutherans. Chanting of psalm verses is slightly more difficult than the Gelineau system, but congregational antiphons are just as easily learned and used.

Reformed Liturgy and Music. Published by the Joint Office of Worship of The United Presbyterian Church in the U.S.A. and the Presbyterian Church in the U.S. in cooperation with the Presbyterian Association of Musicians.

A quarterly journal for ministers and musicians. In addition to articles on worship in the Reformed tradition, each issue contains musical materials, often annotated, for choir or organ. Available from the Joint Office of Worship, 1044 Alta Vista Road, Louisville, Ky. 40205.

The SAB Choral Book. Concordia Publishing House.

Most usable for small choirs with few men or when summer attendance is low; at least one piece for each season of the year.

Peter Waring, *Above the Noise.* Peter Waring, 1972.

This is a privately published guide to the lectionary which integrates Biblical material with hymns (drawn from the *Pilgrim Hymnal* and the 1940 Episcopal *Hymnal*) and rich catechetical materials. Available from the author at 1299 Washington Street, Bath, Maine 04530.

Westminster Praise, ed. and arr. Erik Routley. Hinshaw Music, 1976.

Sixty fascinating entries from the best of contemporary composing and writing, prepared for the Westminster Choir College. Slightly beyond most congregations but eminently useful for choirs. An informative *Westminster Praise Companion* is also available from Hinshaw Music, P.O. Box 470, Chapel Hill, N.C. 27514.

STUDY RESOURCES

Cullmann, Oscar. *Christ and Time.* Rev. ed. Westminster Press, 1964.
Davies, J. G., ed. *The Westminster Dictionary of Worship.* Westminster Press, 1979.
———. *Holy Week: A Short History.* John Knox Press, 1963.
Dix, Dom Gregory. *The Shape of the Liturgy.* London: Dacre Press, 1945.
Flannery, Austin, O.P., ed. *Vatican Council II: The Conciliar and Post-Conciliar Documents, The Constitution on the Sacred Liturgy.* Liturgical Press, 1975.
Fuller, Reginald H. *What Is Liturgical Preaching?* London: SCM Press, 1957.
Jones, Cheslyn; Wainwright, Geoffrey; and Yarnold, E., eds. *The Study of Liturgy.* Oxford University Press, 1978.
Kümmel, Werner Georg. *Promise and Fulfillment.* London: SCM Press, 1957.
Maxwell, William D. *A History of Worship in the Church of Scotland.* London: Oxford University Press, 1955.
———. *The Liturgical Portions of the Genevan Service Book.* London: Faith Press, 1965.
McArthur, A. Allan. *The Christian Year and Lectionary Reform.* London: SCM Press, 1958.
———. *The Evolution of the Christian Year.* London: SCM Press, 1953.
Melton, Julius. *Presbyterian Worship in America.* John Knox Press, 1967.
Moltmann, Jürgen. *The Theology of Hope: On the Ground and the Implications of a Christian Eschatology.* Tr. James W. Leitch. Harper & Row, 1967.
Nichols, James Hastings. *Corporate Worship in the Reformed Tradition.* Westminster Press, 1968.
Old, Hughes Oliphant. *The Patristic Roots of Reformed Worship.* Zurich: Theologischer Verlag Zurich, 1975.
Ritschl, Dietrich. *Memory and Hope: An Inquiry Concerning the Presence of Christ.* Macmillan Co., 1967.

254   Rordorf, Willy. *Sunday: The History of the Day of Rest and Worship in the Earliest Centuries of the Christian Church.* Tr. A. A. K. Graham. Westminster Press, 1968.

Seasons of the Gospel: Resources for the Christian Year. Abingdon Press, 1979.

Thompson, Bard, ed. *Liturgies of the Western Church.* World Publishing Co., 1961.

Von Allmen, Jean-Jacques. *Preaching and Congregation.* Tr. B. L. Nicholas. John Knox Press, 1962.

White, James F. *Christian Worship in Transition.* Abingdon Press, 1976.

———. *Introduction to Christian Worship.* Abingdon Press, 1980.